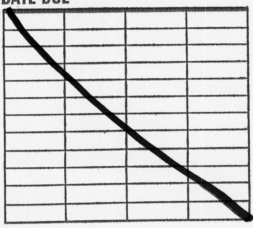

ALEXANDER I OF RUSSIA

Emperor Alexander I in 1805
From a rare unpublished German engraving in the author's collection

ALEXANDER I
OF RUSSIA

The Man Who Defeated Napoleon

By

LEONID I. STRAKHOVSKY

GREENWOOD PRESS, PUBLISHERS
WESTPORT, CONNECTICUT

TO

IVAN

After Bonaparte, Alexander is the
greatest historical figure of the Napoleonic era.
CHATEAUBRIAND

Do you recall our Agamemnon's flight
On eagle's wings from Paris captive?
How great he was, and how attractive,
What ecstasy evoked his sight,
The people's friend, their freedom's savior!
PUSHKIN

CONTENTS

ILLUSTRATIONS

THE MAD EMPEROR

In the dark sky of a March night in the year of grace, 1801, turbulent clouds like evil spirits danced their witch dance about Mikhailovsky Castle, home of the mad Emperor Paul I. The chain bridge was drawn; the steel-like water of the moat glittered grimly in the half-melted snow against the red walls of the heavy turreted castle. Motionless sentries mounted guard.

With the fall of darkness, His Majesty the Emperor and Autocrat of All the Russias had barricaded himself behind the strong walls of his residence, frightened by the howling of the wind through the turrets, by the shimmering of the lights through the trees of his park, by the footsteps echoing along the narrow corridors. He distrusted everyone in his empire, including his son and heir to his throne, Alexander—everyone, that is, with but one exception, Count Pahlen, Military Governor of St. Petersburg. Not for a single moment did he ever forget that his father, Emperor Peter III, had been strangled by the apelike hands of Count Orlov, his mother's lover. Thus he, an emperor, lived the life of a frightened hare, a voluntary prisoner in Mikhailovsky Castle.

The five years of Emperor Paul's reign had terrorized Russia. No one was sure of his future. Officers of the Guards always provided themselves with some ready money when going on duty in the palace lest they should be exiled to Siberia directly from there. Haunted by fear, the emperor suspected his entire entourage. As a result, his orders were often contradictory. After having fought side by side with England against the hated revolutionary, Napoleon, he then turned his hatred against England and suggested to this same Napoleon a plan to invade India. No wonder that a contemporary French print portrayed him issuing diversified orders to his generals under the caption: "*Ordre—contre ordre—désordre.*"

Born in 1754, in the reign of Empress Elizabeth, Paul spent a lonely childhood. He was neglected by his mother, Catherine II, who had to fight her way to the throne through a multitude of court intrigues, full of suspicion, distrust and even high treason. At an early age, nineteen, he had married Princess Wilhelmine, daughter of the landgrave of Hesse-Darmstadt. She was to be known as the Grand Duchess Nathalia Alexeyevna. The abnormal state of affairs prevailing in the Russian Empire where, after the murder of Peter III, Catherine had proclaimed herself reigning empress in place of Paul, the rightful heir, very soon suggested a daring plan to Nathalia Alexeyevna.

With the help of some high dignitaries of the empire—the brothers Panin, Princess Dashkov, Prince Repnin and a number of dissatisfied officers of the Guards—she conspired to overthrow the rule of Catherine and to restore the rights of Paul. The plot failed. One of the conspirators revealed it to Count Orlov. Paul had already approved a constitution, which was drafted by Panin; had signed and sealed it. Then one day Paul

was summoned before his mother and, under pressure, confessed everything, betraying his wife and their fellow conspirators. This marked the beginning of open warfare between the
great empress and her daughter-in-law, which ended only with
the death of the Grand Duchess Nathalia Alexeyevna, less
than a year later, when she gave birth to a still-born child.

Paul did not remain a widower long. As early as 1776 he married Sophie-Dorothea, Princess of Württemberg, who took
the name Maria Fyodorovna. In this second wife Paul found
a worthy companion; but the gulf already existing between
Catherine and her son grew greater. Paul never forgave his
mother the humiliation she caused by forcing him to betray his
first wife. This wound caused him deeper suffering than the
murder of his father. From then on there were two courts, two
opposed camps: that of the empress in St. Petersburg and that
of Paul in Gatchina, situated some thirty miles from the capital.
Everyone who was dissatisfied at the Great Court joined the
Little Court. It was as though the Middle Ages had been revived and a powerful and almost independent vassal were dis-
puting the authority of his suzerain.

Embittered, distrustful, Paul grew more suspicious day by
day. He formed his own guard, a military corps under his personal command, and spent his time drilling, parading, marching, training his troops in the manner set forth by his beloved
hero, Frederick the Great of Prussia. In this little corps everything differed from the rest of the Russian army, even the uniforms which were patterned after those of the Prussians. Paul
loved perfect alignment, the goose step of his regiments passing
by. He loved his officers, who were devoted to him; and as
much as he could be said to trust any group, he trusted this one.

It seems that he had good reason for his suspicions, however. In Gatchina, Paul was surrounded by Catherine's spies, because the great empress knew that she had no legitimate right to occupy the throne of Russia and had never forgotten the rather childish attempt on the part of her son to overthrow her power. Nothing guaranteed her from a renewed attempt by Paul to secure his rightful inheritance. For this reason she deemed it expedient to take precautions to know exactly what was going on at the Little Court. Paul knew that he was spied upon and this knowledge created a feeling of uneasiness which developed later into one of constant fear.

In his younger years Paul had suffered from hallucinations. His unbalanced mind had begun to be touched by the madness which progressed steadily as the years went by. One spring night he strolled through the streets of St. Petersburg, accompanied by Prince Kurakin and two valets. It was one of those indescribable twilight nights of the north, when everything seems unreal, when things assume indefinable shapes, when well-known faces are transfigured by that strange eeriness of the northern light. Paul and Kurakin were conversing with animation. One valet preceded, another followed them. Suddenly at the turn of a street Paul noticed a tall, dark figure, clad in a long military cape and cocked hat. Approaching on his left it fell into step with him. The effect on Paul was terrifying. After some hesitation he started a conversation with the ghost, although Kurakin assured him emphatically that the whole thing was merely a product of his imagination. The stranger called Paul an unhappy prince who would not live long. He told him that he should follow the dictates of his conscience, the best guide for a noble heart. Paul, completely enthralled by his hallucination, followed this creation of his disordered mind through the silent and deserted streets of the capital, until they reached the monument of Peter the Great erected by Catherine. Here Paul heard the last words of the stranger, "Good-by, Paul, you will see me again here and elsewhere," and suddenly recognized in the phantom the features of his great ancestor. In later years this hallucination repeated itself many times. Paul conceived the idea that he had been called by the shadow of his great ancestor to continue Peter's work, to restore chivalry, to fight the evils of his mother's reign. That is why he had ordered a statue of Peter the Great to be erected in the inner court of Mikhailovsky Castle.

When Paul, at the age of forty-three, ascended the throne of Russia following the death of Catherine the Great, the gulf which had existed between St. Petersburg and Gatchina was transformed into one between the emperor and his empire. In the first year of his reign he instituted certain reforms which were both wise and far-reaching. But the twenty years of silent war between St. Petersburg and Gatchina, surrounded by distrust, spying and treason, finally bore fruit. Paul's mind began to fade. He lost himself in details and tried to regulate every phase of life, if not in the whole of his empire, at least in his capital. Not satisfied with giving orders to his army as to how to polish buttons, how to powder wigs and what kind of thread to use for repairs of uniforms, he rigidly prescribed the dress of the civilian population, forbidding under the penalty of imprisonment the wearing of garments that had been introduced into Europe after the French Revolution. His mind, in its delirium, conceived the absurd idea of stopping the flow of time.

His outbursts of anger were terrible. For the slightest mistake or for merely a word that happened to displease him, high dignitaries of the empire were exiled to their estates, officers and officials sent to Siberia. The most careful and tactful, the most wise and skillful of his contemporaries met only abject failure in their diplomatic efforts with him.

Once when residing in Pavlovsk, the country home of Empress Maria Fyodorovna, he signified his desire to go out for a walk. The empress remarked casually that it was going to rain and that it would be better for him to stay in the palace. Paul then turned to Count Stroganov and asked him whether he thought it would rain. The count was the descendant of the famous Stroganov family which in the sixteenth century had won to the Russian rulers territory exceeding that of all the rest of Europe. Stroganov, considered to be the wisest man at court, went out to observe the sky and returned with the answer that the sky was clouded and in consequence it would probably rain. Paul flew into a rage. "Ah," he said, "I see that you are conniving with the empress expressly to annoy me. I am sick of such falsehoods on your part. You never wanted to understand me, to please me. However, I know that you are more wanted at Perm than here, and recommend your urgent departure to your estates. I hope that this time you will understand me." This was a mild way of sending one of the most important and most useful men of the empire into exile.

Paul's anger knew no bounds when anyone had the audacity to appear before him in a uniform differing from the one he had prescribed. Generals, high officials, even princes of the empire, were deprived of their ranks, titles and honors for such disobedience. Even foreign representatives were not immune. Tauentzien, the Prussian envoy, appeared at a court ball in a uniform which displeased Emperor Paul. He had to leave St. Petersburg the same evening, having been given his passports and sent back to Berlin. Nobody felt secure under the rule of Paul I. Alexander, his son, actually trembled with fear whenever he had to lead his regiment on parade before the emperor. He and his brother, Grand Duke Constantine, were very often humiliated by their father in the very presence of their troops, when Paul would send his aides-de-camp to deliver such imperial messages as "brute," "animal," "idiot," "fool" to his sons.

No wonder that the minds of the people were gradually shaped to accept as inevitable the thought that the only way to safeguard themselves and the rest of the country from arbitrary and insane rule was to dethrone the emperor. When Count Pahlen decided to organize a conspiracy, he found many willing to help him and the cause of Russia. There was no better man than Pahlen to be leader of such a plot. Cool reasoning, a talent for organization and boldness characterized this man, a Baltic German by origin, who changed the fate of Russia. By virtue of his position as Military Governor of the Capital, he was in control of the police, and was able, in case of need, to suppress all information about the conspiracy if ever the police were to discover the plot.

It is said that a few days before his murder, Emperor Paul received a complete report on the conspiracy which contained all the names and pointed to Count Pahlen as the leader. Count Pahlen did not deny it, when questioned by the emperor, but said that the very fact that he was a party to the conspiracy guaranteed Emperor Paul's complete safety. Pahlen's ascendancy over the emperor, who trusted him implicitly, was so great that his statement restored Paul's full confidence and thus annihilated the possible disastrous effect of the betrayal.

From the beginning Pahlen proceeded with caution. One by one, men faithful to Emperor Paul were sent away from the capital. Count Arakcheyev and Count Rostopchin, "the men of Gatchina," were exiled to their estates and new persons were appointed to fill their places. At the same time all those who had belonged to Catherine's regime, and who hated Paul for the humiliations he had inflicted upon them when he ascended the throne, gradually gathered in St. Petersburg. Thus, all members of the Zubov family, through the intercession of Count Pahlen, were permitted to return to the capital and re-gained their position at court. Paul believed in Pahlen's loyalty to such an extent that he did everything the latter proposed to him. Barricaded in Mikhailovsky Castle, Paul left all the affairs of the empire in the hands of Pahlen, who was made Minister of Foreign Affairs and Director of the Post, thereby enabling him to control not only the capital, as he continued to be Mili-tary Governor of St. Petersburg, but also the rest of Russia.

During the winter, 1800–1801, the people of St. Petersburg lived under extreme nervous tension. Officers of the Guards and high dignitaries of the empire would gather at dinner parties and discuss politics—a thing unheard of theretofore because of the police system and the time-honored institution of spies. Pahlen attended many of these meetings mainly in quest of men for his conspiracy. He wanted men of action, resolute, bold, but not those who were using their tongues too freely. One day while dining with Count Pahlen, Sablukov, an officer of the Horse Guards who was devoted to Paul and who was suspicious of certain things he had observed in the capital, wanted to put

Pahlen to the test and spoke critically about the emperor without, however, a happy choice of terms and expressions. Pahlen looked at him sharply and said: *"Jean fichu qui parle et brave homme qui agit."* [1]

By February the stage was set, but Pahlen wanted to be sure that the Grand Duke Alexander would not oppose his plans and refuse to occupy a throne vacated by murder. It was obvious to Pahlen that he could not risk the possibility of anarchy in case Alexander proved to be stubborn. So he proceeded to win the heir to the throne of all the Russias to his cause. By pouring salt into the wound of humiliation which had never healed in Alexander's heart, Pahlen succeeded in preparing the grand duke for a possible change of rule in the Russian Empire, intimating that Paul was insane and that it would be best to force his abdication. But even if Pahlen could have counted to a degree on meeting no opposition from Alexander, he was never able to bring the young man to favor the conspiracy openly. To the very last moment he had to be prepared for every eventuality lest Alexander should turn against him.

Living in complete seclusion in Mikhailovsky Castle to such an extent that to avoid going out he had ordered Princess Gagarin, his mistress, to occupy an apartment in the castle just beneath his own which communicated with it by a secret staircase, Paul had insisted that members of his family should share his voluntary prison. Empress Maria Fyodorovna had to submit to this unnatural state of affairs, although it is admitted that Paul never pushed his favorite forward to such an extent as to embarrass the empress. Still, he feared that his wife might become resentful and join hands with his enemies. Therefore, as a

---

[1] "Lost is he who speaks; brave, he who acts."

means of self-protection, a few days before the fatal night, he
ordered the door between his bedroom and that of the empress
to be closed and barricaded. Perhaps this measure cost him his
life.

In the evening of March 23, 1801, the emperor dined with his
family. The meal was eaten in silence except for the bitter words
with which, from time to time, Paul addressed his sons, Alexander and Constantine. The emperor accused them of conspir-
ing against him, and at the end of the dinner, in a rage, arrested
both of them and sent them to their apartments in the castle.
Both Alexander and Constantine had an overpowering fear of
their father. Those tall, strong, young men were simply terrorized by Paul, a short man of no physical strength, whose pale
blue eyes were haggard and whose gestures were nervous and
abrupt.

On this same evening, the conspirators met in small groups
for dinner accompanied by many libations. Later they gathered
for supper at which Count Pahlen and General Bennigsen were
present. Here Count Pahlen said, "*Rappelez-vous, messieurs,
que pour manger d'une omelette il faut commencer par casser
les oeufs.*" [2] The one hundred and eighty conspirators received
this admonition in silence. More wine and champagne were to
give them additional courage, but some had already taken too
much. About midnight most of the regiments on the side of the
conspiracy marched to Mikhailovsky Castle. They were led
by the Semyonovsky Regiment which eventually occupied all
the inner posts in the corridors and passages of the castle. Their
sullen march through the night along the deserted streets was

---

[2] "Remember, gentlemen, that in order to eat an omelette, one first has to
break the eggs."

watched only by the clouds in a somber fury. The conspirators left the table soon after midnight and proceeded in sleighs
across the sleeping town. When they reached the gloomy
castle, Count Pahlen left them and went into Alexander's apartments on the ground floor, assigning the leadership to General
Bennigsen.

The signal for the intrusion into the private apartments of
Emperor Paul was to be given by Archamakov, Adjutant of
the Grenadier Battalion of the Preobrazhensky Regiment,
whose duty it was to inform the emperor of fires breaking out
in the city. On the prescribed hour Archamakov rushed into the
vestibule of the emperor's private apartment and shouted
"Fire!" At the same moment the conspirators made their way
to the emperor's bedroom.

That very evening the emperor had dismissed, on Pahlen's
advice, the men from the Horse Guards on duty at the palace
and replaced them by two valets stationed at the door leading
into his bedroom. These men put up a fight, and one of them
was killed, the other wounded. The door into the bedroom was
a double one, the entrance to the secret staircase that led to the
apartment of Princess Gagarin being between the two doors.
The first was open, the second locked from inside. Having
forced the second door, the conspirators burst into the emperor's
bedroom. It was empty. Yet Paul could not have escaped, as the
only other door to the bedroom leading into the private apartments of the empress had been barred by his express orders.

The conspirators were searching the room in vain when
General Bennigsen, a very tall and phlegmatic German from the
Baltic provinces, went to the open fireplace and, leaning upon
the mantelpiece, suddenly discovered the emperor hiding be-

hind the screen. Bennigsen said calmly, *"Le voilà."* [3] The others
dragged the emperor from his hiding place. Prince Platon Zubov
then addressed the emperor and demanded his abdication. Paul,
entirely composed, began to argue with him. This dialogue
with death as the judge continued for more than half an hour
until the other conspirators, who had had too much champagne,
tired and demanded action. As the discussion became very
heated and Paul raised his voice, Count Nicholas Zubov, a man
of powerful build and enormous physical force, struck Paul on
the hand, saying brutally, "Why do you yell like this?" The
emperor then like a valiant but unfortunate David pushed
Zubov's hand aside. At this Zubov, grasping a heavy golden
snuffbox, administered a terrific blow on Paul's left temple. The
emperor fell to the ground. Zubov's French valet then jumped
on the unconscious man and Skariatin, an officer of the Izmailovsky Regiment, reached for the emperor's scarf which hung
over his bed. So they strangled him, Paul I, Emperor and Autocrat of All the Russias.

[3] "There he is."

II

THE KING IS DEAD—LONG LIVE THE KING

HUMILIATED, his pride repeatedly wounded, hating, still fearing, Alexander did not think of his father, while he lived, as the defender of ancient chivalry, as a man endowed with a noble heart, or as the Emperor and Autocrat of All the Russias by the Grace of God. To Alexander, Paul had become a nightmare, a tyrant, a willful oppressor of all that was so near and dear to the heart of the young grand duke, although Paul had often shown his will and courage and, even more, a chivalrous nature. At the time when war was raging in western Europe and Russia had joined the coalition of powers against revolutionary France, Paul had made an official offer to General Napoleon Bonaparte to settle the dispute by a duel between them in order to stop the shedding of blood of their respective subjects. Notwithstanding the seeming absurdity of such an offer and its untimeliness, most of the crowned rulers of Europe and even Napoleon himself recognized the noble motive of the Russian emperor.

Under arrest in his own apartment in Mikhailovsky Castle,

Alexander must have pondered the fate that awaited him. If the conspiracy succeeded, it meant a crown; but first of all it meant freedom from oppression. If the conspiracy failed, it meant more humiliation and dishonor, perhaps even imprisonment and death. But should he accept a throne upon which he would feel himself a usurper? Would it not be more consistent with his ideals and inclinations to renounce all his rights of succession and to live the simple and uneventful life of an ordinary citizen? He had always dreamed of doing just this. On May 22, 1796, he had written to his friend and confidant, Count Kochubey:

I am thoroughly displeased with my situation. . . . It is far too brilliant for my character, which fits much better with a life of peace and quiet. Court life is not for me. I feel miserable in the society of such people, whom I should not like to have even as my valets. At the same time they occupy the highest offices in the empire. In one word, my dear friend, I am aware that I was not born for the high position I now occupy and even less for that which awaits me in the future and I have sworn to myself to renounce it in one way or another. . . . The affairs of state are in complete disorder; graft and embezzlement are everywhere; all departments are badly managed; order seems to have been expelled from all parts of the country, but notwithstanding all this the Empire tends only toward expansion. Is it possible, therefore, for one man to administer the state, even more to reform it and to abolish the long existing evils? To my mind it is beyond the power of a genius, not to speak of a man with ordinary capacities, like myself. Taking all this into consideration I have arrived at the aforementioned decision. My plan consists in abdicating (I cannot say when) and in settling with my wife on the shores of the Rhine to live the life of a private citizen devoting my time to the company of my friends and to the study of nature.

Alexander had written so when his grandmother, Catherine the Great, was still on the throne. Was this only a dream of a young man of nineteen? It would seem not, for the dream of his youth remained with Alexander during his entire life. But on the eve of Paul's murder, Alexander could not bring himself to any decision as to his own future, because in all the preceding years he had been trained on the one hand to cherish dreams and on the other to act realistically according to circumstances.

Alexander was born on December 24, 1777. Shortly afterward he was taken away from his mother by Empress Catherine, who wanted to give him an education in conformity with the ideas of the French philosophers of the time, i.e., based on the laws of reason and the principles of nature. *Émile* by Jean Jacques Rousseau was the textbook used by Catherine in educating young Alexander. The great empress wanted to mold her grandson for his important mission as ruler after her own ideas rather than those of her son, Paul, whom she wished to thrust aside in order to give the throne to Alexander. He, she believed, would continue the traditions of his grandmother rather than those of Paul, embittered and hateful at his Little Court in Gatchina.

While trying to develop the natural gifts of the child, Catherine wished him to grow up a little Spartan, fully equipped to sustain the physical strain due to fall upon the ruler of a militarized empire. In order to accustom him to the roar of guns she placed Alexander in a room of the Winter Palace with windows facing the Admiralty. The child was forced to hear at close range the cannonade which took place at the Admiralty on every festive occasion—and festive occasions were numerous. Unfortunately for Alexander, although he became accustomed to artillery fire, the membranes of his ears proved too weak to sustain this strain; the result was a deafness in one ear that was to remain with him for the rest of his life. But in other ways the vigorous physical training of the boy proved beneficial.

From his earliest childhood Alexander slept, very lightly covered, in a room with the windows wide open. The mattress in his crib was of morocco leather filled with hay; and all through his life he slept on a similar one, always carrying it with him on his journeys and campaigns. This undoubtedly accounted in no small measure for the extraordinary health and vitality enjoyed by him. It is interesting to compare his childhood training with that of his father. Paul, at birth, was also taken away from his mother by Empress Elizabeth and placed in a room adjoining hers. In this room, which was always kept very warm, wrapped in flannel and covered with three blankets, one of silk, another of fur, and still another of velvet, he reposed in a crib upholstered with the furs of black foxes. No wonder that while constantly perspiring under such covers, Paul grew up a physical weakling, subject in later years to colds with the slightest change of wind or temperature.

Thus Catherine was responsible for the child Alexander's excellent physical upbringing, but his education remained far from adequate. The well-known Russian historians, Kluchev-sky, Shilder, and Grand Duke Nicholas Mikhailovich, concur in the opinion that Alexander did not receive the kind of education that would have best prepared him for the important position to which he was destined. Catherine invited Colonel La Harpe, a Swiss republican, and an enthusiastic though careful admirer of the ideas of the French revolution, to be Alexander's principal tutor. Michael Nikitich Muravyov was invited to instruct the grand duke in Russian and classical studies.

Although Muravyov was a very cultured man, well read, a writer of some repute, he was thoroughly unfitted to be a teacher. He began to read with Alexander and his brother Constantine, two years Alexander's junior, Latin and Greek authors like Demosthenes, Plutarch, Tacitus and the works of French and English philosophers of the time. Throughout his teachings he impressed upon his pupils lofty ideas about supreme human rationality, the welfare of humanity, the origins of society, the equality of man, the evils of despotism, of serfdom, etc. The practical Constantine escaped the influence of this liberal ideology, but the more sensitive Alexander was maimed for life. It must be borne in mind that all this food for thought was given to a boy between twelve and fourteen years of age— to a youth who could not possibly digest it and had to accept it as it was. At such an early period of life when boys live almost entirely by direct impressions and manifestations of their instincts, abstract ideas are transformed in their minds into concrete images, moral principles into actual feelings. The sort of instruction that La Harpe and Muravyov were giving to young Alexander gave him no real knowledge; neither did it train his mind logically nor introduce him to the historical present. In a word, it could not yet stimulate and seriously direct his thoughts. The elevated ideas of his two tutors were transformed in the mind of the twelve-year-old boy into a political fable which filled his imagination with images and moved his heart with feelings too mature for one of his tender years.

Alexander was taught how to feel and how to behave and not how to think and act. He was never given scientific or everyday problems to solve. He received for every question a ready-made answer—political and moral canons, indisputable truths which he had but to follow blindly. His brain was never put to the exercise of individual thinking but on the contrary absorbed like a sponge the distilled essence of western European thought. The grand duke never knew actual schoolwork with its tiny but important miseries and joys; he never experienced the strife of a schoolboy with his textbooks, the victories and defeats on the cold white pages of a copy book—those victories and defeats which alone, perhaps, give to the school its real educational importance. Alexander had read a great deal, had listened to even more, but he had never studied. It is easy, therefore, to understand why with the passing of years the idyllic picture painted for his youthful imagination by La Harpe and Muravyov gradually became a dream, all the more cherished because the realities of life with which Alexander came into contact were so far removed from all that had filled his heart and mind.

Alexander was not only the grandson of Catherine, but also the son of Paul, and his position between the two courts was a very awkward one. Every Friday, Alexander and his brother Constantine had had to go to Gatchina. There every Saturday

a parade of troops took place. It consisted in a merciless drilling
of men in which both grand dukes were forced to participate.
The first battalion was commanded by Paul himself, the second
by Alexander and the third by Constantine. After the parade,
the grand dukes returned to St. Petersburg. From military
maneuvers on a parade ground to the refined salons of Catherine,
from an almost puritan atmosphere such as prevailed in Gatchina, to the libertine, *fin de siècle* surroundings of the Court of
St. Petersburg, where high politics were discussed between
the showing of the latest French play and the telling of the
latest French joke, Alexander had to move smoothly, to be one
with his father, another with his grandmother—the eternal
Janus, adding to the two faces of the Greek god a third, his own.
How remote was this school of life from the idyllic school
through which Alexander went under the direction of La
Harpe and Muravyov. No wonder that leading such a dual life
Alexander sooner or later had to pay its price.

The years spent between Gatchina and St. Petersburg, instead of strengthening his character, weakened it, made it flex-
ible, adaptable to such an extent that Alexander himself did
not know sometimes what he wanted to do. Bogdanovich, the
Russian historian, wrote:

The character of Alexander I was composed of different
and even sharply contrasting elements: Christian humility
and pompousness, frivolity and studious activity, kindness
and resentfulness, persisting in his opinion about people who
once displeased him. But with all these different and changeable elements of his character, the dominating note was an

extraordinary art of knowing the right way to approach people, a remarkable ability to charm the hearts of all with whom he came in contact.

Such ability to charm, however, was attained only after long schooling in which affairs of the heart also played an important part. When Alexander reached his fifteenth year, the great Catherine deemed it expedient to have him married. She was aware that in the peculiar atmosphere of her court the young prince's passions had been aroused earlier than was usual, and she considered it necessary to protect Alexander from the court *amourettes* by giving him a wife. The youthful bride chosen for the future Emperor of All the Russias was Louisa-Augusta, Princess of Baden-Durlach, third daughter of Prince Karl-Friedrich, heir to the throne of the Duchy of Baden, and of his wife, Amalia, Princess of Hesse-Darmstadt. Princess Louisa, who was to be known as Elisabeth Alexeyevna, very soon won everyone's heart. Not only did Alexander gradually fall in love with her, but Empress Catherine, all her court, and even Paul and Maria Fyodorovna, Alexander's parents, could not find enough praise to express their delight at having found such a worthy companion for the young grand duke. Indeed, according to the testimony of contemporaries, Elisabeth was extremely attractive. "I have not seen anything more delightful and sylph-like than her waist, her agile movements and her pleasing behavior," wrote Count Komarovsky. Others stated that her features were fine and regular—a classic profile, large blue eyes, a perfect oval-shaped face. She had beautiful blonde hair, a graceful figure and an extraordinary lightness in all her movements. In addition to all these qualities she possessed also a very soft and melodious voice. No wonder Catherine called her a siren and remarked that her voice had the faculty of enveloping one's very heart.

On October 10, 1793, the two young people were married. Alexander was sixteen, his bride barely fifteen. Catherine wrote to Prince de Ligne: "It was the wedding of Psyche and Cupid."

The first years of Alexander's married life seem to have been fairly happy. The young couple had two children—two daughters, who died in infancy. The son whom all Russia desired was never born. With years, however, the "ideal" match, like so many similar ones, proved to be an unfortunate one.

One evening at one of the *soirées intimes,* so much favored by Empress Catherine that they had almost replaced the big receptions except upon extraordinary occasions, Alexander conversed with his friend and aide-de-camp, Prince Adam Czartoryski, in the winter garden at Catherine's palace. The soft music of a distant string orchestra reached them in a faint melodious whisper. Exotic plants exhaled a strange, penetrating aroma. Their unfamiliar forms stretched high to the glass ceiling through which one could see the cold glitter of the northern stars. The air was warm and damp. A small fountain mixed its gentle splashes with the strains of the music. The garden was lighted by softly shaded candles, well hidden behind the large leaves of tropical plants. One could imagine himself in distant lands where life seemed the more attractive because unknown, where people had not the worries of young princes already bent under the burden of future leadership, where eyes and smiles were frank and open and need not assume the rigidity of the mask, where women chose their lovers and men their wives, where blood ran faster and the joy of living mingled with the deep languid notes of passionate music. Alexander must have been under such impressions that evening; his glance was vague and his heart beat faster than usual, although the theme of his conversation with Prince Adam was hardly exciting—a comparison of the uniforms adopted by the Court of St. Petersburg and those of Gatchina!

Suddenly, Alexander heard approaching footsteps, and thinking he was about to be reprimanded for his isolation in the winter garden, he rose quickly. The next minute he realized his mistake. He heard a woman's voice and saw two young girls appear in the open space near the fountain. They were both very beautiful, but it was the elder who captured Alexander's fancy. At the sight of the grand duke they became visibly embarrassed and after performing a deep curtsy, they retired in haste to the salons of the palace. Alexander remained motionless and stared long in the direction they had taken. His mind retained the vision of a slender figure, of beautifully shaped, statuesque shoulders revealed by the court dress, of a mass of black hair and a pair of dark fiery eyes. Blood rushed to his head and a crimson flush colored his cheeks. He sat down again on the bench and covertly scrutinized the face of his friend to see if Prince Adam had noticed what had happened. But the prince's face revealed nothing to alarm Alexander. Prince Adam was not only a gentleman but also a born courtier. Reassured, Alexander asked Czartoryski whether he knew the young women. "The one with the black tresses is Princess Maria Sviatopolk-Chetvertinsky, lady in waiting to Her Imperial Majesty," was the reply. "She is my compatriot. Her father was hanged by the mob two years ago because he was a faithful friend of Russia.

She is an orphan and Her Imperial Majesty has taken her under her protection."

Late that night Alexander evoked the fugitive beauty of Princess Maria; her deep voice, somewhat veiled, sounded in his ears like exotic music from distant lands. The large dark eyes and long black tresses of the young Polish princess almost erased from his heart the angelic beauty of Elisabeth, and very soon they were to occupy an important place there for many years to come.

It is interesting to note that both Alexander and Napoleon, the man whom he was destined to fight and to defeat, found solace from their unhappy marital ventures in the embraces of two beautiful daughters of Poland. But the fair Alexander was less fortunate in his choice of Princess Maria Chetvertinsky, who was unfaithful to him, than the dark-haired Corsican with his blonde Countess Maria Walewska, who even followed him in his exile at Elba.

Princess Maria Antonovna Sviatopolk-Chetvertinsky became the wife of Dimitry Naryshkin, who belonged to one of the noblest families of Russia. Sometime after her marriage, in 1804, Maria Naryshkin became Alexander's mistress and remained his official companion not only with the tacit consent and knowledge of her own husband but also with that of Elisabeth. Maria Antonovna bore three children to Alexander, two daughters and one son. The eldest daughter, Zinaida, died as a child, in June, 1810; the second, Sophia, whom Alexander adored, and who had inherited her mother's beauty, died from consumption at the age of seventeen in 1824, on the very eve of her marriage with Count Andrey Shuvalov; the son, Emmanuel, enjoyed a long life. He died as Chief Marshal of the Household in the reign of the last emperor of Russia, Nicholas II.

Throughout his life Alexander captivated the imagination and captured the hearts of the fair sex. His charm was irresistible. It would not be an exaggeration to state that there was not a single young woman who, meeting Alexander, did not fall in love with him either secretly or openly. Even in his own family, his charm had disastrous effects. Although all his sisters were extremely fond of him, it was Catherine whom he preferred to all the others. The feelings which Alexander had for this sister of his were out of the ordinary and the relations which were established between them are revealed by their correspondence. These letters, a few excerpts from which follow, are extraordinary human documents.

Alexander to Catherine

Dear Bissiam,[1] your charming letter has given me the greatest of pleasure. I cannot express to you how sensible I am to all your friendship. I also love my dear Bissiam with all my heart and, oh! God knows, how anything coming from her touches me beyond expression.

My good friend, your letters are each one more charming than the preceding ones and I cannot tell you what real pleasure they give me. If you say that you are mad, at least you are the most delightful mad girl that has ever existed. At first I must declare that you have completely conquered me and that I am mad about you. Do you hear that? Goodby, Bissiamovna. *I adore you.*

Foolish little thing, put it out of your head that to answer

[1] Catherine's nickname.

your letters annoys me; on the contrary it is a real pleasure, because there are few things in this world which I love as much as my Bissiam. . . . Good-by, charm of my eyes, adoration of my heart. . . . All yours of heart and soul.

Catherine to Alexander

Dear Alexander, when taking hold of my pen in order to write to you, I felt somehow like a schoolgirl appearing before her teacher: she scratches her head not knowing her lesson and especially not knowing in what sort of humor her master is. However, I say to myself, if he wants it, all is well, if not he will tell me his reasons and then we shall see. Anyhow I say to you now: *Let us be friends, Cinna, it is I who invite you to this!* . . . Good-by, Dearest, all yours.

Alexander to Catherine

If my letters give you pleasure, my good friend, I assure you that yours are really a good deed. But you are absolutely ridiculous when you ask me not to write to you. Be assured that whenever I have a free minute it is a delight for me to write to you. Good-by, dearest friend, all yours for life.

Catherine to Alexander

Forgive my foolishness, Dearest, but as you have probably wished me in Jericho after the last two mails, I want to regain your favor again by this one; I have told you *my way of thinking.* Be angry, be wild! Let God preserve you from being cross, because the one who is cross usually suffers all the pain, but love me a little always. . . .

Alexander to Catherine

Dear Biskis,[2] how good you are to have written me again. I cannot tell you how much your letters please me, especially when I see from them that you behave yourself, because you insist upon being crazy without which you have *no value* (you know what this means) and then this is painful to me. It is indispensable to my happiness to be loved by you, because you are the most beautiful creature that has ever existed in this world. Good-by, dear foolishness of my soul, *I adore you and am only afraid lest you will despise me.*

. . . Alas! I cannot use my former rights (it's your feet that are in question, *do you understand?*) to press most tender kisses on them in your bedroom at Tver. . . .

Not only women experienced Alexander's charm and fell prey to its spell. When soon after his accession to the throne Alexander first visited Moscow, he was the object of a touching manifestation of the love that his people had for him. One morning when the sun shone bright and lighted the domes of Moscow's churches and the turrets of the Kremlin with multi-colored fires, Alexander called for his horse and rode alone down the Tverskaya, the principal street of the ancient capital. He saw the busy street open before him like the unfolding of a panorama. East and West mingled in the shops, both in the costumes and in the faces of the people. At first no one seemed to take any notice of the young officer in the simple green uniform without any decorations. Soon, however, people recognized their ruler whose attempt to imitate Harun-al-Rashid

[2] Catherine's nickname.

did not succeed. The news spread like wildfire down the street, into the shops, into the houses, and very soon Alexander found himself surrounded by a crowd which grew larger and larger with every minute.

The people pressed round him as strongly and at the same time as carefully as a passionate mother would press her beloved child to her breast. There were no shouts, no noise. A gentle whisper floated over the heads of the assembled people, and in it the emperor could distinguish their salutations: "Little Father," "Our Own," "Bright Sunshine" and many others which represented in the language of simple people of Russia everything that was most dear and most tender. The emperor's horse, the reins, the saddle, the emperor's clothes, everything that was close to his person became sanctified in the people's imagination. They kissed therefore his horse, his boots, his stirrup, as they would have kissed a holy icon or the relics of a saint. In the East the people used to fall to the ground terror-stricken before their rulers, in the West some centuries past they used to gaze upon their kings in respectful silence, but only in Russia have the tsars been so boldly and openly adored.

Thus to the title of Emperor and Autocrat of All the Russias Alexander was to add also that of Charmer. In fact this is the surname that the people of Alexander's immediate entourage gave him, as reported in the memoirs of Countess de Choiseul-Gouffier. But Alexander the Charmer was only a mask to cover his complex nature.

While the murderers of Emperor Paul were committing their infamous deed, Count Pahlen conversed with Alexander. The grand duke was under arrest and the visit of the Military Governor of the Capital at such a late hour was anything but usual. When Count Pahlen appeared before young Alexander, the latter was still under the spell of the latest scene he had had with his father. He was nervous, almost trembling. He had not been able to sleep. Very few could sleep in Mikhailovsky Castle. But Pahlen reassured him and explained that he wanted to consult the grand duke on a question of great importance.

It happened that the post of Military Governor of St. Petersburg had formerly (in the first years of Paul's reign) been occupied by Alexander himself. Pahlen told the grand duke that he wished to resign his military governorship, but that he did not dare do so unless he knew with certainty who would succeed him. Pahlen wanted to know whether Alexander would accept this office again. Alexander understood, of course, that this was nothing but a pretext, and refused to commit himself in any way.

As for Count Pahlen, his nocturnal visit had a very definite purpose. In the event that the conspiracy was successful, he wanted to be the first to announce the news to the new emperor; on the other hand, should it be a failure, he was determined to sacrifice Alexander in order to save himself. He would have arrested the grand duke and accused him of leading the conspiracy. Throughout, he counted on the unlimited trust of Emperor Paul in his own faithfulness and on the strained relations existing between father and son.

They talked—a wise fox and a frightened hare. Suddenly the door flew open and one of the conspirators jubilantly entered

the room. Before he had had time to speak, Count Pahlen arose
and said: "His Imperial Majesty Emperor Paul is dead. I con-
gratulate Your Imperial Majesty upon Your Majesty's accession to the throne of his ancestors. The king is dead—long live
the king!"

III

DREAMS AND REALITY

TEN DAYS had passed since Paul's death. The new emperor was holding his first big reception in the Winter Palace, his new residence, which had also been that of Catherine the Great. Brilliant lights flooded the large building. Sleighs and coaches drawn by powerful horses deposited at the main entrance of the palace high dignitaries of the empire, generals, staff officers, officials of the state. Resplendent uniforms embroidered in gold and silver, contrasting strangely with the deep mourning of the ladies, glittered in the light of thousands of candles. All eyes were radiant and rested with admiration and hope upon the new emperor.

Alexander's slender figure in the green uniform of the Semyonovsky Regiment, his own regiment—the same that had helped the conspirators—moved among his guests with a shyness natural to a young man hardly accustomed to all this manifestation of admiration. His beautiful open face looked like that of a young Greek god, and everything about the twenty-four year old ruler of the mighty Russian Empire seemed to promise fulfillment of the expectations of his subjects and to raise great hopes for the coming of a new era. A festive spirit,

a feeling of joy, animated everyone who came to this reception.
People greeted each other with exclamations of happiness, with
congratulations; some of them even kissed each other as if it
were the night of Holy Easter.

After the reception was over, Alexander, tired, his ears still
ringing with mellow, servile words, his eyes still dazzled by the
brilliancy of uniforms, by the shimmering stars and crosses of
Russian and foreign decorations, went to his own study and
sank into a chair before his desk. He closed his eyes. When he
opened them he saw with amazement a large, sealed envelope in
the middle of his desk. It was addressed to him. He wondered
how it could have been placed there in his own study, to which
no one but himself had access. He broke the seal and began to
read. What he read was new to him and appealing. For the first
time in his life, someone had dared to write to him openly,
freely, making suggestions, giving advice, expressing hopes that
the new emperor would fulfill his subjects' expectations. But
the letter was not signed. The author did not have enough confidence in the young emperor to disclose his identity. This
saddened Alexander, but he determined to find the one who
had been bold enough to write him in this vein.

When later Count Pahlen and Troshchinsky, then Minister
of State, entered the emperor's study, Alexander rose and said:
"Gentlemen, an unknown man placed this letter on my desk;
it is unsigned. I want you to find him and bring him to me."
Having dismissed them, Alexander read the letter over once
more. The author appealed to the emperor's noble heart. He
evoked the dreams Alexander had cherished for so long. He
gave a brilliant description of the situation in which the new
emperor would find his empire, and continued:

Passing in the night by your palace, I imagined this picture of your blessed political situation and wondered what ways you will choose. Is it possible, I said to myself, that he will destroy deliberately this perfect harmony of heaven and earth in his favor and will leave the work of one-half of a century unfinished? Is it possible that he will calmly sacrifice for the simple pleasure of autocracy the hope of nations, the immortal glory and that reward which after a long, serene and happy life awaits benevolent rulers in the country of felicity? No! He will finally open that book of our fate and that of our descendants which Catherine but indicated. He will give us nontransgressable laws. He will establish them now and forever by an oath of all his subjects. He will tell Russia: "Here are the limits of my own autocracy and of that of my heirs, immovable and forever."

Then at last Russia will enter into the family of constitutional monarchies and the iron scepter of personal despotism will never be able to destroy the tablets of her scriptures. . . . Nations will always be what the governments want them to be: Ivan the Terrible wanted to have speechless slaves, obedient to him, cruel to themselves. And he had them. Peter wanted to see us modeled after foreign patterns; unfortunately we became foreigners in our own country. Wise Catherine began to form real Russians; Alexander will complete this great task.

It is easy to understand why Alexander was so moved by this message. The dreams of his youth, the teachings of La Harpe and Muravyov found their echo in this anonymous epistle. All that was best in the emperor's heart was revived, brought

forth by this sincere address of an unknown subject. The appeal
to Alexander in the name of Catherine the Great, the admiration that the author expressed at viewing the work of his grandmother, touched the emperor the more because in his first
manifesto, announcing his accession to the throne of his ancestors, the young monarch had already promised "to rule over
his people on the throne conferred on him by God, in accord
with the laws and heart of the Great Catherine." And the very
name of that empress, after the terror of Paul's reign, was a
symbol of liberal and humanistic ideas.

The next morning Troshchinsky reported to the emperor
that he had found the culprit, and brought him to face his
sovereign. It was an employee of one of Troshchinsky's chanceries, a young man by the name of Basil Nazarovich Karazin.
Having thanked Troshchinsky for his zeal, Alexander dismissed him and invited Karazin to his study. When he was left
alone with him he asked: "Did you write this letter to me?"

"I am sorry, Your Majesty," Karazin replied.

Then the emperor came close to him and said: "Let me embrace you for it. I thank you and wish I had more subjects like
you. Please continue to tell me the truth." Alexander pressed
him to his heart and Karazin, moved to tears, fell to the emperor's feet and swore that he would always tell him the truth.
Alexander invited Karazin to sit down, and conversed with him
at great length. He told Karazin to communicate directly with
him by personal letters thereafter and to use his study at any
time the young man desired to do so. When the interview came
to an end there stepped out of the emperor's study a new
Marquis Posa who for a time was to help a new bewildered Don
Carlos.

Karazin came from a distinguished noble family of Little Russia. Like all young men of his class, he had entered the army and had become, in due course of time, an officer in the Semyonovsky Regiment of the Imperial Guards. But he did not remain in the army for long. Moved by a desire for knowledge, he had abandoned his military career at the age of twenty-five in order to study Russian conditions and the natural sciences. This was at the time when Paul's despotism had reached its heights. Russia was actually tortured by her ruler. When Karazin had seen enough of his country's martyrdom, he decided, in disgust, to leave it and to seek a better life in foreign lands. But Paul had forbidden his subjects to cross the frontier, so Karazin was refused a passport. He then decided to follow a daring plan and to cross the frontier illegally. While crossing the Niemen River, he was seized by dragoons and taken to Kovno. It seemed that there was no hope left for Karazin, as such infringements of Paul's orders were severely punished. But as a drowning man grasps even at a straw, Karazin turned to the one chance he still had left, notwithstanding its apparent hopelessness and obvious danger. Preceding the official report, he wrote directly to Emperor Paul on August 26, 1798. In this letter he confessed his crime of disobedience to the emperor's orders. Then he explained his reasons for doing it:

I wanted to hide from your rule, fearful of its brutality. . . . Many examples of your arbitrary rule are reported throughout your empire, and, although they are perhaps exaggerated tenfold, they trouble my thoughts and imagination day and night. I was not aware of committing any fault. In the seclusion of country life I had no occasion nor any reason to insult you. But my liberal ideas were already a crime. . . . Now it is in your power either to punish me and thus give a manifest realization to my fears or to forgive me and make me shed tears of repentance because I had such false ideas about my great and merciful ruler.

Strangely enough this frank appeal had a salutary effect. Not often did Paul hear the truth from his subjects. Fear of his despotism, which had decided a young man to flee his empire, puzzled the emperor. He received the "criminal" and said: "I shall prove to you, young man, that you are mistaken, that service in Russia cannot be bad even under my rule. In which department do you wish to serve?" Although service in Russia was not exactly Karazin's aim when he attempted to leave the country, he had no choice at the time. So Karazin named the department directed by Troshchinsky, the most enlightened of Paul's ministers. The emperor commanded him to be appointed and to be left in peace.

Such a man, of course, was a treasure for Alexander. Karazin's untiring activity and his profound scientific education were far above ordinary. He was an astronomer and chemist, a scholar of agronomy and of statistics, an economist and a talented student of finance. But above all he was alive, bringing to every problem discussed an original point of view. Alexander showed his appreciation. He called for Karazin and discussed state reforms; with him he sought measures for the amelioration of the Russian people's sufferings. Karazin elaborated in great detail measures to free the serfs. He drew up a project for the creation of a ministry of education. From the nobles and wealthy merchants of Little Russia he obtained vast sums of money for a gigantic project of a university in Kharkov, the principal city in that part of the Russian Empire, although to accomplish this he often had to humiliate himself by begging, almost on his knees. Alexander was more than satisfied with Karazin's work, but already some unknown force had begun to build barriers in the path of Karazin's success.

The ministry of education was founded, but it was far from Karazin's original project. The university in Kharkov became a reality, but instead of a central institution of learning to serve not only for all of Little Russia but for the southwestern Slav nations as well, it materialized into nothing more than a provincial German *Hochschule*. Karazin had sought the greatest minds of the scientific world for this university. Laplas and Fichte had consented to come, but the government found them too expensive. It seemed that all Karazin's wonderful projects were to share the fate of these two. His brilliant career was envied by many. Some of them were close enough to the throne to have the ear of the emperor. They tried to prejudice the young sovereign against his faithful collaborator by painting the latter as a vain and ambitious man who was gradually usurping Alexander's autocratic power.

Alexander was accustomed to organizing literary *soirées* in the Winter Palace to which were invited only a selected few. At one of these gatherings they listened to the reading of *Don Carlos*, a new tragedy by Schiller. After the reader had completed his task, silence pervaded the room. The emperor seemed to be engrossed in his thoughts. His eyes looked vaguely at the painted ceiling. Did he think about his own life which seemed to resemble so closely that of Don Carlos? Or did he recall his own Philip? Suddenly in the complete silence a loud whisper was heard. Prince Alexander Nikolayevich Golitsyn said to Count Kochubey in a whisper, but intentionally loud enough so that everybody, and especially the emperor, should hear it: "We have our own Marquis Posa." Kochubey grinned and turned his eyes upon Karazin who sat at a little distance. Everybody in the room did likewise.

Alexander stared at the gathering, then looked at Karazin. A sudden suspicion seized his mind. He frowned, obviously displeased, and after bowing to the persons present, left the room. Prince Golitsyn smiled. The future Minister of Education and of Spiritual Affairs, a mason and an inquisitor, Director of the Biblical Society and of the State Post, an intimate friend of Alexander—to such an extent that in the space of ten years he had dined with him over three thousand times—was pleased. Knowing Alexander's suspicious character, he was sure that his word would bear fruit, and he was not mistaken. He did not himself know why he was preparing the downfall of the talented young Karazin, but as a thorough courtier he deemed it wise and expedient to put aside one who had such a hold on the monarch.

The break soon came. In 1804, Karazin had just returned from a tour of inspection upon which he had been sent by the emperor to investigate the activity of Governor Lopukhin. He had uncovered terrible abuses, and the governor was brought to justice. Karazin went with his report to Alexander. The emperor received him frowning. "You show my letters to others," he said. "*Sire*," began the unfortunate man, but Alexander did not allow him to speak. "Others," he said, "know what I have written only to you and have never spoken to anyone else. You may go."

It was the dismissal, the final break. Alexander did not know that even an emperor's messages were not immune from the eyes of postal officials, a fact he was to learn only some years later. And so ended one of the most fruitful collaborations that has ever existed between a sovereign and one of his subjects. And for Alexander, particularly, the break was perhaps a disastrous one.

As a whole, the first four years of Alexander's reign completely transformed life in Russia. It is almost impossible to enumerate all the decrees that were enacted by the young emperor, but a few of them will suffice to show the trend of that new era which dawned in 1801. The freedom of the cities and the personal liberty of the nobility were restored. Ten thousand civilian and military servants whom Paul had discharged and deprived of civil rights were returned to their posts. The frontiers were thrown open and Russians could go abroad again and foreigners could enter Russia. The secret police, the famous Secret Expedition, founded by Empress Anna Ioanovna, was abolished. Torture was strictly forbidden. Although Paul had already abrogated this survival of the Middle Ages, the order had never been enforced and torture had been practiced in Russian courts throughout his reign. Private printing offices were again permitted to exist and foreign books were allowed to be brought into the country. The arbitrary system of censorship which had prevailed during the reign of Paul and even during that of Catherine was completely reformed. Based upon a set of liberal rules, its supervision and enforcement were not entrusted to narrow-minded bureaucrats, but to a committee of university professors. This reform, and Alexander's personal interest in literature, were responsible to a great extent for the appearance of much literary talent in Russia.

It is seldom [wrote the Russian historian Bogdanovich] that a sovereign gives such encouragement to literature as did Emperor Alexander. Worthy literary productions by people in active service of the State were rewarded by advancement, decorations and pensions; writers who were not in the government service often received valuable presents and gifts of money. As the circulation of books, particularly of a scientific nature, was still so small that it could not offer sufficient royalties to compensate adequately many authors, the emperor often gave these authors important sums of money in order to encourage them to further literary activity.

Many writers began to send their manuscripts directly to the emperor and if they had any value at all, Alexander usually ordered their printing at his own expense and then presented the whole edition to the author. When Karamzin, the well-known Russian historian, expressed a desire to undertake the writing of a history of the Russian State, the emperor conferred upon him the title of Official Historiographer of the Empire, gave him a pension of two thousand rubles, and ordered the publication of the voluminous work at the expense of the State.

Whilst he plunged himself into the tremendous activity which gave birth to so many reforms, Alexander attracted new men who were eager to give him their utmost co-operation.

These were his personal friends, companions of his youth, who had been scattered over the almost endless expanse of the empire during Paul's reign and who now returned to St. Petersburg to join the intimate circle surrounding the young monarch. They were Nicholas Novossiltsov, Count Victor Kochubey, Count Paul Stroganov, and Prince Adam Czartoryski. These men came from noble families with a tradition of service to the crown. They had also received an education similar to that of the emperor himself. Count Stroganov's tutor had been a Frenchman by the name of Rosque, a republican, member of the Convention and author of the French republican calendar. Rosque's influence on Stroganov was as great as that of La Harpe on Alexander. Kochubey and Novossiltsov had lived in England where they became converted to English constitutional ideas. As for Czartoryski, his Polish ancestry and French education made him a typical liberal of the time.

At first these men did not occupy official positions, but later Kochubey was Minister of the Interior; Czartoryski, Minister of Foreign Affairs; Stroganov, Minister of Public Instruction; and Novossiltsov, Secretary of State. They would gather together in Alexander's study to discuss with him the important problems the new regime was facing. Society people of the capital and experienced old courtiers laughed at them and considered their gatherings more an emperor's fancy than a serious attempt to reform Russia. Alexander himself gave this unofficial committee a republican name, calling it the Committee of Public Welfare. However, it was precisely in this committee that most of Alexander's early reforms were elaborated, discussed and prepared for execution. Among these were the creation of ministries under responsible heads and the first timid step toward the emancipation of the serfs in the law of 1803, which established a new peasant class of "free farmers."

All these measures seemed designed to wipe from the memory of Russians the evil recollections of the former reign.

At first Alexander did not know what steps to take against Count Pahlen, the Zubov brothers, and the other leaders of the conspiracy. Perhaps he still feared them. But when he found support in La Harpe, his former tutor and friend, who had returned to Russia on the express invitation of the young monarch, he felt he was not alone. Moreover, he began to realize that public opinion would condemn him if he suffered the presence of his father's murderers any longer. On October 30, 1801, La Harpe had written a long letter to Alexander expressing himself on the subject. He reassured his former pupil on the question of the latter's participation in the conspiracy, but exhorted him to take stern measures against the assassins, for in committing their crime they had overreached themselves, as their new legitimate ruler had never agreed to bloodshed but had given his approval only to a forced abdication. He then continued:

> As Your Majesty asks my opinion I shall tell you that you have only two ways before you. To follow the first is to admit that the murder was accidental, which is a hard thing to believe. But even in this case all persons connected with it should be compelled to leave the capital, a thing they themselves should have done long ago. The second way is to let the law follow its course.

There was at that time an important group of Russian people who considered Emperor Paul as their benefactor. These were the *raskolniki*, the "old believers," a religious sect which had been persecuted since the time of Peter the Great and had had no legal standing in the Russian Empire. Paul had granted them the freedom of their belief, authorized them to have their own houses of worship and to enjoy the practice of their particular rules of life. After the news of Paul's murder had reached them, they felt that a great wrong had been done them and, to express their protest, they sent to Paul's widow, Empress Maria Fyodorovna, holy images with texts from the Scriptures, which were of a character to alarm Count Pahlen. Pahlen approached Alexander in a highly nervous state and said that the dowager empress was setting the people against him and the other members of the conspiracy (meaning Alexander also) by the display of these holy images. Emperor Alexander demanded to see them and found that the incriminating text was taken from Chapter IX of the Second Book of Kings, and read: "Had Zimri peace, who slew his master?" When Empress Maria Fyodorovna heard about this step of Pahlen's, she expressed to Alexander her utter displeasure at the way he had dared to blacken her in the eyes of her son.

This was the opportunity Alexander had waited for. The next morning when the count arrived on the parade ground in his coach drawn by six horses and was ready to alight, an aide-de-camp of the emperor invited him by order of Alexander to retire to his estate in Kurland. Without a word Pahlen obeyed. The same evening Count Nicholas Zubov suffered a similar fate.

The new emperor adopted a remarkably simple mode of life. He appeared in the streets of his capital alone, without the usual protection of police or of a bodyguard. He dressed without extravagance, usually wearing the simple green uniform of the

Semyonovsky Regiment, without decorations, even without a watch. He was quite satisfied when passers-by simply lifted their hats to greet him. Nor did it matter when people ignored him completely during these lonely promenades. This impressed his subjects, particularly when they compared his ways to those of the late Emperor Paul. Paul had ordered that everyone who should meet him in the streets, with no exception even for ladies, should greet him with a deep bow; and if the people were riding in a coach, they were to step out in the road to perform the curtsy. It happened one day, when it was raining and the unpaved streets of the capital were transformed into rivers of mud, that a young lady riding in her coach met the emperor. Knowing Paul's rigorous enforcement of his rules, the young lady stepped out quickly into the mud. Paul was so embarrassed at the sight of a pretty girl knee deep in the muddy river of a St. Petersburg street, that he shouted to her: "Sit down, sit down!" meaning, of course, that the young lady should re-enter her carriage. But the spell of terror was so great in Paul's capital that the lady obeyed literally and sat herself down in the mud.

One can understand, therefore, the feeling of relief that pervaded the minds of the Russian people after the accession of Alexander. The young, handsome, and amiable monarch won every heart. Russia was ready to serve him, to give him all her support in everything he might attempt to do for her progress. Karazin's first appeal to Alexander seemed to have borne fruit. The emperor expressed openly his desire to end once and for all the era of arbitrary rule and to base the life of the nation on firm and immutable laws. When a titled lady of the court addressed a request to him in which she asked for an exceptional favor and said that the emperor could grant it if he pleased since he stood above the law, Alexander replied that he did not recognize any power on earth which did not originate in the existing laws.

Despite the far-reaching reforms conceived by Alexander and his collaborators, the enactment of these measures met with stubborn resistance on the part of the conservative class of nobility. This opposition forced Alexander more than once to compromise and to sacrifice his ideals for the sake of expediency. Gradually overpowered by the opposition, the dreams of Alexander and his Committee of Public Welfare for completely reforming Russia faded. Their enthusiasm and zeal were no match for the practical experienced men who opposed them so persistently. Alexander's friends had hoped that he would follow resolutely the path which they had traced in the meetings of the committee. They now began to realize that Russia under Alexander had no chance of becoming a second England with its traditional liberty under a strictly constitutional and parliamentary government. Dreamers themselves, they could not visualize the necessity of facing reality. So one by one they left the emperor. Novossiltsov went to live in his beloved Albion; Count Stroganov exchanged the pen of a reformer for the sword of a soldier; Count Kochubey retired to his estates to lead the life of a country gentleman; Prince Czartoryski applied his activity to his native Poland as Curator of the Educational District of Vilno. Alexander remained alone. He would have liked to follow the example of his friends and to retire to a quiet life, as he had dreamed when a youth. But one cannot abandon the inherited responsibility of a throne as easily as one can relinquish a public office. In 1803, he wrote in one of his letters to La Harpe:

When Providence shall bless me with bringing Russia to the degree of prosperity that I desire, I shall deem it my first duty to cast aside the burden of rule and to retire to some remote corner of Europe wherefrom I shall be able to watch and to enjoy the felicity of my country.

Equipped as he was with an armor of ideals, enveloped in a cape of dreams, Alexander was easily vanquished by the solid weapons of stern reality, weapons that had been forged for centuries. Heir to a mighty empire, he brought with him no experience to fulfill the difficult task of ruling, nor any strong desire to persevere in the task. He faced his responsibilities with the lightheartedness and enthusiasm of a schoolboy at his first class, but found only too soon that the problems requiring solution were not so simple as he had imagined; that, perhaps, they were even beyond his capacity. Realizing that he would eventually have to concede victory to the reactionary forces strongly entrenched in his realm, Alexander gradually abandoned his reforming activities and retired more and more within himself.

In the time to come, however, he was to recall more than once the first happy years of his reign. Notwithstanding their feverish activity, they were peaceful years as compared with those that fate had in store for him, the shadows of which were already visible on the horizon. The thunder of marching French grenadiers was even then echoing over the expanse of Europe.

The ambition of a single man was set against the historical heritage of a whole continent. Little did this man know that a handsome young sovereign of a distant land was to be his nemesis. Alexander the Dreamer had been vanquished by the forces of reality because he could not cope with them. A new Alexander, fortified by a knowledge of men, was ready to resume the struggle. And fate gave him a new and powerful opponent, worthy to be an emperor's antagonist. It was—Napoleon.

IV

THE RIVALS

THERE is no doubt that Napoleon had a better chance of development than Alexander, hampered as the latter was by inherited responsibilities, driven from one extreme to another, first by his educators and later by the circumstances which beset him. He said himself: "I am accused of being suspicious, but, is it not known that from the time I began to reason I have seen nothing but misfortune around me? Everything I have undertaken has turned into disaster against me."

From the time of his childhood Napoleon played the leader with his playmates at Ajaccio. In his youth, in Brienne, he seized every opportunity to perfect himself, to prepare himself for his future role of leader of men. He developed great will power. He did not know what fate had in reserve for him, but it seems that he always governed his actions in order to be ready when his hour would come. He chose his own subjects to study, and early in his youth he abandoned as unnecessary all humanistic branches of learning in order to devote all his attention and capacity to the service of mathematics and of the exact sciences. He trained his mind by efforts of will for this purpose, and all through his extraordinary life he was able to use his fantastic memory to remember dates, dispositions of battles, columns of statistics—unable at the same time to memorize even a few lines of poetry. He prepared even his imagination to work for him as a faithful and reliable servant. Nature, and not art, was the stimulus for his imagination, and he was able to recall the exact topographic characteristics of a landscape years after having seen it, although at the time he might not have attached much importance to it. His brain registered everything that could be useful to him at some later date, as if it were the film of a photographic camera.

He learned how to dominate his moods, how to conceal his temper, because he knew that such a mastery would become useful to him. He became proficient in the science of ruling men. He brought his own physical nature under control—he needed only three hours of sleep and almost nothing to eat—thus gaining more time for work. All this was possible for him to achieve because no one disturbed him, no one intervened in his everyday life with advice, recommendations or demands. He was unknown then, still in the shadow of history, left alone and in peace to become the young man who attained prominence with his first appearance in Toulon.

Alexander's childhood and youth were crowded with too many advisers. They unwittingly dissolved amid disorder all that was orderly and solid in his character. Napoleon gathered his forces into one whole; he prepared himself, like a block of steel, by gradual tempering. Alexander moved between pleasure and disappointment. Napoleon worked hard and thought much; Alexander gathered knowledge like a butterfly, choosing that which was beautiful and elevated. Napoleon accepted for himself only that which was practical and useful; Alexander came out of school years an idealist. Thus, when they started their careers, Alexander was soon lost in contradictions, lofty though they were, while Napoleon showed himself in Italy to be such a master that he received immediate recognition and respect from older and more experienced men, like Massena and Augereau.

Both Alexander and Napoleon had to fight for their thrones. Both obtained their thrones through violence. But the conspiracy of 1801 was purely of a palace nature, while the overthrow of the Convention, in 1799, was a real coup d'état. Though Alexander did nothing but take a little earlier that which belonged to him by right of birth, Napoleon really usurped the power of the people. Nevertheless, Alexander's act carried with it a more personal and deeper moral effect than Napoleon's. Both received punishment and made expiation: Napoleon at Saint Helena and Alexander in Siberia.

It may be recalled that Victor Hugo, one of the greatest admirers of Napoleon that ever lived, could not forgive his hero the violence of the 18th Brumaire. And Napoleon realized himself how unstable his power was so long as it rested upon usurpation. The 18th Brumaire was a success, but it had an unfortunate result in that from then on the people demanded success from Napoleon. Once the crown was given for saving the country from anarchy and foreign invasion, it was obvious that the people would refuse their support to the emperor of the French in case of any failure however small. Everyone knew it, everyone including Napoleon himself. He said to Metternich:

Your sovereigns, born on the throne, have the privilege of letting themselves be beaten twenty times and are still able to return to their capitals as rulers. I cannot afford it, because I am a soldier of fortune. My power will end on the day when I shall cease to be strong and awe-inspiring.

That is why Napoleon strove continually to achieve spectacular effects in order to hold the imagination of his people in a state of continuous wonder. It is the reason also that led him to attempt to intimidate his opponents. He succeeded so long as he had to deal with men upon whose imagination and feelings he had influence, but the day he encountered a man who was not afraid of him, who opposed the crudeness of a conqueror with the skill and finesse of a born diplomat, and who was in his own faith as fanatical as Napoleon in his, the spell was broken.

Metternich has said: "Alexander's character represents a strange blending of the qualities of a man and the weaknesses of a woman." And La Ferronays, at one time French ambassador in St. Petersburg, added: "If Alexander were to be dressed in woman's clothes he would have made a shrewd woman." Napoleon went further when he said that all the affinities of Alexander's character "lacked something" to make them "the qualities of a man." That is why, perhaps, they resembled much more "the weaknesses of a woman." There is no doubt that precisely these attributes of "a shrewd woman" were responsible for molding Alexander into a great diplomat. In the struggles of the conference room, where shrewdness, hypocrisy, and the ability to hide the truth were the accepted weapons, Alexander was really a great figure. The well-known Russian historian, Alexander Kiesewetter, has said: "Alexander was a born diplomat, as much as Napoleon was a born general."

Although apparently very different in character, Alexander and Napoleon shared a mutual distrust of men. Alexander once said to General de Sanglain: "I do not trust anyone; men are scoundrels." Chapsal reported in his memoirs that "Napoleon did not believe in either virtue or honesty. He often termed these two words 'abstractions.'" And General Mathew Dumas wrote that Napoleon had once said to him: "You cannot be different from other men; all of them think first of their personal interests." As a result of this attitude on the part of the two rivals, each surrounded himself with bureaucratic mediocrities, and their struggle held, therefore, more the aspects of a personal duel than of a fight between two nations, between two empires.

In the first years of Alexander's reign, Russia's relations with France, though never cordial, were at least outwardly friendly. Alexander was feeling his way carefully in the complicated game of diplomacy. Napoleon was eager to win the young sovereign to his side, as France was still engaged in a war with England. The First Consul of the French Republic sent the trusted Caulaincourt as his first ambassador to Alexander's court with instructions to revive the talks of an alliance which were held in the last months of Paul's reign. But Alexander refused to commit himself, turning a deaf ear to accusations that his collaborators, and particularly Novossiltsov, were making him a tool of England.

When in 1802, the war between France and England was ended by the Peace of Amiens, the urgency of obtaining Russia's help vanished and Napoleon's diplomacy turned to other quarters. It was then that Alexander, following a romantic meeting at Memel with beautiful Queen Louisa of Prussia, decided to espouse Prussia's cause and help her wrest from Napoleon the last territories on the Rhine.

The opportunity for a break with Napoleon presented itself in 1804. The unwarranted execution of the Duke d'Enghien revolted Alexander. He sent two vehement notes: one to the German diet in Regensburg in which he invited all the German states to protest against the violation of German territory, because the unfortunate last Condé had been captured by the French on the territory of the Duchy of Baden; and the other to France in which Alexander expressed his indignation at the unlawful act perpetrated by agents of the French Republic. This note, delivered to Talleyrand, then Napoleon's Minister of Foreign Affairs, by the Russian chargé d'affaires on May 12, received an unexpected reply. On May 16, Talleyrand handed the Russian representative a counter note dictated by Bonaparte in which the first consul unequivocally reminded the Russian emperor of the latter's participation in the murder of Paul, and expressed his surprise that a person whose hands were stained with the blood of his own father should presume to protest against an execution which had been necessary for the political tranquillity of France. The note also accused Alexander of having made his protest under the influence of the British government.

This, naturally, led to an open break between France and Russia. On May 17, Bonaparte recalled his ambassador at the Court of St. Petersburg, and on May 18, the Corsican was proclaimed emperor. Bonaparte disappeared and Napoleon made his entry on the stage of Europe.

Grand Duke Constantine in Polish uniform

Grand Duke Alexander at the age of 18

View of the Winter Palace from across the Neva River
From an eighteenth-century engraving in the author's collection

Alexander then proceeded to form a coalition against France. The timid king of Prussia refused to enter the field at the time as Prussia was not prepared for a campaign. Alexander turned to Austria. On November 6, 1804, Austria signed an alliance with Russia. On January 14, 1805, Russia signed a treaty of alliance with Sweden, and on April 11, one with England. On August 9, Austria joined the Anglo-Russian alliance by means of a special declaration. War was now inevitable. On September 21, 1805, Alexander left his capital in order to join the army stationed on the Austrian frontier.

It was a gray, foggy day. Clouds hung low over St. Petersburg, dark and menacing. A strange feeling of fear, almost of awe, gripped Alexander's heart. Two days before, he had visited a venerable hermit by the name of Sevastianov, who had implored the emperor not to start a war against the "accursed Frenchman," because it was too soon and would do no good. "Your time has not come yet," the old man had said. "He will beat you and destroy your army; you will have to flee in shame. Wait, get stronger, your hour will still come, then God will help you to destroy the power of the enemy of mankind." Alexander felt that perhaps the hermit was right, that he should not attempt to do what seemed to be beyond his power. But the die was cast—Napoleon had already opened his brilliant campaign against Austria. He had defeated the Austrian army under General Mack at Ulm; he had occupied Vienna, crossed the Danube and advanced as far as Brünn.

On November 18, Alexander reached Olmütz where Emperor Francis of Austria with the remnants of his army awaited his ally and protector. The military situation seemed to be precarious. Kutuzov, the Russian general who was appointed commander in chief of the allied armies, advised caution and urged the opening of negotiations for peace with Napoleon. However, the younger generals, led by Prince Peter Dolgoruky, assured the emperor of the imminence of victory. This young nobleman, more than anyone else perhaps, should be held responsible for the disaster of Austerlitz.

A descendant of one of Russia's most illustrious families, Prince Peter was born on December 19, 1777. As was customary at that time, he was inscribed on the lists of the Izmailovsky Regiment of the Guards almost from the day of his birth and, while not actually serving, received promotions so that at the age of fifteen he was already a captain. The next year he started his military service with the rank of major, having been appointed aide-de-camp to his uncle, then governor general of Moscow. Three years later he was a colonel in the Arkharov Regiment. He was then not quite twenty years of age.

In spite of this brilliant career, Prince Peter was not satisfied with his garrison duties. He addressed a petition to Emperor Paul to be given a more active appointment. This petition was refused. Undaunted he sent another one, this time receiving an admonition "not to bother His Majesty any further."

He then took a dangerous step by appealing to the heir to the throne. Alexander became interested in the case of Prince Peter, as it was unusual for a young officer to seek something to do at a time when the almost universal desire in the empire was to do nothing. He was able to intercede for Dolgoruky whom Paul appointed commandant of the fortress of Smolensk. In less than three months the young colonel brought order into the affairs of his command which had been thoroughly neglected by his predecessor and, on December 23, 1798, he was rewarded by an appointment as General Aide-de-Camp to His Imperial Majesty.

Alexander took him under his wing and, after ascending the throne, entrusted him with a number of special missions which Dolgoruky carried out successfully, thus gaining greater favor with the young emperor.

On the eve of Austerlitz it was really Dolgoruky, the Austrian general Weiroter, and Alexander who gave orders to the allied armies instead of Kutuzov, the commander in chief.

In Olmütz, Alexander received the visit of General Savary whom Napoleon had sent to open negotiations for peace. This, and the fact that a few days prior to the French general's visit the allied armies had had a successful encounter with Napoleon's troops at Wischau, completely turned the heads of Alexander's advisers who now felt sure that Napoleon was afraid to give general battle and that, consequently, victory for the allies was assured. Savary returned to his master with a report stating that Prince Peter and the young generals surrounding Alexander were determined to fight and would inevitably commit blunders, while the experienced and wise generals against whom there would be less chance for victory were kept inactive. In order to gain time for the concentration of his troops, Napoleon sent Savary to the allied camp again, requesting a personal meeting with Alexander. In answer to this, the emperor sent Dolgoruky to Moravia to meet the emperor of the French.

Napoleon, surrounded by a small group of generals, was riding down the road in order to inspect the advance posts when he saw a Russian general advancing toward him on horseback. He drew up his mount and began to converse with Alexander's messenger. After inquiring about the health of the Russian emperor, he continued:

"How long have we to fight? What do you want from me? What does Emperor Alexander desire? If he wants to enlarge his states let him do it at the expense of his neighbors, Turkey especially, and then he will have no disputes with France."

Prince Dolgoruky openly showed his contempt in talking to Napoleon. His answers were haughty and insolent. He said that no one had the right to dictate to the Russian emperor concerning his conduct; that Alexander had no animosity toward France, but that he was determined to free Europe from French subjugation. "Russia should follow a different line of policy and think of her own interests first," Napoleon interrupted the young messenger of Alexander. Then, visibly annoyed, he said, "Well, if you wish it, we shall fight." Prince Dolgoruky remounted his horse and galloped back to the Russian lines without even taking leave of Napoleon. During the entire conversation he did not address Napoleon with the customary "Your Majesty." He spoke to the emperor of the French as if he were a vulgar *parvenu*. One can understand in what a fury this left Napoleon. In his 30th Bulletin he mentioned this meeting and said that he would not have accepted Russia's conditions even if Russian troops were occupying the heights of Montmartre. He called Alexander's envoy: *"un fréluquet impertinent, ce polisson de Dolgoruky,"* [1] and complained that Prince Peter

---

[1] "An insolent nincompoop, this mischievous Dolgoruky."

had spoken to him as if he were a Russian subject about to be exiled to Siberia. This was one of the blunders of which Savary had spoken and one which had a catastrophic effect, because Prince Peter Dolgoruky had had a chance to avoid the defeat at Austerlitz, which opportunity he did not seize.

The morning of December 2, 1805, was cold. The allied armies started to execute the detailed disposition of General Weiroter in a dense morning mist. Many of the detachments lost their way and encountered the enemy where, according to the Austrian strategist, the enemy should not have been. By noon the battle was lost, but the fighting continued.

Alexander had remained with the Fourth Army Group. During the battle he was lost from sight by most of the persons attached to him. Only his court surgeon, Sir James Wylie, Bt., and four aides remained with him throughout the long hours of the battle. Toward evening, Major Tohl, following the fleeing detachments of the defeated armies, suddenly discovered the emperor with his little escort in the middle of a field. Alexander was ill. The defeat was so unexpected that it had shaken his entire being. He stopped his horse, dismounted, threw himself on the ground under a tree and, covering his face, began to cry like a child. Soon a violent attack of indigestion caused him to be seized with convulsions. That night he stopped in the small hamlet of Urjitz, where the Austrian emperor had already taken up quarters. Wylie found a peasant's hut for him, and it was there on the floor, hastily covered with some straw, that Alexander spent the night after the defeat of Austerlitz. Only toward morning, after a long and patient search through the hamlet, did Wylie find some red wine in order to prepare a soothing potion for Alexander. During this search Lamberti, the Austrian Marshal of the Court, had refused to supply wine for the Russian emperor, because, he said, he could not do so without the permission of Emperor Francis who was asleep and could not be disturbed. Not even to soothe the pain of his ally and recent protector, Alexander, Emperor and Autocrat of All the Russias, could Emperor Francis' slumbers be disturbed.

Tormented by his conscience, shaken by a nervous fever, and doubled up by convulsions, Alexander suffered the agonies of shame attending his first defeat. He recalled the strange prediction of the hermit, Sevastianov, and an awe-inspiring fear clutched at his heart. It seemed that he had uttered the sheer truth when he said: "Everything I have undertaken has turned into disaster against me." This indeed was a disaster. His own and the Austrian armies defeated, thousands of men slain, himself covered with shame. Was this a warning of destiny not to attempt the impossible? Was the hated Napoleon the chosen man? Should he submit to the dictation of fate? Or was this only a test of his strength of character? After all, Sevastianov warned him not to undertake the destruction of the Corsican at that time only; the venerable hermit assured him of a future victory. This was, then, only a lesson, and a warning not to underestimate the strength of the one who boasted of being the "unconquerable." Gradually Alexander felt his hopes revived. A determination to continue the struggle grew steadily. Austria was defeated, but he would find new allies. He would force Prussia to keep her part of the bargain; he would induce England to render more effective help; he would call upon the resources of his own great Russia, and with God's help he could and would free Europe from the "accursed Frenchman."

THE DUEL OF TILSIT

THE SECOND campaign which Alexander led against Napoleon, this time with the help of Prussia, ended for the two allies in the disasters of Jena and Friedland in 1807. Following these defeats it became clear that Russia could not fight any more at this time, and that Prussia, which had been entirely overrun by Napoleon's troops, could not be counted on for any assistance. King Frederick William III of Prussia was indeed a king without a kingdom, having taken refuge in Memel, the only city of his realm as yet not occupied by Napoleon.

The news of Friedland came as a heavy blow to Alexander. Under the circumstances there was nothing for him to do but to open negotiations for peace with the dreaded enemy, and this he proceeded to do. Russia's offer to negotiate was met with open satisfaction by Napoleon. Although, as he said at a later date, his armies were ready to march on Vilno and would have occupied the city within twelve days, nevertheless he was well aware that the occupation of Vilno would not have ended the war with Russia; it would have been just the beginning of a new campaign, as it was to be in 1812, and he was not prepared for it. On the other hand he welcomed peace with Russia because it fitted with his plans to find a strong ally in Europe in order to make his continental system, directed primarily against England, effective. The battle of Marengo had assured Napoleon's predominance in Italy; Austerlitz had brought Austria to his feet; Jena broke the resistance of Prussia; and Friedland assured him of an ally whose acquisition he had sought since 1801. "It is essential," he wrote to Talleyrand, "that all this end with a system of close alliance either with Russia or Austria." Vienna was still undecided when Emperor Alexander made his offer, placing the welfare and interests of Russia above his personal ambition.

It seemed, therefore, that from now on the two rivals, instead of grappling at each other's throats, would combine their forces for the division of their spoils—Europe. The haughty words of Prince Dolgoruky, addressed to Napoleon on the eve of the battle of Austerlitz, stating Alexander's desire to free the world from a tyrant, seemed to belong to another century, so different was the situation now.

On Napoleon's invitation, suggested by Alexander himself, the two rulers of the mightiest empires of the time were to meet at Tilsit on the banks of the Niemen River in East Prussia in order to discuss personally the terms of peace and alliance. Destiny had turned a new page. Whether Alexander or Napoleon would fill this page depended upon the trial of their skill in the forthcoming meeting: the combat on the field of battle was about to be replaced by a duel, a duel with much more subtle weapons than pistols and swords—a duel of diplomacy.

The day of June 25, 1807—the day of the fateful meeting—

was heralded by a beautiful sunrise. The trees of the distant woods shone like the rarest of emeralds. The mighty waters of the Niemen River, in the middle of which floated a large raft bearing two pavilions, flowed like a broad mass of aquamarines, and the sand of the shores was of pure gold. It seemed that nature clothed itself in a festive garb for the historic meeting of the Gallic Mars and the northern Apollo. Tilsit, then Napoleon's headquarters, lay on the left bank of the river. Early in the morning troops and civilians moved from the town to the high cliffs overlooking the Niemen in order to acclaim the Corsican, their demigod. All the Guard was there, lined up facing the river, and thousands of townsmen with their wives and children. On the Russian side there were no special preparations, no display of multitudes was made. Only a boat was held ready, the rowers of which were hurriedly found among the local fishermen; and half a squadron of Russian Horse Guards and a squadron of Prussian cavalry were to serve as an escort to Emperor Alexander and King Frederick William.

Toward eleven o'clock in the morning, Alexander, accompanied by the king of Prussia, the Grand Duke Constantine, and members of his household, left his headquarters in the village of Amt-Baublen and proceeded down the Tilsit road to the Niemen. When they reached the banks of the river at a point opposite the French headquarters, they entered an old abandoned inn. There Alexander sat down near a window and gazed at the picture spread before his eyes. Directly in front of him he saw the raft in the middle of the river, prepared by the French. The two pavilions were covered with white linen. The larger one, intended for the two emperors, was decorated with huge initials painted in green: N on the

French side, A on the Russian. To the great disappointment and anger of the Prussians the initials of their king were not displayed.

Alexander sat in silence awaiting the arrival of Napoleon on the other side of the river. He was entirely master of himself, as reported by more than one person present at the time, but his head was filled with alarming thoughts. He feared that he would find Napoleon a stern and exacting victor. Although he had communicated to the French emperor that he would not cede a foot of Russian soil, he realized that with this forthcoming meeting, the policy he had pursued since ascending the throne of Russia was coming to an end. He had wanted to bring about the liberation of Europe—his youthful ideal— but had failed. He was bitter against his allies: first Austria, then Prussia, had shown that they were of no assistance in a battle of titans. At the same time he recalled Sevastianov's prophecy, and an uneasy feeling crept into his heart.

He argued with himself. There had really been no other way out of the situation. Were not his reasons for seeking peace with Napoleon, as he explained them to Prince Kurakin, perfectly sound? Russia had lost an enormous number of officers and men; all her best generals were either wounded or ill; the army had only five or six lieutenant generals left, most of whom were still young and inexperienced, thus in reality leaving no one to command the troops if hostilities were to continue. Then, too, Russia was now alone, since her allies, Austria and Prussia, had been decisively overcome and England remained thoroughly unreliable. She had promised to send a detachment of from ten to fifteen thousand men, which in itself was a meager help, yet she had never fulfilled her promise; and the financial assistance she offered was pitifully inadequate. The English government had announced that England could supply not more than 2,200,000 pounds sterling a year to be divided among the three continental allies, a sum entirely insufficient. Everything indicated that he had made the right decision. Besides, had he not said that there were circumstances when one has to look out for one's self, to be selfish, guided exclusively by the welfare of one's own country? All this was sound reasoning.

But Alexander knew that there was something else that troubled him: a wound inflicted by the hand of the Corsican which would never heal. Blood rushed to his face and he turned more to the window in order to hide his emotion. After all, the brutal reminder by Napoleon of Alexander's tacit participation in the murder of Emperor Paul could never be forgotten. Alexander might declare his friendship to the victor of the hour, he might accept him as an ally, but all this only so long as he himself remained weak and unable to strike the vengeful blow. Yes, revenge! With this sacred duty in mind and heart, he was sure to win the forthcoming duel, a duel fought with words. There is an old saying: "Words are given to men in order to conceal their thoughts." Alexander, a master in concealment, was confident of victory!

An aide-de-camp hurriedly opened the door and announced: "He is arriving, Your Majesty." Alexander rose slowly, took his hat and gloves and left the room. His face was calm, almost serene, when he walked down to the waiting boat. On the other side of the Niemen, Napoleon galloped along the front of his Old Guard. A colorful group of his marshals and generals followed him. The soldiers and people shouted in a frenzy: "*Vive l'Empereur!*" Their acclaim was so loud that its sound was carried over the water to the Russian side. In comparison with this scene, the little group surrounding Alexander seemed almost negligible.

The two emperors took their places in their respective boats simultaneously. Alexander wore the uniform of the Preobrazhensky Regiment of the Guards. The ribbon of the Grand Cross of the Order of Saint Andrew was his only decoration. Napoleon was clad in the uniform of the Old Guard with the scarlet ribbon of the Legion of Honor across his shoulder and the historic little tricornered hat on his head. He stood in the prow of his boat, his arms folded on his chest, silent, statuesque, the conqueror of the world, "the greatest military leader since the time of Alexander the Great and that of Julius Caesar." Slowly the two boats approached the raft. With a sudden effort the French rowers brought their boat to moor first. Napoleon landed a few seconds before Alexander and hurried forward to greet the Russian emperor as he set foot upon the raft. The two rivals shook hands, embraced, and without saying a word disappeared into the imperial pavilion. Alexander was the first to break the silence.

"I hate the English not less than you do," he said, "and I am ready to support you in anything you will undertake against them."

"If it is so," Napoleon answered, "then everything can be arranged and the peace consolidated."

Alexander, the diplomat, scored the first touch: he had found Napoleon's weak spot. From that point on the duel was nothing but a game. After discoursing at length on the "perfidy of Albion," Napoleon realized that, after all, the reason for this meeting was not the preparation of war against England but the mutual desire for peace. He then praised the Russian soldiers whom he had seen in action at Austerlitz, Eilau, and Friedland. He compared them to the legendary heroes of ancient Greece and said that the combined armies of Russia and France could rule the world, establishing at last an era of peace and prosperity. Finally, Napoleon offered Alexander quarters in Tilsit, for which occasion the town would be proclaimed neutral, in order that the Russian emperor and he could discuss the terms of peace and possible alliance unhampered by chanceries and secretaries. "In one hour," he said, "we shall accomplish more than our plenipotentiaries could do in several days. I shall be your secretary and you shall be mine." Alexander accepted the offer and, on this, the first interview between them ended. It had lasted for one hour and fifty minutes.

During this time, King Frederick William remained on the Russian side of the Niemen. Napoleon did not want to include him in the negotiations. Nevertheless, he had accompanied Alexander in a faint hope that the emperor of the French might change his mind. On horseback, he looked longingly toward the raft where, perhaps, the fate of his kingdom was being decided. At one time he even directed his mount into the water and stopped only when it had touched his boots. He then returned ashore, his head bent low, dejected, his whole unprepossessing figure expressing shame and despair.

In the evening of the next day, Alexander moved into Tilsit. Although the town was proclaimed neutral and divided into two parts—one under French and the other under Russian command—Napoleon took measures to greet Alexander as a guest. As soon as Alexander set foot on shore after crossing the Niemen, the French artillery saluted him with a hundred shots.

Napoleon waited for his new ally at the river. He escorted Alexander personally through the lines of the French troops which formed a long corridor from the bank of the river to Napoleon's residence. During this march along the lined troops, although the enemy of yesterday, Alexander was given the same honors as would have been accorded an ally. The glorious banners, many of them dark from powder smoke and torn in battle, were lowered to the ground at his passage. After dinner, still accompanied by Napoleon, Alexander proceeded to his own residence. That first day, parole, recall, and passwords were given to the troops by Napoleon. They were: Alexander, Russia, Greatness. The next day it was Alexander's turn and he gave: Napoleon, France, Bravery. Thus began the historic days at Tilsit during which a new map of Europe was carved out.

Every morning Count Tolstoy presented himself at Napoleon's house, while Duroc went to Alexander's, to inquire how the emperors were feeling and how they had spent the night. Then until midday Alexander and Napoleon, like two friends, spent their time in inspecting and reviewing the French troops quartered in Tilsit and those stationed in the neighborhood of the town. They were accompanied by all the marshals and a number of generals. Upon returning from these tours Napoleon often detained Alexander in his residence and had a change of clothes brought for the emperor of Russia. Often, too, Napoleon would lend Alexander his cravats and handkerchiefs. When one day Alexander happened to admire Napoleon's beautiful traveling toilet set of pure gold, the French emperor hastened to present it to him.

Alexander dined with Napoleon every day. King Frederick William had repeatedly asked to be admitted to Tilsit—after all, the future of his kingdom was at stake. He at last obtained the requested permission, but began to annoy both Alexander and Napoleon with his unending lamentations. Napoleon openly showed his dislike for the Prussian king and more than once said that he intended to give Prussia to his own brother, Jerome. Once he even told Alexander of his attitude toward the latter's unfortunate ally in the following bitter words: "He is a nasty king, it is a nasty nation, a nasty army—a power which has betrayed everyone and should not even exist." After dinner Alexander and Napoleon would part in order to rid themselves of the presence of King Frederick William. Toward ten o'clock in the evening Napoleon would go to the house occupied by Alexander, alone, unaccompanied even by his personal aide-de-camp, and the two emperors would begin their conversations which lasted far into the night.

Although, officially, the *pourparlers* for peace were conducted by Prince Kurakin and Prince Lobanov-Rostovsky, representing Russia, and Talleyrand, representing France, Alexander and Napoleon really settled between themselves the terms of the treaty of peace and those of the treaty of alliance. Unfortunately, Napoleon's offer to be Alexander's secretary and the suggestion that Alexander serve in the same capacity for him had its important drawbacks. No record was kept of these conversations; so that in years following the Tilsit meeting, Napoleon was able to instruct Talleyrand to follow the terms of the written treaties and to ignore "*les belles phrases que j'ai debitées à Tilsit.*" [1] Thus it might appear at first glance that Alexander was defeated in the diplomatic duel which he had determined to win. In reality he was victorious because he

---

[1] "The pretty words that I said at Tilsit."

achieved his aim: to blindfold his opponent, if it were only for a short time and this by all possible sacrifices, in order to prepare quietly for the final and open struggle on the field of battle.

During these days in Tilsit both Alexander and Napoleon made comments in writing on the strange meeting of a "soldier of fortune" and of an "emperor by divine right." Napoleon wrote to Empress Josephine: "My dear, I have just seen Emperor Alexander. I was very well pleased with him; he is a very handsome, good, and youthful emperor, and he is cleverer than he is usually thought to be."

While Alexander wrote to his beloved sister, the Grand Duchess Catherine Pavlovna:

> God has saved us; instead of sacrifices we have come out of the fight almost gloriously. But what will you say to all these events? *I! to spend my days with Bonaparte,* to be whole hours engaged in conversation with him! I ask you: does not all this seem like a nightmare? It is past midnight and he has only just left me. How I wish you could be an invisible witness to all that is happening. Good-by, my dear, I do not write to you often, but, on my honor, I have hardly a moment in which to breathe.

What completely different people Alexander and Napoleon appear from these quotations! Napoleon's writing has that satisfied parental tone of a person who has expected to meet a weakling, an unbalanced youth with conflicting ideas in his head, but who has actually encountered a man who "is cleverer than he is usually thought to be." On the other hand, Alexander is filled with surprise to find his opponent easy to handle, but he attributes it exclusively to Providence—"God has saved us." Before going to Tilsit he wrote to his sister, Catherine, "Bonaparte thinks I am only a fool. *He who laughs last laughs best!* And I place all my hope in God." In 1812, this feeling of gratitude to divine powers was transformed in Alexander's soul into an assurance that God had selected him not only to save Russia but also to avenge the whole world.

The nightly conversations continued between Alexander and Napoleon until July 7, when the peace treaty comprising twenty-nine articles, with the addition of seven secret ones, and the treaty of alliance were signed. On July 4, Napoleon sent Alexander a memorandum accompanied by a short letter in which he said:

Sire, and brother, I am sending to Your Majesty a note concerning our discussion. Your Majesty will see from it that I desire to hold myself always in a position of friendship and alliance with Russia and to avoid anything that could find itself directly or indirectly in opposition with this great and beautiful idea.

NAPOLEON

The note attached described a new system for the division of Europe: the west, together with Egypt and Syria, to be under the domination of France; the east, including the Balkans and Constantinople, under that of Russia. However, the final text of the treaty differed very much from this memorandum which raised for the first time the question of Constantinople in the light in which it was to be considered by Russia in later years. Before the conversations in Tilsit, Alexander had looked upon

Turkey as rather an inoffensive neighbor. He lacked the ambition of his grandmother, Catherine II, to drive the Turks out
of Europe. After listening to the flattering words of Napoleon,
however, he suddenly realized the importance of Constantinople for Russia. "The key to my house," he was to refer to
it later. Although Napoleon repeated more than once with
reference to Turkey that "one should end the existence of
a state which cannot survive by itself," and notwithstanding
his personal proposal of July 4, he maintained through Talleyrand that it was impossible for him to hand Constantinople
over to Russia, because "the possession of Constantinople
assures the control of the whole world."

The heaviest obligation imposed upon Russia by the treaty
of Tilsit was to join Napoleon's Continental System directed
against England, which constituted a severe blow to Russian
trade, since England was one of her best customers. However,
Russia was compensated somewhat for the loss of the British
market by gaining that of the United States, when two years
after Tilsit she signed a commercial treaty with the young
overseas republic. Russia also gained a definite advantage from
this treaty in her relations with Sweden. Napoleon gave his
formal sanction to Russia's annexation of Finland, explaining:
"St. Petersburg is too close to the Finnish border; the belles
of St. Petersburg in their palaces should not be forced to listen
any more to the roar of Swedish guns."

On July 9, the treaty was ratified by the two emperors in a
brilliant and most impressive ceremony at which both Russian
and French troops assisted. That morning Alexander entrusted
Prince Kurakin with a mission of honor: he was to present to
Napoleon five insignia of the Order of Saint Andrew to be

given to Napoleon himself, to his brother Jerome, king of Westphalia, to Murat, Talleyrand, and Marshal Berthier. At the same time Duroc presented Alexander, through the intermediary of Count Tolstoy, with five insignia of the Grand Cross of the Legion of Honor for Alexander, the Grand Duke Constantine, Baron Budberg, at that time Alexander's Minister of Foreign Affairs, and the two Russian plenipotentiaries— Prince Kurakin and Prince Lobanov-Rostovsky.

At noon Emperor Alexander, wearing the scarlet ribbon of the Legion of Honor, and Napoleon, decorated with the blue ribbon of Saint Andrew, left their respective residences on horseback to meet halfway up the main street, one side of which was occupied by a battalion of the Preobrazhensky Regiment and the other by one of the French Guard. From there the two emperors proceeded to Alexander's house where the ratification took place. In the same evening Alexander left Tilsit. Napoleon accompanied his new ally to the Niemen and there the erstwhile enemies embraced in the midst of the jubilations of the troops and of the civilian population. Napoleon remained on the bank of the river until he saw that Alexander had crossed it safely.

Thus ended the historic days of Tilsit. From the beginning, Alexander had set for himself a very difficult task. He knew that for the time being he was unable to face his foe in open battle, that he needed time and, for the sake of this, he was ready to do anything and everything in order not to arouse any suspicion in Napoleon's mind—anything, even if it were to be humiliating. His hatred for Napoleon was not lessened in the least; on the contrary, it had received a new incentive in his desire for revenge. However, Alexander succeeded in hiding his own feelings, playing his chosen role brilliantly to the end.

Unfortunately, not only the court and the nobility, but even the members of his own family did not appreciate Alexander's aim. In their eyes, and in the eyes of his former allies, he had consorted with the hated Napoleon to the detriment of all Europe and the shame of his own country.

VI

CAT AND MOUSE

THE DAY of July 17, 1807, was one of the hottest days of that eventful summer. Alexander had returned to his capital from Tilsit on the day before, and stopped at the Tavrichesky Palace, where it was a little cooler than in the Winter Palace. That morning he rose early in order to have time to receive the reports of his ministers before going to assist at a solemn *Te Deum* in the cathedral.

At eleven in the morning he left the palace and proceeded in an open carriage to the cathedral. Along the way he did not meet many people, but when he reached the square before the cathedral he saw that it was thronged with his subjects. He smiled and acknowledged greetings, although he was conscious that the reception was considerably cooler than that to which he was accustomed. Still smiling, he scrutinized the faces of people lined up all the way to the main entrance of the cathedral and noticed that they did not light up when their emperor's glance rested upon them, as they had done during the first years of his reign. This discovery slowed his gait. He reached his place finally, and the *Te Deum* began.

Alexander stood alone, his ministers grouped some fifteen or twenty feet behind him. The familiar stoop of his shoulders seemed to shorten his stature. He stood with his weight resting upon his right foot which was slightly advanced. He kept this characteristic pose throughout the duration of the religious service, often making the sign of the cross and the customary genuflections, apparently deeply engrossed in prayer. What a turmoil of thoughts must have whirled in his head! The ruler of the mightiest empire of his time, he had already suffered two shameful defeats: Austerlitz and Friedland. More than that, he felt that his recent friendship with the man who had so grossly insulted him three years before was a sacrifice which his people did not praise because they could not understand. For the first time in the six years of his reign he had given up his personal ambition and, deeply humiliated, had followed a policy intended exclusively to benefit his country. And now his country had turned against him. He had seen it in the attitude of the people outside the cathedral; he had heard it in the hypocritical voices of his ministers when they had congratulated him only that morning, in the most flattering manner, for having concluded such an advantageous peace. He was conscious that the same feeling pervaded the congregation that filled the vast cathedral behind him; he was almost certain that even the best and most loyal among them were now praying that the Almighty would enlighten their ruler and bring him back to the path which, he alone seemed to know, meant only ruin to the country.

He recalled the prophecy of Sevastianov on the eve of his departure from the capital to the army in the field where he was to witness the shame of Austerlitz. Suddenly another recollection fixed itself in his mind. He saw the grim structure of Mikhailovsky Castle. Laden with heavy turrets, surrounded by a deep moat, somber, sinister, it towered. The chain bridge was drawn, the steel water of the moat peered grimly through half-melted snow. The silent figures of the sentries, rigid, almost statuesque, kept close watch. In the midst of this picture appeared a small, forlorn-looking man in a long nightshirt, trapped in his own bedroom. Alexander passed a hand over his eyes and shuddered. Then he turned to the glittering altar in silent quest of an answer to his troubled thoughts. "Is this the punishment?" But neither the golden cross on the altar nor the sad eyes of the holy images responded.

The new policy inaugurated upon the raft on the Niemen River was very unpopular with the most influential members of the Russian aristocracy as well as with the people. Admiral Shishkov wrote in his diary:

The Tilsit peace lowered the head of mighty Russia by the acceptance of the most humiliating conditions which transformed the despised Bonaparte, fearful of our force, into the dreaded Napoleon.

When on August 21, an Imperial Manifesto announced the terms of the Tilsit treaty, Admiral Mordvinov wrote to Alexander:

Well, the peace terms which have been kept secret for so long are known at last. Your new ally was in a hurry to announce to the world through the press the shame which has fallen on our heads. The sons of Russia would rather have given the last drop of their blood than have bowed in disgrace under the yoke of one who has nothing to his credit except that he knew how to use weakness, incapacity, and treason.

Count S. R. Vorontsov, former Russian ambassador at the Court of Saint James, went so far as to propose that the dignitaries who had signed the Tilsit peace should ride into the capital on donkeys; and Nicholas Novossiltsov dared to throw openly into Alexander's face the threat that the emperor was not immune but should remember the night of March 23, 1801.

General Savary, who, immediately the treaty of Tilsit was signed, was sent to represent Napoleon at the Court of St. Petersburg, has left a plaintive record in his memoirs of the difficulties with which he had to contend and of the slights he had to bear. While Alexander treated him with an affectionate cordiality and missed no opportunity of displaying publicly the esteem with which he regarded him, the doors of the fashionable world were resolutely closed against him.

The common people were no less antagonistic. The anti-Napoleonic propaganda spread by order of the government during the previous years through the medium of church organizations of all denominations now bore its fruit—every peasant in Russia believed that Napoleon was the anti-Christ. As, in addition, they suffered from the economic effects of the Continental System, they opposed the new policy vigorously and blamed Alexander for all the ills. A contemporary, F. F. Viegel, characterizes the effects of the Tilsit meeting in the following way:

This was the time when the most tender love that subjects can have for their sovereign was suddenly transformed into something worse than enmity—into a feeling of disgust. . . . All that a man who was not born to be a great general could do was done by Alexander. What could he do when he saw the innumerable armies of the enemy facing his own defeated troops with only one fresh and intact division—that of Prince Lobanov-Rostovsky—and the all-dreaded Napoleon standing on the very border of the Russian State? What would these Russians have said if he had permitted Napoleon to cross that border? . . . I come to the conclusion that nations can be as villainous as individuals.

Such was the situation which Alexander had to face during the years that followed the meeting at Tilsit, the years of Franco-Russian friendship.

The immediate result of the Tilsit agreement, apart from the open break with England, perhaps as a consequence of it, was war between Russia and Sweden. King Gustav IV refused to join the Continental System directed against England, and returned to Emperor Alexander the insignia of the Order of Saint Andrew, explaining that it was incompatible with his dignity to wear a decoration similar to that granted to Bonaparte. Alexander, having obtained by the Tilsit treaty a free hand in Finland, seized this opportunity and declared war. Strangely enough, this war against an age-old enemy of Russia was very unpopular among Alexander's subjects. The reason for this lay in the fact that this war meant an indirect thrust at England and an affirmation of Russia's friendship with revolutionary France.

In the meantime, General Savary was replaced at the Court of St. Petersburg by a regular ambassador. This was another of Napoleon's generals—Caulaincourt. He had been in St. Petersburg in 1801 when he was sent by the first consul to the Russian court with a friendly mission, though without much success. In 1804 he was employed by Napoleon to seize some agents of the English government in Baden, which led to the unfounded accusation that he was concerned with the abduction of the unfortunate Duke d'Enghien. Since this accusation was in a way true in the case of General Savary, it gave opportunity for some influential Russians to use it as an excuse for receiving neither Savary nor Caulaincourt—as indirect murderers of the youthful prince. Caulaincourt had, therefore, to fight a serious handicap from the very beginning of his stay in Russia.

It was only through the action of Alexander himself that the new French ambassador's mission turned out to be slightly less an ordeal than that of General Savary. However, this situation gave Alexander the opportunity to make use of Caulaincourt for his own ends, because his marked friendship and Caulaincourt's gratitude for it made the marquis of Royal France and general of the revolution a tool in the clever hands of the emperor-diplomat. Thus Caulaincourt's reports to Napoleon throughout the years of his mission in St. Petersburg reveal that he was not at all aware of Alexander's secret plans, for these reports breathe optimism even on the eve of the fateful year of 1812.

At this time Napoleon fed his ally with fantastic projects for dividing the Ottoman Empire, even for an expedition in common to India. Alexander, however, was shrewd enough to listen to his ally without giving any serious thought to his words. As for Napoleon, once more he had changed the map

of western Europe; he had invaded Portugal, penetrated in
the guise of a friend into Spain, and obtained at Bayonne the
abdication of the Bourbons in his own favor. By a decree he
named his brother Joseph, then king of Naples, to be king of
Spain, and gave the vacant throne of Naples to his favorite—
Murat. Napoleon's decrees creating rulers did not differ in
their general form from his military ordinances appointing
colonels and generals in the army. For example, the decree
nominating Murat ran as follows:

> The throne of Naples and Sicily being vacant by the
> accession to the throne of Spain and the Indies of our dear
> and beloved brother Joseph Napoleon, we have ordered:
> our dear and beloved brother-in-law Prince Joachim Napo-
> leon, grand duke of Berg and Cleves, to be king of Naples
> and Sicily from August 1, 1808.

Russia took cognizance of these changes, but very soon
Napoleon found himself in a difficult position. The Spanish,
helped by England, drove the French out of Spain. Joseph
had to leave Madrid, once more a king without a country.
Taking advantage of this situation Austria was openly preparing for a new war against the ambitious Corsican. Napoleon felt that he must find support in his Tilsit ally, if he wished
to maintain his powerful position in Europe. Besides, affairs
in Russia herself did not look so very encouraging. True,
Caulaincourt's reports continued to be enthusiastic, but Napoleon knew through his secret agents that Russia steadily opposed
the new alliance and he was afraid lest Alexander should be in-
fluenced by the voice of his people. Therefore, Napoleon con-

sidered a personal meeting with the Russian emperor impera-
tive.

The *pourparlers* were entrusted to Caulaincourt.

After prolonged negotiations, Alexander finally agreed to
meet Napoleon. The place chosen for this meeting was Erfurt,
a town in Prussian Saxony. This decision brought a new outburst of protests from influential Russian circles. When Alexander announced his intention to go to Erfurt at a meeting of
the Imperial Council, the old Count Alexis Sergeyevich Stroganov declared that as a Russian subject and faithful servant
of His Majesty he deemed it his duty to rise against such a
decision of the emperor because, although he was not at all
opposed to maintaining peace between the two empires, such
a close alliance was ruinous to Russia's commercial interests.
As for the Dowager Empress Maria Fyodorovna, she sharply
observed to Count Nicholas A. Tolstoy, Chief Marshal of the
Court, upon his bidding her good-by before leaving for Erfurt,
that she considered him responsible before God and Russia for
the journey that her son was undertaking.

On September 14, 1808, a little more than a year after the
Tilsit meeting, Emperor Alexander left St. Petersburg for
Erfurt. Caulaincourt was personally invited by Alexander to
accompany him. After stopping in Königsberg, where he had
to listen to the lamentations of the king of Prussia, and in Weimar where he spent two days with his sister, Grand Duchess
Maria Pavlovna, Alexander reached Erfurt on September 27.
Napoleon met his ally on the outskirts of the town. He was
surrounded by a brilliant suite of kings, princes, and marshals.
When he saw Alexander's carriage, he galloped forward, dismounted and embraced Alexander. The two rulers then entered

Erfurt on horseback, riding side by side, whilst all the guns of the French artillery stationed in the town and all the bells of the numerous churches of Erfurt greeted the visitor. Napoleon accompanied Alexander to his residence. The finest house in town had been chosen for Alexander by the express orders of the French emperor.

Napoleon took all possible pains to give to this meeting the appropriate setting. Not only were most of his distinguished marshals present, but he had permitted all the German princes who desired to do so to come to Erfurt. The kings of Bavaria, Saxony, Westphalia, and Württemberg, a number of dukes and ruling princes, not to mention a crowd of petty princes who hoped to get something out of this gathering, swarmed to Erfurt. The guard of honor was composed of the best soldiers of the Imperial Guard and a number of the best French regiments were called to the little German city to reinforce its garrison. Some of the best actors from Paris came to produce for a *parterre de rois* the classical plays of the French repertoire.

In the great game that the two allies-enemies were playing, Napoleon took the greatest care to mask his real intentions. He tried to arouse Alexander's vanity by showing him that nothing was too good for the pleasure of the northern Apollo. He sought to overwhelm Alexander by the flattering display of royalty, gathered by Napoleon's magic wand. Most of all he wanted Alexander's help, and to attain this aim it was necessary for him to allay every possible suspicion. Napoleon knew he had not played fairly since the pact of Tilsit, but he did not know whether Alexander was aware of it. As a matter of fact, Alexander did have knowledge of his "friend's" plotting, especially with regard to French propaganda in Little Russia.

As far back as 1802, when Napoleon was first consul, he had entertained the idea of creating trouble for Russia in her southwestern territories. Émile Godin, French agent in Constantinople, had worked out a plan for him by means of which French influence would be extended in Little Russia in "opposition to English influence in Great Russia." He recommended the establishment of French trading posts directed by government officials or army officers on the coast of the Black Sea. Foreseeing a possible war between Russia and Turkey for the possession of the Straits, Godin recommended the exploitation of the budding nationalist movement in Little Russia. This plan was adopted by Napoleon in later years and developed particularly after the Tilsit meeting. According to this enlarged plan, Little Russia was to be established as an independent state under the personal rule of the French emperor. It was to be called *Les Napoléonides* and to serve as "a most powerful barrier to Russia's aspirations with regard to the Black Sea and the Bosporus."

After 1807, this plan was revived and a number of French agents sent into Little Russia. It shows that Napoleon also looked upon the Tilsit agreement as only temporary, and used all possible means to undermine the power of his ally and inevitable enemy. With this in view, he had also ordered General Savary, his personal representative at the Court of St. Petersburg, to provide himself with a die in order to be able to manufacture Russian bank notes. All this only a few days after the embraces at Tilsit! Savary fulfilled his mission and Napoleon ordered the manufacture of Russian counterfeit bank notes which, in 1812, he imported on thirty-four carts into Russia. It was of no avail. The Russians refused to trade with the invaders in any form or manner and Marshal Mortier had to burn his load before evacuating Moscow.

Thus the two allies who met in Erfurt were both playing the little game of cat and mouse, in which each believed himself to be the cat. Following the example of Tilsit, the two emperors renewed their meetings alone, unhampered by ministers and secretaries. But this time Napoleon found in Alexander a very different man from the one he had known a year ago. While at Tilsit it was Alexander who wanted to soothe Napoleon's irritability by all possible means, because he had to save his empire from invasion, at Erfurt it was Napoleon's turn to use all his diplomacy to win Alexander over to his cause, because this time it was he who needed Alexander's help.

Fearing the inevitability of a war with Austria, Napoleon suggested joint action on the part of France and Russia in order to exercise pressure on the Vienna cabinet even to the extent of demanding complete disarmament. Alexander refused to accede to this plan. He preferred to use an amicable way of inducing Austria not to violate the existing peace. An exchange of ideas on this subject ended with the following incident: Napoleon became furious and throwing his hat on the floor began to trample on it. Alexander smiled and said quite calmly: "You are violent and I am stubborn; with me rage does not gain anything. Let's talk and reason or else I shall go."

As Alexander turned to the door, Napoleon controlled his temper and kept his ally for a continuation of the discussion. To Caulaincourt he later said: "*Your* Emperor Alexander is as stubborn as a mule: he does not listen to what he does not want to hear."

On another occasion, however, it was Alexander's turn to

beat a retreat when he asked Napoleon to evacuate Prussia
completely as a token of his peaceful attitude toward Russia
and Europe at large. This Napoleon refused to do because it
would have placed him in a strategically inferior position to
Austria. He then proposed to settle his dispute with Austria
right away, and this time Alexander had to yield and to withdraw his proposal. It was obvious that the two emperors had
ceased to be allies, but they both continued to maintain the
subterfuge because neither was then ready for the final struggle.

Alexander became completely persuaded at Erfurt that it
was not Austria with her military preparations that threatened
the peace of Europe, but Napoleon's secret plans for further
and still more extensive conquests. He was confirmed in this
opinion by Talleyrand. The cleverest foreign minister that
France has ever had is said to have betrayed his master because
of a desire to marry his nephew and heir into the Russian imperial family, preferably to Alexander's youngest sister—Grand
Duchess Anna Pavlovna. He did not fully succeed in realizing
this ambition; still he obtained for his nephew the hand of the
Duchess of Kurland. At his first opportunity, in Erfurt, Talleyrand approached Alexander and gave him the following advice:

You are predestined to save Europe and you will be
able to do it only if you do not give in to Napoleon. The
French nation is civilized, but its sovereign is not; the Russian
sovereign is civilized, whilst his people are not. Therefore,
the Russian emperor should be an ally of the French people
and not of the French emperor.

Empress Elisabeth Alexeyevna

Grand Duchess Catherine

Prince Peter Dolgoruky

Prince Peter Volkonsky

Count Paul Stroganov

Count Victor Kochubey

Nicholas Novossiltsov

Prince Adam Czartoryski

At another meeting he spoke even with greater precision: "The Rhine, the Alps and the Pyrenees are conquests of France. The rest is only a conquest of the emperor. France does not care about it."

These treacherous words, spoken by the former Bishop of Autun, served only to fortify Alexander in his belief that Napoleon was a menace to civilization. It was obvious to him that he should hasten the coming of the final struggle.

The Erfurt meeting ended with the signing of a secret convention between Napoleon and Alexander which was of no material importance except that it gave Russia a free hand in Turkish affairs and engaged Russia to stand by France in a war against Austria. On October 14, Alexander and Napoleon left the town together and parted on the road to Weimar never to meet again. Alexander was no longer afraid of his opponent.

He returned to St. Petersburg on October 28. The capital received the return of the emperor under the same cloud of suspicion that had prevailed since the signing of the Tilsit treaty. The people did not know the results of the new meeting, the secret convention not having been divulged. And Alexander found himself in a position even more difficult than that which had existed before his departure to Erfurt. Something had to be done to pacify the passions of the people—first of all their passion for material gain so common to every nation and age. Since trade with England was prohibited, and France together with the other members of the Continental System could not offer a convenient market for Russian goods, it was necessary to find new customers. Alexander turned to the new but promising overseas republic, the United States of America, as a solution of this problem.

In 1806, Alexander had met and conversed at length with Joel R. Poinsett, who was probably the greatest American traveler of his time. Thus America and the American people were not unknown to the Russian emperor. At that time the United States was finding it difficult to continue her trade under the effective blockade by England of most of the ports of western Europe, and when Alexander suggested to President James Madison the exchange of diplomatic representatives between Russia and the United States, the proposal was promptly accepted by the young republic. John Quincy Adams became the first American envoy accredited to the Court of St. Petersburg. When he arrived in the capital of the Russian Empire, he had already heard much of the Russian emperor. But all his greatest expectations were surpassed by the gracious simplicity and democratic friendliness with which Alexander greeted the envoy plenipotentiary of the new republic, which many people of the time still considered to be nothing more than a revolted colony of Great Britain.

There can be no doubt that Alexander wished to attach to himself this newcomer from beyond the seas, because he already realized the importance of the role the United States was to play in the life of nations. So he arranged to meet John Quincy Adams in the mornings when the latter took his daily walk along the embankments of the Neva. Knowing the hour and the itinerary of the American envoy, who methodically changed neither, it was easy for Alexander to meet Adams "accidentally" and to talk to him about the weather, about Russia, and the United States, about Europe and the political situation. For more than an hour the two "republicans" would converse, apparently pleased with each other. These conversations benefited both the United States and Russia to a far greater extent than a number of conferences would ever have done, because the friendship that grew up between Alexander and Adams, and between Adams and Alexander's chancellor, Count Rumiantsov, led to the conclusion of a very favorable commercial treaty. This treaty relieved the tension in Russia, at least for a time. The end of the war with Sweden also pleased the people. But the danger of an Austro-French war was once more a threat to Russia's tranquillity.

In February, 1809, Prince Schwarzenberg arrived in St. Petersburg with a special mission from Emperor Francis to explain to Alexander the reasons for Austria's anti-French attitude and to ask the Russian emperor for the maintenance of a benevolent neutrality in the forthcoming conflict. This Alexander was unable to promise in view of the Erfurt convention, but he assured the Austrian envoy that he would do everything possible to weaken the blows intended for Austria. He added that his situation appeared to him to be hopelessly unnatural, since he could not help wishing all success to the Austrians although he belonged to the opposite camp. At the same time Alexander assured Caulaincourt that he would stand by Napoleon in case of a war with Austria. Nevertheless, when the Austrians declared war on April 10, 1809, and Caulaincourt demanded action, Alexander used all sorts of excuses to delay the inevitable entrance into a war in which his sympathies were with the enemy. It was only on June 3, many weeks after Napoleon had beaten the Austrian army and captured Vienna, that thirty-two thousand men of the Russian army crossed the frontier into Austria. Napoleon raged at the way Caulaincourt was led to believe in Russia's effective help, and expressed it to his ambassador in a furious letter; but Caulaincourt was helpless in the clever hands of Alexander the Charmer.

When Austria met with defeat, Alexander became worried. He felt the approach of the hour for his own open struggle with Napoleon. At that time, Alexander's personal friend, Prince Peter Volkonsky, whom he had sent upon a mission to Napoleon, reported that at a dinner the all-powerful Bonaparte took an apple and said: "The world is like this apple. We can cut it into halves and divide it between ourselves. Tell your sovereign that I am his friend and that he should avoid those who want us to quarrel." To this the pupil of La Harpe remarked: "At the beginning he would be satisfied with one half, then he would work up an appetite for the other half also."

The estrangement between Alexander and Napoleon grew rapidly. An unsuccessful attempt on the part of Napoleon to marry Alexander's sister, the Grand Duchess Anna Pavlovna, the future queen of the Netherlands, only made matters worse. On November 22, 1809, Napoleon ordered Caulaincourt to request the hand of the grand duchess, and demanded an answer within forty-eight hours. Alexander, however, was not ready to refuse at once. He placed the whole matter in his mother's hands, thus delaying an answer. The dowager empress conferred with the Grand Duchess Catherine and finally decided, on February 4, 1810, to accept the offer but only on the condition that the marriage should not take place for two years as the Grand Duchess Anna was barely fifteen years of age. In the meantime, foreseeing a refusal, Napoleon had turned to Austria. There the matter was settled within twenty-four hours. While the courier bearing Alexander's conditional acceptance of Napoleon's proposal was on his way to Paris, Napoleon's betrothal to the Archduchess Maria-Louisa was officially announced, and the marriage ceremony followed shortly.

The game of cat and mouse was coming to an end.

On the eve of his epic struggle with "the enemy of mankind" Alexander tried desperately to regain the confidence of his people without whose wholehearted support he could not possibly carry out his plans. To achieve this end he had to make many sacrifices including the expiatory offering on the altar of the god of war of the last and most brilliant of his enlightened collaborators—Michael Speransky, whose far-sighted policy of reform dominated the internal affairs of Russia during the years after Tilsit.

Unlike Alexander's earlier collaborators, Speransky, born on January 12, 1772, was not of noble birth. The son of a village priest, he was expected to follow his father's career, as was customary in those times. But an ecclesiastical career did not tempt young Speransky, and when he had completed his studies at the seminary in St. Petersburg he sought a position in the civil service. At the outset of his career he had the good fortune to obtain a position as tutor to the children of Prince Kurakin. He knew Latin and Greek perfectly as well as French, but his particular talent revealed itself in the flawless mastery of his native tongue, both written and spoken. His career as a tutor soon came to an end when Prince Alexis Kurakin, Attorney General in the reign of Emperor Paul, became aware of Speransky's talent and placed him in his own chancery. There the young clerk soon rose to the predominant position of an invaluable Chief of Chancery whose services were appreciated not only by Prince Kurakin himself, but also by his successors in office.

The creation of ministries in 1802 assured Speransky's brilliant future. He was transferred to the new Ministry of the Interior and immediately taken under the wing of such a powerful man as Count Kochubey, then Minister of the Interior—the emperor's personal friend of long standing. All the projects of reforms concerning the new ministry were written by Speransky and because of their exceptional brilliance were published for general circulation. This had never been done before. Under Speransky the Ministry of the Interior also started another undertaking which was considered almost revolutionary by reactionary contemporaries. Beginning with 1804 the Ministry of the Interior began to publish an official monthly review under the title, *The Review of St. Petersburg*. This publication contained the most important imperial and ministerial decrees, reports, and projects of reforms, most of them composed by Speransky or at least revised by him. An unofficial part of the review contained original and translated works on state administration.

It was only in 1806 that Speransky became personally known to Alexander. In that year Count Kochubey had been ill for a long time, so that it was Speransky who presented the reports of the Ministry of the Interior to the emperor. Very often Alexander would retain the young reformer beyond the usual time alloted an official audience and would discuss with him the numerous projects for the betterment of the people's life in general, for the perfection of the machine of state, etc. Speransky's clear and calm reasoning, his perfect mastery of the Russian language, the evident appearance of a future statesman, respectful but without flattery, appealed to Alexander. Speransky was so different from the rest of the employees of the state. One of his bitter enemies had said of him, "If I had but one-third of Speransky's brains I would be the greatest man of my time." And so, in the difficult years after Tilsit, when Alexander needed a helping hand after his enlightened but theoretical friends of the first years of his reign had left him, it was to Michael Speransky that he turned.

In 1808, Nicholas Novossiltsov, the last of the group of "reformers," definitely abandoned his active participation in the government. After this Alexander called for Speransky whose official status became "attached to the person of His Imperial Majesty for special affairs" and whose work consisted in presenting reports on the functioning of the government. On December 27 of the same year Speransky was appointed Assistant Minister of Justice with a special assignment to take over the codification of Russian laws which had been started in 1803 by an appointed commission. At the same time he was entrusted with the delicate task of preparing a constitution for Russia, one of Alexander's cherished dreams. Speransky plunged headlong into this immense undertaking, and very soon not only all legislation but all the affairs of state in general became centered in his hands. He became, according to the saying of a contemporary, that spot of light toward which all the beams of the empire converged.

Having started with the codification of laws, Speransky soon found himself discussing with Alexander the idea of a general reorganization of the state. This idea appealed to both the emperor and his minister. A new and vaster field of activity was thrown open for Speransky, the reformer. For two years he worked like a slave carrying out a tremendous task concerned not only with the regulation and control of the machine of state but also with a complete change of the most important parts of the structure of the state. By November, 1809, the work had been completed in all its details. The project was based mainly on the *Code Napoléon* and partly on the French constitution of 1799. The guiding thought governing the project was the centralization of power. From the emperor through the State Council, which was to serve as a link between the autocratic power of Alexander and the state adminstration, the power of government was to be exercised by three principal institutions: the State Duma (legislative), the ministries (executive) and the Senate (judiciary). From these institutions, branches went down the pyramid joining it to the top, the emperor, with its base, the people.

Speransky's work seemed perfect and easily applicable to Russia if he had not stood alone, if he had had collaborators, men of vision like himself, who would have been capable of filling all the posts in his vast project. This, combined with Alexander's personal fear of breaking completely with all the past institutions, prevented Russia's great statesman from carrying out his gigantic plan. Alexander agreed only to the establishment of the State Council which was opened with great solemnity on January 13, 1810 (Russia's New Year). On this occasion Alexander delivered a speech (written by Speransky and only slightly edited by the emperor) "full of a feeling of dignity and of such ideas as have never as yet been pronounced from the throne in Russia." Speransky was appointed Secretary of State and Count Joseph de Maistre, envoy plenipotentiary of the king of Sardinia, characterized him in one of his reports as "the great and almighty Speransky, secretary general of the empire and in fact prime minister, if not *the* minister."

The years 1810 and 1811 marked the zenith of Speransky's career. It is perhaps paradoxical that the very greatness of his position in the empire contributed to his downfall. On the heights that he had reached he was alone, since he was a statesman and not a politician, a reformer and not a diplomat, because he despised the idle crowd of courtiers and valued above all else intelligent work. He forgot that politicians or courtiers very often have more power and influence than the real builders of the state. The Grand Duke Nicholas Mikhailovich tells, in his monumental work on Alexander I, of the reasons which contributed to Speransky's downfall:

It is in the personal relations between Alexander and Speransky, daily sincere relations full of living trust, that one should look for the root of the misunderstanding which led to the final disgrace. By showing such an extraordinary favor to one person, by granting him such extensive power, having placed Speransky at the head of numerous institutions beginning with the Chancery of the Empire and ending with the Chancellorship of the University of Abö, Alexander had alienated all people without exception. Speransky found himself isolated. He had no friends while enemies surrounded him. But he paid not the slightest attention to his enemies (in fact, he did not know how to fight intrigue) and did not look for friends; all of his talent, all his creative energy, the whole of himself he gave to his emperor, firmly trusting in his protection and giving no thought to the possibility of losing it. For two years everything went smoothly, everything and everyone submitted and bowed to the tsar's favorite, a former seminarist and son of a poor village priest. At that time Speransky indeed governed Russia.

The unpopularity of the Tilsit alliance had its direct bearing on the final events that led to Speransky's downfall. The fact that Speransky had largely used French legislation as a basis for his state reforms sufficed to throw in his face the ignominious accusation of treason. Alexander resisted the constantly growing pressure of attacks on his favorite until he felt that he could do so no longer as his own popularity was at stake. At the same time the formidable array of accusations piled up against Speransky were convincing enough to create in the emperor's mind a feeling of doubt as to the complete innocence of his minister.

On March 29, 1812, a Sunday, Speransky came down to dinner in an excellent frame of mind. He had aged considerably during the last two years. His hair had become sparser and silver strands appeared on his temples. He looked much older than his forty years. He had worked all that morning notwithstanding the fact that the day was one of rest.

During the dinner a messenger from the palace brought an order that the emperor would see him that very evening at eight o'clock. It was not the first time that Speransky had thus been called to the emperor, so that this evening he left his home without suspecting what awaited him in the Winter Palace. On reaching the emperor's anteroom, Speransky found waiting there a general aide-de-camp and two cabinet ministers. He was called into Alexander's study. Alexander was standing in the middle of the vast room in semi-darkness. Only two chandeliers placed on the emperor's large desk lit the room. Alexander seemed to be worried. His face was stern, but he did not lift his eyes to Speransky. He was not prepared to meet the frank look of his collaborator and favorite, because he knew that Speransky was not guilty of that which he was about to be accused. For two hours the three men in the anteroom waited. From time to time they heard through the closed doors the sound of voices. At the beginning, Speransky's voice was heard more clearly; at the end of the interview it was reduced almost to a whisper, while Alexander's tone grew louder and louder. Then the door opened and Speransky stepped out of the emperor's study. He was very pale and visibly moved. Hastily he assembled his papers and placed them in his brief-case, bade good-by to the two ministers and departed. The all-powerful minister was no more.

When Speransky reached his home he found waiting for him General Balashov, then Minister of Police, and General de Sanglain who were among the leaders of the campaign against him. They were both very much relieved when they saw Speransky, for they were not at all sure that he would not be able to persuade the emperor of his innocence, and this would probably have meant their own banishment. General Balashov sealed all Speransky's papers and invited him to proceed to his place of exile—Nizhni-Novgorod. Speransky left the capital an hour after his return home without even bidding good-by to his family; he did not have the courage to face them.

When Speransky had left the emperor's study, one of the waiting cabinet ministers—Prince Alexander Golitsyn, Minister of Cults, and Alexander's personal friend—was called to the emperor. He found Alexander in tears. He inquired the reason for such display of emotion. Alexander answered, "If you had your arm cut off, you would probably scream and howl from pain. I have lost Speransky and he was my right arm."

The banishment of Speransky marked the end of the last period of reform in Alexander's reign. This period was apparently but an interlude in the Russian emperor's struggle to assure peace to Europe by defeating Napoleon. That spring of 1812, which witnessed the dismissal of one of Russia's greatest statesmen, was pregnant with the approaching thunder of combat. The game of cat and mouse was ended. A battle of titans was to begin.

VII

"EN GARDE"

In 1812, Emperor Alexander was thirty-five, but he looked much younger than his age. Notwithstanding his fine and regular features and good complexion, his physical beauty was less striking at first glance than the expression of benevolence which captured all hearts and instantly inspired trust. His noble, tall and majestic figure, often inclined in graceful posture reminiscent of ancient statues, was threatened by corpulence although he was exceptionally well built. His eyes, of the color of a cloudless sky, were clever and alert; he was a little nearsighted, but he was a master of the smile of the eyes (*le sourire des yeux*), if one can thus characterize his expression which was filled with kindness and affection. His nose was straight and finely shaped, his mouth small and agreeable, the contour of his face and his profile reminded one of his beautiful mother. A slight baldness over his forehead made his face look open and even serene. His golden blond hair, carefully dressed like that on the heads of beautiful cameos or of ancient medals, seemed to have been predestined to be crowned by a triple crown of laurel, olive and myrtle leaves.

Although this fervent description of Alexander was made by an ardent admirer of the Russian emperor—Countess de Choiseul-Gouffier—it is corroborated by the testimony of other contemporaries. Alexander was, in 1812, in full possession of his mental and physical faculties, no longer the enthusiastic inexperienced young man of Austerlitz or even of Friedland. After Tilsit and Erfurt he discovered not only what Napoleon's ambitions and desires were but also how to oppose them by what he himself wanted. Napoleon was to find a worthy opponent in Alexander this time.

Toward the middle of 1811, Napoleon's preparations for war had already progressed to such an extent that he was able to show his temper with regard to Russia. It was his custom to let Europe know whenever he was on the eve of another war. In the evening of August 15, at a solemn reception in the Tuileries Palace, in the presence of the entire diplomatic corps, he made a scene with the Russian ambassador, Prince Kurakin, which bore extraordinary resemblance to the comedy he had played with the British ambassador, Lord Whitworth, in 1803, and with the Austrian ambassador, Count Metternich, in 1808. In a loud voice, so that everyone could hear him, for two solid hours Napoleon piled up an imposing array of accusations against Russia.

Previous to this outburst, Napoleon had relieved Caulaincourt of his ambassadorial post in St. Petersburg and had replaced him by Count Lauriston. When Caulaincourt was received in a farewell audience by Alexander, the Russian emperor frankly indicated to him what he thought of the situation and what he was ready to do:

I have not such generals as yours, and I am not such a military leader and administrator as Napoleon, but I have good soldiers, a faithful people, and we would rather die in combat than allow ourselves to be dealt with as the people of Holland or Hamburg. Still, I assure you on my honor that I will not fire the first shot. I will let you cross the Niemen and I will not cross it myself. Be assured that I will not declare war on you. I do not want a war; my people, although insulted by the attitude of your emperor toward me, are opposed to war as much as I am, because they know its dangers. However, if we are attacked we shall know how to defend ourselves.

These words reveal exactly Alexander's plan of the time. Notwithstanding Napoleon's threats, Alexander was determined to wait for his aggression.

As for Napoleon, he counted on a wavering Alexander and was sure he would win by a sudden attack with all his forces. His plan had already been elaborated on March 16, 1810, in a secret memorandum. Napoleon's marital alliance with the Hapsburg family was at the bottom of this plan. The memorandum stated the inevitability of an understanding between Russia and England that would lead France to undertake severe measures directed against her Tilsit ally. The war against Russia was to be the beginning of a new rearrangement of the map of Europe including the restoration of Poland. The empire of Charlemagne was to appear, not only re-established, but considerably "enlarged and fortified in the light of the civilization of ten centuries." Furthermore, to General Wrede of the

Bavarian army Napoleon declared: "In three years' time I will be master of the universe."

Alexander awaited the coming war with confidence. He took all possible measures to assure himself of as great an advantage as possible. For this purpose he opened negotiations with Sweden and assured himself of the alliance of this age-old rival of Russia in the north of Europe. This was achieved mainly because Alexander knew how to flatter the ambitions of Napoleon's former marshal, Bernadotte, then crown prince of Sweden.

The prohibition of trade with England, which Napoleon imposed on Sweden in 1811 as part of his Continental System, had the same ruinous effects on that country as it had on Russia. Under these circumstances the natural step for Sweden to take, in order to protect her interests, was to join France's enemies, foremost of whom were Russia and England; yet the Swedish people recalled only too vividly the recent war with Russia which had ended in the annexation of Finland by Sweden's neighbor. As for England her government was suspicious of Bernadotte, because of his past connection with Napoleon, and was reluctant to open negotiations unless the crown prince should manifest his change of views in some very obvious way. It seemed, therefore, that the first step for Sweden to take would be to come to some understanding with Alexander, a step which should solve the entire problem because it would not only guarantee Sweden's security along its northern frontier but it would also be that obvious manifestation the English expected. When early in 1812 the French marshal, Davout, occupied Swedish Pomerania, Bernadotte hesitated no longer; and on April 5, Count Löwenhielm, special envoy of Sweden to the

Court of St. Petersburg, signed a treaty of alliance with Russia. In order to divert popular ambition from the reconquest of Finland, lost in 1809 to Russia, Bernadotte's policy was to acquire Norway. Alexander readily agreed to this demand on the part of the prince royal of Sweden, because Norway then belonged to Denmark and the Danish king was a staunch supporter of Napoleon. Alexander was now assured that in the forthcoming struggle against Napoleon his right wing was secure.

The successful solution of the Swedish problem was outbalanced by Alexander's failure to win Poland to his side. Notwithstanding the bitter disappointment in Alexander that the Poles felt when, in 1805, he had failed to fulfill their desires to restore an independent Poland, Alexander began once more to discuss the whole Polish question with Prince Adam Czartoryski, who had served in previous years as intermediary between the Russian emperor and the leaders of the Polish nation. It seems that as late as June, 1812, Alexander was still under the impression that he might attract Polish sympathies to his side. On June 4, however, Prince Adam wrote a pathetic letter in which he described his difficult situation because his own father and other members of his family had openly embraced Napoleon's cause. "If Napoleon were really to do something magnificent for Poland, what fate awaits those Poles who did not follow him?" Czartoryski exclaimed; adding, "Only an imperial manifesto (*by Alexander*) announcing the complete restoration of Poland in her territorial limits of 1772 could meet the necessities of the moment. A partial restoration would not satisfy anyone." Nine days later, having decided to espouse Napoleon's cause, Prince Adam wrote to Alexander again:

Before this letter reaches you, Sire, something important will have happened with regard to my country. Any proclamation of Your Majesty having a similar aim in view will be belated. . . . I can foresee its timeliness only in the event that victories and conquests would place Your Majesty in a position to be listened to.

Far gone were the days of 1805 when even Poniatowski, the pretender to the Polish throne, was ready to acclaim Alexander as king of Poland. At present, it was a careful bargaining in which both sides wanted to gain most and to pay least. Alexander's position was decidedly less favorable than that of Napoleon; the Poles had been disappointed by the Russian emperor, while the disappointment in Napoleon was still to come.

Meanwhile, the situation between France and Russia grew more tense day by day. In November, 1811, Alexander wrote to his sister the Grand Duchess Catherine Pavlovna: "We are constantly on the alert; hostilities may break out at any moment." In the same letter Alexander added: "I have never as yet led such a dogged existence; I arise from my bed only to sit down to my desk and I leave my desk only to eat a bit all alone."

A month later hostilities started in Naples where the Russian envoy, Prince Dolgoruky, and Baron Durand, Minister of France, fought a duel. By February, 1812, both the Russian and French armies were ordered to occupy their positions near the frontier. To a question of Count de Saint-Julien, Ambassador of Austria, as to what Alexander expected from an encounter with such a terrible opponent, Alexander observed: "I am ready to suffer some defeats at the beginning, but they

will not discourage me. In beating a retreat I shall place a desert
between our armies: I shall evacuate everyone and everything."

In March, 1812, Bernadotte recommended that Alexander
should persevere and should not fear to use retreat as a weapon
against his enemy. He wrote: "The end of Napoleon will
come from Alexander as that of Charles XII came from Peter
the Great." In the same month, Alexander assured General
Knesebeck that "he would rather retreat to Kazan than sign
a dishonorable peace"; and on July 4, when Napoleon had
already penetrated deep into Russia, Alexander wrote to Bernadotte in answer to an anxious letter from the prince royal
of Sweden: "Let Your Highness be assured now that this
struggle has started, I am determined to make it last for years
even if I have to fight on the banks of the Volga."

It seems that as much before the fight as after it had started,
Alexander's decision was to make it a struggle for life or death.
He remained firm in this decision and thus saved not only his
throne but also Russia and the rest of the world.

At the same time, Napoleon opposed Alexander's military
plan or, more exactly, lack of any plan, with an elaborate and
logically thought-out campaign. He said to Metternich:

My enterprise belongs to those which are achieved by
patience. The triumph will belong to the most patient one.
I shall open my campaign by crossing the Niemen. I shall end
it in Smolensk and Minsk. There I shall stop. I shall fortify
my position in these two towns and shall proceed to Vilno
where I shall hold my general headquarters for the winter
and organize Lithuania which is longing to throw off the
Russian yoke. We shall then see which of us will be the first

to tire: I from keeping my army supplied at Russia's cost or
Alexander from having to keep my army on Russian soil.

When Metternich inquired what Napoleon would do if the
occupation of Lithuania did not bring Alexander to terms,
Napoleon replied: "Then after spending a comfortable winter
I shall march to the center of Russia and in 1813 I shall be just
as patient as in 1812. The whole issue is only a question of time."
Unfortunately for Napoleon he had to change his perfectly
balanced, strategical plan because of political considerations.
In order to be able to stop in Minsk and Smolensk it was necessary that this campaign be as brilliant as those of 1805, 1806,
1809. Otherwise Paris and Europe might feel disappointment.
The prestige of his name and of the entire empire demanded
that this war should be a *grand coup*. Napoleon feared that
if the war should drag along, France might become turbulent
and his vassal states rise in open revolt—and who knew what
all this might lead to? So Napoleon, after he had crossed the
Niemen, decided to cut the Russian armies in two in order to
produce one of these desired *grands coups*. This plan failed.
Prince Bagration, commanding the Second Russian Army,
escaped the danger of being surrounded and joined the First
Army below Smolensk. Napoleon then tried to break through
Smolensk and appear in the rear of the Russians. This would
have been a *grand coup* too. This time Nevierovsky in the
battle of Krasny prevented its realization. Even the capture
of Smolensk which had cost an enormous price in men was of
no great strategical importance at this moment. Europe was
waiting and Napoleon simply could not afford to stop in Smolensk. Consequently he decided to push farther into the heart

of Russia, still hoping for a definite and brilliant success. He was certain that the Russians would defend Moscow, that in doing so they would meet a crushing defeat, and that once Moscow was in his hands he would have Alexander at his feet begging for mercy. This second plan was to be realized perfectly except for its last part: Alexander remained steadfast in his decision, notwithstanding all the difficulties he had to overcome.

On April 21, 1812, Emperor Alexander left St. Petersburg on his way to Vilno in order to be nearer to his troops, since Napoleon's army had now reached Königsberg on its way to the Niemen. The same day Count Rumiantsov assured the French ambassador:

> His Imperial Majesty begs to communicate to the French emperor that he remains his friend and his faithful ally in Vilno as much as in St. Petersburg and that his journey has but one aim: to prevent his generals from making some rash decision which might provoke the opening of hostilities.

At the same time Napoleon's ambassador, Count Lauriston, had received orders from his master to make any engagement— not in writing, however—to the effect that the French army had no intention of crossing the Russian border, going even so far as to issue an order to the army when it would reach the Niemen to stop its advance, with the understanding that such an order would not be complied with because the ambassador had no authority to command the armed forces. With his plan based upon patience, Napoleon wanted to gain a strategic position from which to strike best.

On April 26, which day was Palm Sunday, the firing of guns and the ringing of bells at two o'clock in the afternoon announced to the people of Vilno the arrival of Emperor Alexander. The capital of Lithuania tendered Alexander a most magnificent reception. It seemed that Napoleon was misinformed when he spoke about Lithuania "longing to throw off the Russian yoke," but time was to show that these same people would greet Napoleon just as enthusiastically as they were now greeting Alexander. True, perhaps, was F. F. Viegel's remark that "nations can be as villainous as individuals."

In Vilno the ruling class was composed of Poles, and Alexander proceeded to win them to his cause. Distinctions of all sorts were heaped upon them. Not only did many Polish nobles and officials receive decorations and court titles, but a number of fiscal measures were revoked by the emperor, thereby freeing estates and estate owners from seizure and taxation legally imposed upon them by the Russian administration. At the same time, Alexander took pains to exercise his charm on the Polish patriots, dancing with the ladies and flattering the ambitions of the men.

In the meantime, hearing of Alexander's journey to Vilno, Napoleon also left his capital, and proceeded to Dresden. In order to gain more time, which was necessary for the concentration of his troops, he dispatched a special envoy to Alexander—Count de Narbonne—whom he entrusted with a confidential mission: to obtain information about Alexander's plans under the pretense of a last offer for peace. Napoleon was afraid lest the Russians should invade East Prussia and the Duchy of Warsaw before he had time to be ready for this eventuality. Napoleon chose Count de Narbonne for this mission for he felt certain this envoy would mislead Alexander.

Count de Narbonne was not a new man born of the revolution. A former minister of Louis XVI, former knight of honor of Madame Adélaide, he belonged to Royal France much more than to Napoleon's empire. Alexander, not to be disarmed, treated this "relic of the past" with all the attention and consideration due to him. However, when Narbonne revealed the extent of Napoleon's peace proposals, he found Alexander firm and unyielding. Having rejected Napoleon's offer for a personal meeting, the Russian emperor turned to a map unfolded on the table and said:

I am not blinded by unreasonable dreams. I know how great a military leader Napoleon is, but on my side I have space and time. In all this land hostile to you there is not one single spot, no matter how distant it may be, to which I would not retreat, which I would not defend rather than conclude a dishonorable peace. *I will not start the war, but I will not disarm so long as a single enemy soldier remains in Russia.*

Referring to this meeting, Count de Narbonne commented: "The emperor was so firm on his ground, his reasoning was so strong and logical, that I was able to entrench myself only behind some banal court phraseology."

That evening Count de Narbonne was invited to dinner by Alexander, but when he left the table he was informed that his horses were awaiting him. As for the Russian war plans, Napoleon's envoy wrote to Marshal Davout: "We are not lucky enough to have them even think of crossing the Niemen."

When Count de Narbonne reported the results of his mission to Napoleon in Dresden, where the French emperor was surrounded by all the sovereigns of the Rhine alliance, the emperor of Austria, and the king of Prussia, the fiery Corsican said: "They want a war—I will start it." The troops then received an order to accelerate their march to the Niemen, and Napoleon himself left Dresden to follow his armies to the Russian border.

Storm clouds gathered over Holy Russia. Six hundred thousand men, inspired by the genius of the Corsican, marched across Prussia to the Niemen. Like the armies of a modern Attila they were to bring ruin and disaster to the vast empire of Alexander. They were composed of the best fighting material that western and central Europe could produce, and they were commanded by the Little Corporal, whose place on the modern Olympus would have been assured had it not been for his lust for power.

Alexander seemed almost helpless in the face of this invasion. Austria and Prussia, his former allies, for whom he had sacrificed not only the interests of his empire, not only his personal ambition, but the precious blood of thousands of sons of Russia, had deserted him and joined the ranks of his enemy. Frederick William III concluded an alliance with Napoleon on March 7, 1812, and informed Alexander of it by a tender letter in which he said that it had been necessary to sacrifice his heart's inclination upon the altar of necessity. Seven days later Austria also became an ally of Napoleon. Both their armies were now marching toward Russia.

Though Alexander had been able to bring Bernadotte and Sweden to his side, it did not mean effective help, for Napoleon's former marshal did not intend to sacrifice the life of a single one of his soldiers in a cause the issue of which was not yet sure. On the other hand, the aged Kutuzov, after defeating the Turks in November, 1811, had finally signed a treaty of peace with the Ottoman Empire on May 14, 1812, the day before he was relieved of his command in the Balkans by Admiral Chichagov. This treaty was ratified on May 25, thus freeing a Russian army which could now be used against the main enemy. Still it was with barely two hundred thousand men that Alexander had to face Napoleon's force. So by necessity, he relied mostly on his invisible allies: space and time.

On June 24, Napoleon's armies began crossing the Niemen. That same evening Alexander attended a ball given outside Vilno in Zakret, the country home of General Bennigsen. Since this residence did not contain a large ballroom, a local architect was ordered to erect a covered gallery in the garden. On the eve of the ball, Alexander received an anonymous message warning him that the gallery was insecure and would collapse as soon as the dances started. Alexander dispatched General de Sanglain, director of military police, to verify the contents of the note. No sooner had de Sanglain reached Zakret than the gallery actually collapsed. The architect fled and later committed suicide. When Alexander was informed of what had happened, he gave immediate orders to clear the floor of the gallery; he had no intention of postponing or countermanding this ball lest people should think that he was afraid. "We will dance in the open air," said he, dismissing de Sanglain.

The ball was a great success. The night was exceptionally warm and the melodies of the music mingled with the aroma of linden trees in full bloom. Dark masses of trees formed a vast colonnade supporting the dome of the star-covered sky. The gay assembly in which the gorgeous uniforms of officers contrasted with the dark coats of civilians and the light frocks of ladies refused to acknowledge that the country was on the eve of war, that soon the brilliant uniforms would be marred by gunpowder and blood, that the light frocks would be replaced by the black garments of mourning. Alexander moved among the dancers with perfect poise as though unaware that his empire was being threatened. His simplicity, his desire to be nothing more than one of the guests, his charming smile, added to the success of the evening. Just before supper was served General Balashov brought the news received from Kovno that the French army had started crossing the Niemen. Alexander ordered Balashov to keep silence so that the festivities might not be disturbed.

The emperor left the ball at the end of the supper. He did not sit down at table, but moved from one table to another with an appearance of perfect enjoyment. I say "appearance" because he played his role marvelously, having already been notified that at this very moment while the ball was going on at Zakret, a scene much more magnificent and solemn was being enacted twenty miles from there. Napoleon crossed the Niemen with six hundred thousand soldiers of whom only thirty thousand were to return to France.

So wrote the Countess de Choiseul-Gouffier.

Upon his return to Vilno, Alexander spent the rest of the night at his desk. Toward morning an imperial manifesto announcing to Count Soltykov, left in charge of the empire in

St. Petersburg, and through him to the rest of Russia, the beginning of hostilities by Napoleon without a declaration of war, was ready to be dispatched. This historical document ended with the following words: *"I will not lay down arms so long as a single enemy soldier remains in my empire."* An order to the troops was also prepared. Napoleon had said in the order to his armies before crossing the Niemen: "Russia is enticed by fate." Alexander's order to his troops ended with the words: "God's wrath be on the one who starts." The great struggle of the century had begun.

VIII

SPACE AND TIME

NAPOLEON's six hundred thousand men safely crossed the Niemen in three days. Like so many huge waves they rolled over the plains of Lithuania finding the country deserted, the Russian army retreating to the interior. On June 28, Napoleon entered Vilno which had been evacuated by the Russians the night before. Here he was approached by Alexander's last messenger of peace. It was General Aide-de-Camp Balashov who brought to the French emperor a personal letter from the sovereign of Russia. Alexander wrote to Napoleon saying that it was not yet too late to maintain peace if the latter would re-trace his steps and recross the Niemen to its western bank.

Napoleon thought differently. To Balashov he said, "Even God could not undo now what has been started." Then as if to emphasize his final decision he asked Alexander's envoy which was the best route to Moscow and St. Petersburg. Bala-shov accepted the challenge and looking straight into the Corsican's eyes, answered: "There are many, sire. One can take also the one of Poltava." This reference to the defeat of Charles XII of Sweden, who a century before had also invaded

Russia, threw Napoleon into such a rage that he forgot the elementary rules of courtesy and dismissed Balashov as if he were a mere subaltern officer. When Balashov reported the results of his mission, Alexander remarked, "I did not expect you would meet with any success, but at least now Europe will know that we are not beginning this slaughter." Later he added, "The charm is broken; now we shall see what brings better results: to be feared or to be loved."

Days went by and Napoleon marched farther and farther into the depths of Russia. The great machine of war which he had put into action was handled by inexpert hands. Notwithstanding the enormous supplies of provisions which followed the troops, already in Lithuania the soldiers remained more than once without bread for days on end while the retreating Russian armies destroyed everything behind them. In addition, this time Napoleon did not have the same sort of army that he had had in Italy in 1796. His generals of 1812 as well as himself had been spoiled by luxury, and so were most of the subordinate officers. They needed comfort and demanded it. When they were unable to obtain it from a legitimate source, they plundered. Soon the enthusiasm which had met Napoleon in Lithuania and Poland gave way to a bitter disillusionment. The rich country became a prey to the vultures into which Napoleon's eagles had become transformed. Many a Polish patriot sighed heavily at the realization of the mistake he had made in linking his fate to that of the Corsican. Yet this was long before the final defeat.

As for Alexander, his situation grew more precarious with every passing day. His presence with the army became the subject of open and bitter criticism. Nominally he was commander in chief, but virtually the army had no supreme command. People remembered the fatal days of Austerlitz when, through him, youngsters like Prince Dolgoruky had upset the wise plans of a Kutuzov. So they began to express openly their desire to see the emperor entrust command of the army to a responsible officer. As a first step toward this goal, they urged him to abandon military affairs to those actually in charge of operations, i.e., to Prince Bagration and to Barclay de Tolly. The Grand Duchess Catherine Pavlovna wrote:

For God's sake do not decide to assume command yourself. . . . There is no time to lose to give the armies a chief in whom the men would have confidence. As for you, you cannot inspire them with any.

Reluctantly Alexander left the armies and proceeded to Moscow. Count Rostopchin, who had been appointed governor general of that ancient capital of Russia through the influence of Alexander's sister, Catherine, prepared a magnificent reception for him. When Alexander saw the genuine enthusiasm of the people of Moscow he felt that his sacrifice had not been made in vain. He still represented that symbol which in the eyes of the Russian people embodied the greatness and magnitude of their country. During his stay in Moscow he received news of the conclusion of a peace treaty with England in Cerebro on July 18, and two days later that of a treaty of alliance signed in Velikie Luki with the representatives of the Spanish Cortes. Russia was gradually gaining friends who were primarily enemies of Napoleon.

Upon his return to St. Petersburg the question of appointing a commander in chief for the armies was pressing. Alexander listened first to the voice of the army and found to his great astonishment that the name of the army's favorite was Count Pahlen. The specter of March 23 reappeared and plunged Alexander into consternation. Was it possible that the man who had not held an active command for the last twenty years could be the real choice of the army? Or was it a reminder and a challenge? Then he listened to the voice of the people and heard the name of Kutuzov. This choice, though less unpleasant, was also unsatisfactory to Alexander because he could not forget the days of Austerlitz when "the old fox of the north," as Napoleon had called Kutuzov, proved to be more of a courtier than a military leader. But the voice of the people clamored louder and louder until Alexander was practically forced to make a decision. After consulting a committee of military and government leaders, he appointed Kutuzov commander in chief on August 20. At the same time he told his intimate friends that in so doing he had complied only with the popular demand. "As for myself," he added, "I wash my hands of it." But the choice proved to be a wise one.

The Most Serene Prince Kutuzov was sixty-seven years old in 1812. Early a lieutenant of the famous Field Marshal Suvorov, he had become aged as much by a number of wounds and the exhaustion of numerous campaigns as by his rather licentious life. Fat, somnolent, having only one eye, the other torn by an enemy bullet, he had difficulty in mounting a horse and once in the saddle could not remain in it for very long. He usually spent his days on a divan, his one eye half closed by a heavy eyelid, inert and panting, changing his position only in order to go to bed. However, his intellectual faculties remained intact. His mind was sharp and discriminating, and he possessed sure tact and a great deal of common sense. He replaced the defect of a lack of scientific knowledge, which he had never acquired because of his laziness, by the fruits of his long experience. His theory of war matched his temperament perfectly. He was slow, but tenacious, generally careful, perhaps to excess, but fertile in stratagems. During actions and engagements he remained impassive, as if having nothing to do with the development of the battle. However, he usually foresaw its ultimate results and had given orders which had to be executed, even if nobody understood them, but which generally proved to be the best. Almost invariably he gave his orders orally because he hated the task of writing—after ten signatures he was out of breath. But he knew how to talk to the soldiers and his paternal ways were universally liked.

Such was the new commander in chief. All Russia had placed its hope in him and was sure that the veteran of so many wars would offer standing battle to the invader. However, when Kutuzov reached the army he continued to retreat to the great astonishment of those who had backed his candidacy, since from him they expected the so long desired action. Meanwhile Napoleon's six hundred thousand men continued their inexorable march toward Russia's holy shrine—Moscow.

Alexander now spent dreary days in the capital of Peter the Great. Notwithstanding his decision to fight to the end, the terrible trial which had befallen his country frightened his imagination and troubled his heart. Visions and recollections of the past began to haunt his soul although he tried to drive them away. More often than ever the disfigured head of Paul appeared before his sleepless eyes. His tormented conscience whispered in his ears words of reproach, accusing him of being the source of the evils that had befallen his Russia. With every passing day Alexander became more and more afraid of life, of that terrible responsibility that life had placed on his stooping shoulders. He had no one to talk to, no one to share with him the burden of his conscience. The world seemed dark and fearful.

Dark and mysterious seemed also that splendid St. Petersburg, clad in marble and granite, with its high embankments which were constantly fighting against the elements to retain the furious onflow of the Neva River that threatened the very existence of the imperial city. True, the marvelous palaces, churches, squares and monuments were of magnificent beauty, but they seemed to be nothing but a vision—a fantastic scenery hiding the real Russia stretched over immense and mournful spaces. Alexander had expressed a hope that "space and time" would break down the force of the indomitable Bonaparte, but at times he had felt that he would like to be absorbed, to be lost, in their fugitive mirage. He had once said to Countess de Choiseul-Gouffier:

At times I have a desire to bang my head against a wall and if I could honorably change my position I would do it without hesitation, because there is no more difficult profession than mine. I have no vocation whatsoever for the throne.

This thought now recurred with ever-increasing tenacity: to abandon the throne, to leave everything and to live the rest of his life "somewhere on the Rhine" in peace and calm.

But could he do it? The struggle that had been started was of such a nature that he could not "honorably change his position." The only thing left to him was to continue his suffering in silence and to profit by the teachings of his youth to conceal his real feelings.

Napoleon still advanced and the guerrilla warfare of the Russian army, though making the great conqueror and his generals feel uneasy, was not of a nature to halt this advance. In St. Petersburg a diversion of the enemy toward the capital was feared. Its inhabitants feeling insecure began to prepare themselves to leave the town at a moment's notice. The government began the evacuation of valuables. Everyone looked upon residence in the northern metropolis as temporary. Yet at this very time Prince Alexander Nikolayevich Golitsyn began the construction of a new palace. Rumors were immediately spread in the city that the emperor's personal friend was a traitor and therefore feared not the invader. These rumors also reached Alexander, but did not move him: he knew his friend too well. However, he went to visit the site of Golitsyn's new palace and inquired, for curiosity's sake, why he was starting such a magnificent edifice in such troubled times.

Golitsyn, who had been known to Alexander from his early youth, when as a page at court he had the reputation of an accomplished Lovelace, had now become a mystic. Abandoning the frivolous writers of eighteenth-century France, the prince at present read only the Bible. He told Alexander that he did not fear Napoleon, because he had confidence in divine Providence. He assured the emperor that the Scriptures contained answers to all problems. Golitsyn then stretched out his hand to take from the table a heavy volume of the Bible, but the book slipped. In falling to the floor it opened at the page containing Psalm XCI. Moved by curiosity, Alexander read: ". . . I will say of the Lord, He is my refuge and fortress: my God: in Him will I trust . . . He shall cover thee with His feathers, and under His wings shalt thou trust . . ." Golitsyn then explained to him that the opening of the book at this particular page was not a coincidence but the expression of the will of God, and Alexander, much impressed, reread the psalm with great eagerness.

When at one of the next church services he attended, Alexander again heard this psalm read in old Slavonic, he became convinced that it was really the expression of God's will. He felt a growing desire to read the Bible which was unknown to him, but the library of his palace did not have a single copy of the holy book. Alexander found instead the complete works of Voltaire, Rousseau, Diderot, Montesquieu, Mably, La Fontaine, even the libertine verses of Parny. The Bible apparently was not in demand at the imperial palace. Then Alexander remembered that his wife had seemed to be interested in religion so he went to her in quest of the desired book. Indeed, Empress Elisabeth Alexeyevna did take an interest in religion and possessed a copy of the Bible but it was in French. Thus it was in a Catholic vulgate that Emperor Alexander sought an answer to his mystic quests. Referring to this time Alexander said in later years:

I simply devoured the Bible, finding that its words poured an unknown peace into my heart and quenched the thirst of my soul. Our Lord, in His infinite kindness, inspired me in order to permit me to understand what I was reading. It is to this edification, to this internal light that I am indebted for all the moral well-being that I have acquired by reading the divine Scriptures.

It was in the fiery prophecies of Jeremiah, Isaiah and Ezekiel that Alexander found astonishing revelations. It seemed to him that the Jewish prophets had foreseen the invasion of orthodox Russia by a little French corporal. Alexander found what he considered exact descriptions of his implacable foe:

His heart is like a stone, the sight of his grinning teeth is terrible, his eyes burn like coals aflame . . . He decided in his mind: I will climb up to heaven, I will place my throne above the stars of the firmament, I will seat myself on the top of the highest mountains beyond the highest of clouds, I will be equal to the Supreme Being . . . I am the king of kings, I will lead against thee people of different languages which like the advancing waves of the sea will break the walls of thy towns.

Was it not a true picture of what was happening? Alexander was deeply moved by the thought that almost countless centuries before, extraordinary men had spoken in a flaming tongue about the impious conqueror, who, forgetting God and sacrificing his immortal soul, dreamed of enslaving all the people and of becoming a god himself. Indeed, Napoleon had told General Wrede that he was going to be the master of the universe. He had reiterated his intentions when, in 1811, he said to Abbé de Pradt, "In five years I will be the ruler of the world." Alexander had no hesitation at present: the Bible truly meant Bonaparte, the man who was stamping out everything that was sacred in order to create new institutions sanctified by himself. This enemy of truth, this enemy of humanity was vain and proud like Satan himself. He was already a demigod, but he aspired to become the Son of God, God Himself.

Thus Alexander spent his days plunging deeper and deeper into a sort of superstitious mysticism. But in reading the Bible he found not only an explanation of the terrible events which like a nightmare enshrouded Russia but also he persuaded himself of his own weakness and moral inferiority. What was he before these formidable forces gathered against Russia? Had he the right to be the ruler of this empire, the master of this valiant nation? Was he not predestined to expiate the sins of past generations? His own sins? No wonder that he had met with no success in his previous attempts. Would things change now? The old hermit Sevastianov was right when he had predicted the disaster of Austerlitz. But had he not also told the young emperor that a day would come when he would triumph over his enemy? Lost in contradictions, deep in a mystic haze, Alexander struggled with himself, while Russia struggled with Napoleon.

As Napoleon's armies were nearing the heart of Russia—Moscow—Kutuzov suddenly halted the Russian retreat. Upon his orders the army began to entrench itself along a vast field near the village of Borodino. Redoubts were hastily built, cannons were moved into position. The men who had begun to grumble not understanding the reasons for such a lengthy retreat were whipped into action by the spirit of battle. Everyone on the Russian side was confident of victory and satisfied that the long desired encounter was now near at hand.

Napoleon was satisfied too. He needed a spectacular victory badly as news from France was far from reassuring. And here was his opportunity. The "old fox from the north" had finally decided to fight in order to defend Moscow from invasion. The Corsican was certain of victory. Proudly he recalled the occupation of Vienna, of Berlin. He pictured to himself already a delegation of Moscovites presenting to him the keys of the city as the municipalities of other European capitals had done before. That, he was sure, would bring the French to their senses, stop their grumbling at excessive taxation and permit him once more to saddle them firmly.

By the evening of September 6 the two enemies had occupied their positions across the broad expanse of the field. All was quiet on the Russian side. On the French side, Napoleon made a last tour of inspection. The Russians could hear the distant shouting: *"Vive l'Empereur!"* as the Little Corporal rode along the lines. They could see the flicker of numerous torches which, added to the shifting flames of bonfires, transformed the calm autumn night into a gruesome picture of some ghastly witch meeting. Soon, however, all was quiet on the French side also. The two armies were now awaiting the break of dawn.

With the first glimmer of light in the east, Napoleon's troops launched their attack, thus starting one of the greatest battles of all times. Furious fighting continued for fifteen hours with changeable fortune. When night fell, the Russians still held most of their positions, although eighty thousand men from both sides were left on the field.

That evening Kutuzov held a council of war. He had previously given an order to resume fighting in the morning, but when the reports of the Russian losses arrived, he was so appalled that he decided to continue the retreat and to abandon Moscow to the enemy. Wearily his generals left the peasant hut where the council had been held to transmit the order to the troops. That very night the Russian army left its blood-drenched redoubts and withdrew beyond Moscow, setting a trap for the "impious conqueror" who had dared to threaten the heart of Russia.

Alexander received the news of the great battle on September 11. Kutuzov's report was short and vague. It seemed as if he had been tired when writing it. To any military man it was obvious that it was a victory for Napoleon since the Russian army continued its retreat. However, Alexander did not want to tell Europe at large of the defeat suffered by his army. He wrote a personal letter to Bernadotte in which he described the battle of Borodino as a brilliant victory for Russia, adding that Kutuzov did not see fit to profit by the fruit of his victory and continued his retreat. A similar message was read to the people of St. Petersburg. On the other hand, Napoleon did not fail to announce his great victory, but he called it the battle of the Moskova, whilst the Russian report named it the battle of Borodino. This confused the contemporaries for a time, but very soon they learned the truth. On September 14, Napoleon's troops entered Moscow. When General Michaud arrived with the news of the occupation of the ancient capital of Russia by the enemy, Alexander said:

This will not decide the struggle. When I shall have used all the means in my power, I shall let my beard grow and live like the poorest peasant eating potatoes, but I will not sign the dishonor of my country and of my dear subjects, whose sacrifices I do appreciate.

The five weeks of Napoleon's stay in Moscow were for Alexander the worst trial he had suffered since the terrible night on March 23, 1801. He felt that all his solemn resolutions "to retreat to Kazan," "to fight on the shores of the Volga," to "let my beard grow and to lead the life of the poorest peasant" could not undo the wrong done, could not heal the mortal wound which the country had received.

On the twenty-seventh of September when Alexander went to assist at a *Te Deum* in the cathedral of Our Lady of Kazan, on the occasion of the anniversary of his coronation, the crowd which had gathered in the cathedral square maintained a hostile silence. He recalled a similar attitude on the part of his people after the Tilsit meeting, but this time he felt that the animosity toward him was greater. Countess Edling née Princess Sturdza, a lady in waiting to Empress Elisabeth Alexeyevna, wrote in her memoirs:

Never shall I forget those minutes as we were ascending the steps of the cathedral. One could have heard a pin drop and I am sure that a single spark would have put this crowd aflame. I glanced at the emperor; I understood what he was undergoing and my knees trembled.

In the meantime terrible news arrived from Moscow. The ancient city was burning and entire quarters were nothing but smoking ruins. The French plundered undisturbed. The holy shrines of Russia were transformed into stables. The people who had not fled were terrorized. But this debauch of the Grand Army was also a sign of its own untimely end. As the supply trains were often captured by Russians on their long way from the Prussian frontier, Napoleon's army in Moscow began to suffer from hunger. The French emperor then decided to break through the Russian lines south of Moscow in order to reach the provinces of Little Russia, rich in foodstuffs. But his army under Murat was beaten at Tarutino on October 18, and Napoleon decided to evacuate Moscow. He had offered peace to Alexander more than once. He had sent a personal letter to his "brother and friend" through a Russian nobleman, Yakovlev, the father of Alexander Herzen. He had appealed to Kutuzov through Count Lauriston who was permitted to cross the lines. He did not understand that Alexander could no longer dream of peace even if he had wanted such an issue himself: Russia was determined to punish the intruder.

The people now took the matter into their own hands and fought a people's war. Men and women alike armed themselves with what they could find and harassed the French troops along the long line of communication. Many a Frenchman who had reached his homeland after the ordeal of the Great Retreat continued to shudder at the recollection of Russian peasant women who were as merciless and revengeful as the ancient furies. This people's war strengthened Alexander in his decision not to conclude peace "while a single enemy soldier remains on Russian soil." But even more than the manifestation of popular sentiment, the justification for his conduct as revealed to him in the Bible gave him strength to oppose all proposals of peace, notwithstanding the fact that these were backed by such persons as his brother, the Grand Duke Constantine Pavlovich, his chancellor, Count Rumiantsov, and last but not least his own beloved sister, the Grand Duchess Catherine Pavlovna. Count Joseph de Maistre wrote: "The emperor is firm and will not even hear anything about peace."

When Alexander received the news of Moscow's evacuation by Napoleon, he realized that the danger was over. A week later the Corsican himself suffered an important defeat at Maly-Yaroslavets. The Grand Army was still imposing, but it was doomed. Alexander's allies—space and time—at present received support from the elements: early frosts mowed down Napoleon's soldiers like grass. A thick white frosty mist enveloped the retreating columns. Frenchmen, Poles, Italians, Germans were lost from the high road and, if they escaped the torturing clutches of the frost, they perished at the hands of the Russian people in arms. They disappeared, they melted—these wonderful soldiers. Napoleon's army seemed to be engulfed by the endless plains of Russia. His proud declaration at the beginning of the campaign that "Russia was enticed by fate" seemed now more applicable to himself.

Alexander watched this phenomenon with a feeling close to religious awe. The idea that miraculous forces were saving Russia embedded itself strongly in his mind. He felt that the Almighty was not forcing him yet to expiate the blood of his father, but he took it as a timely warning. The ancient prophets were right. From now on he was to devote himself to the triumph of everything that was sacred: truth, justice, and the fear of God. The words of Isaiah resounded in his ears like a solemn and mysterious pledge:

The Almighty Jehovah punishes impious kings. He makes the princes fall, reduces them to dust and makes the mighty of the earth seem futile. . . . He breathed on them—they dried out and a wind carried them away like straw. . . . The people and the kingdoms which will not hear Him will perish and disappear forever.

IX

ALEXANDER THE BLESSED

On Christmas day, 1812, Alexander issued an imperial manifesto in which he announced that the patriotic war was ended since "not one enemy soldier remained on Russian soil." But the emperor was not content to let the struggle rest there. Convinced of his own divine mission to rid Europe of Napoleon, he was determined to fight the Corsican until the latter's downfall. Consequently, on New Year's day, 1813, Alexander inaugurated the campaign for the liberation of Europe by crossing the Niemen River at the head of his troops.

Kutuzov, who was still in command of the Russian army, strongly opposed the continuation of the struggle, insisting that Russia's interests had been protected when Napoleon and his formidable army were driven out of the country, and that Europe should find by herself the solution of her difficulties. Although Alexander had honored the aged soldier by conferring upon him the Grand Cross of the Order of St. George—the highest Russian military decoration—and had created him Field Marshal of the Russian army and given him, after Napoleon's manner, the title of Prince of Smolensk, he announced to Sir Robert Wilson, the English general attached to his head-quarters:

I know that the field marshal did not accomplish any-thing that was necessary. All he did against the enemy was what he could not possibly avoid doing, being driven to it by the force of circumstances. He won victories in spite of himself. He played more than one of his tricks on us. Never-theless, the nobility upholds him because it wants to sym-bolize in him the national glory of the last campaign. I will not leave the army anymore, because I do not want to aban-don it to the dangers of such a command.

And to Count Soltykov he wrote: "Thanks be to God, everything goes well with us, but I have some difficulty finding a way to get rid of the field marshal. However, this will have to be done."

The opposition to Alexander's continuation of the struggle was removed, however, by the untimely death of Kutuzov. In a final effort to save Russian armies from defeat, he had opposed Alexander's plan to cross the Elbe River, saying: "Nothing is easier at present than to go beyond the Elbe. But how shall we return? With a bloody nose." Kutuzov knew what he was talking about. The main portion of the Russian army numbered only eighteen thousand men, and Napoleon was gathering fresh forces. But Alexander ignored the wise advice of his field marshal. On April 7, he gave orders to his troops to advance to the Oder. At Steinau he was presented with a crown of laurels by the inhabitants who acclaimed him the victor of Napoleon. Alexander did not keep this crown, however. Notwithstanding his severe criticism of the commander in chief, he knew that at the time it was more fitting for Kutuzov to receive such homage. So he sent the crown to his field marshal with a note: "The laurels belong to you." But this crown was to become a funeral wreath. On April 28, Field Marshal the Most Serene Prince Michael Illarionovich Kutuzov of Smolensk died. His death gave Alexander the opportunity to follow his own policy unhampered by opposition, a policy which was to carry him to the heights of glory though at the cost of many lives and to the detriment of Russia's real interests.

When Alexander began his European campaign, Austria and Prussia were still allied to Napoleon. Prussia was the first to break away from France and to join Alexander. On February 28, 1813, she signed a treaty of alliance with Russia and, on March 16, declared war on France. This alliance brought England once more into the anti-French coalition. Friendly relations between Berlin and London were re-established and even before a diplomatic agreement was signed enormous quantities of war materials were shipped to the mouth of the Elbe River. At the end of April the Marquis of Londonderry paid a visit to the Allies in Dresden and promptly signed a treaty which assured Russia and Prussia of an advance payment of two million pounds sterling in addition to a subsidy of half a million pounds for the maintenance of the Russian fleet in fighting condition. In return for this financial aid, Russia and Prussia promised to maintain in the field an army of from one hundred thousand to two hundred thousand men each. "The sword lifted against Napoleon thus received from the English smithy the tempering and sharpening which it had previously lacked."

Meanwhile Napoleon, having gathered a new army, reached Weimar on April 26, leading his troops in person. In starting this new campaign he had announced to his soldiers: "I will conduct this campaign not as the emperor but as General Bonaparte." Indeed, as General Bonaparte, Napoleon had been invincible. The first battle of the new campaign was fought at Lützen. With only seventy-two thousand men at their disposal, Alexander and the Prussian king attacked Napoleon's army, one hundred twenty-five thousand men strong, and met with defeat. They retreated then to the fortified position at Bautzen, but were promptly overtaken by the Corsican and defeated again. The king of Prussia lost courage and kept on repeating: "I see myself in Memel again." Then Napoleon made a tactical blunder by offering peace to his enemies. Austria lost confidence in him and, although still his ally in name, was now willing to listen to Alexander's proposals. Metternich declared himself ready to negotiate.

On June 27, Russia and Prussia signed a secret convention with Austria at Reichenbach. Notwithstanding this agreement, Austria continued to negotiate with Napoleon. Metternich went to see the French emperor in Dresden, but was handsomely rebuked by him. Napoleon asked the man who had arranged his marriage with Maria-Louisa: "How much did they pay you for betraying me?" And to Caulaincourt, whom he had entrusted with the *pourparlers* for peace with the Allies in Prague, he wrote:

Russia has every right to favorable terms of peace. She has bought them with the heavy price of two campaigns full of hardships, including the devastation of part of her territory and the loss of a capital. Austria, on the contrary, does not deserve anything. Nothing would be more painful to me than to see Austria obtain the advantages and the glory of having restored peace in Europe in reward for her betrayals.

However, Austria was to reap a rich harvest this time, a harvest which she had not sown. Feeling that she could gain more with Alexander than with Napoleon, and having lost much confidence in Napoleon's military genius, she cast her lot with Russia and Prussia. In the night of August 10, woodpiles were set aflame on the heights surrounding Prague, and their sinister glow in the darkness of a clouded night marked the end of the armistice with France, which had been concluded after the battle of Bautzen, the resumption of hostilities against Napoleon, and the entrance of Austria into the coalition.

The three allied armies now numbered collectively 492,000 men and 1,383 pieces of artillery, while Napoleon's army comprised 440,000 men and 1,200 cannons. But the French army was under a single command whereas the Allies could not decide upon the nomination of a commander in chief. The Russian and Prussian armies were both nominally under the command of the Russian general, Barclay de Tolly; the Austrian troops, on the other hand, were entrusted to the leadership of Prince Schwarzenberg. And the presence at the allied headquarters of Emperor Alexander, Emperor Francis, King Frederick William, and the French generals, Moreau and Jomini, who had deserted Napoleon, complicated the conduct of operations.

Napoleon was aware of this state of affairs and counted on the continued lack of unity and centralization in the enemy camp when elaborating his military plans. The practical and well-organized plans of the Corsican, based upon the assumption that the enemy would not be able to check him with similar practical and well-organized plans, failed completely, however, because the French emperor could not count upon the unexpected: the sudden development of Alexander into a military leader.

In the midst of the confusion of ideas and actions in the allied camp, Alexander moved about calmly. Thoroughly convinced of the righteousness of his cause, he discovered in himself unsuspected sources of energy and resourcefulness. He naturally attributed this new-found strength to the intervention of divine forces. This mystic belief in his own mission, together with the petty jealousies and ambitions of his Allies, were decisive in Alexander's assumption of the leadership at the critical moment.

The first battle that the three Allies gave Napoleon turned into a disaster. Alexander had recommended a march with all the combined forces on Leipzig, but Schwarzenberg, after learning that Dresden was defended only by the small corps of Saint-Cyr, led the Austrians to the capital of Saxony in quest of an easy victory. Alexander submitted to Schwarzenberg's plan, because he did not desire to impose his ideas in the face of Austria's opposition right at the beginning of the new campaign when Austria was far from having been completely won to the allied cause. When the troops arrived before Dresden, Schwarzenberg lost twenty-four hours in deliberations, which exasperated General Moreau to such an extent that he threw his hat on the ground in disgust and exclaimed: "Damn it, sir, I am no longer surprised that during the last seventeen years you have always been beaten!" Alexander pacified the excited Frenchman, but could not bring Schwarzenberg to listen to reason. When the battle was finally started it was too late.

A cold penetrating rain, driven by a sharp wind, fell on the combatants. Alexander, on horseback, watched from the top of a small hill where he could see Napoleon's troops coming to the rescue of Saint-Cyr. Here an incident occurred which Alexander interpreted as a miracle, confirming him in the belief of his mystic mission. Toward three o'clock in the afternoon Alexander noticed that his horse was continually beating the ground where its shoe struck a stone. He then moved his horse a few feet aside. General Moreau, also on horseback, followed the emperor. But no sooner had he occupied the place where a few seconds before Alexander had stood than an enemy cannon ball wounded him mortally. He died two weeks later.

Toward evening the Allies were beaten and had to abandon the hope of capturing Dresden. During the retreat into Bohemia, the Allies won a spectacular victory in annihilating the corps of General Vandamme and taking him prisoner. It was the battle of Kulm. It was won when at the decisive moment Alexander took command of the troops and surrounded the French by means of a clever maneuver. This victory was followed by two others, when on August 23, the northern army of the Allies defeated Oudinot, and on August 26 the Prussian general Blücher crushed MacDonald. This succession of victories had an important moral effect upon the troops as well as on constantly wavering Austria. After the defeat at Dresden, Metternich had almost decided to withdraw Austria from the coalition and to throw himself and his country once more upon the mercy of the Corsican. But now that the Allies were gaining victories, he was willing to give them another chance.

Notwithstanding the defeats suffered by his lieutenants, Napoleon was determined to continue the struggle. The Allies, encouraged by their recent victories, were equally determined to face Napoleon in person in order to inflict upon him the final blow. They adopted Alexander's original plan and marched on to Leipzig. Here on the morning of October 16 started the Battle of Nations which lasted three days. It cost nearly one hundred thousand lives, freed Germany, and hurled Napoleon across the Rhine back into France to fight, this time for the preservation not of his empire but of his very existence.

At the beginning of the battle the command of the Allies still lacked unity. Schwarzenberg refused to listen to Alexander and conducted a separate engagement which ended in defeat when General Merfeldt was taken a prisoner. Frederick William was not able to take command of the Prussian troops because he waited to be informed by Alexander which was the proper uniform for him to wear for this occasion. When pressed by his aides to wait no longer, he replied: "After all I cannot appear before my troops in underwear." It devolved, therefore, upon Alexander to assume responsibility for the fight. In doing so he proved to be an able commander. He saved the Allies from ignominious defeat at the end of the first day of battle when at the decisive moment he put into line the one hundred twelve pieces of Russian artillery, which until that time he had kept in reserve. On October 17, Napoleon offered peace, but it was refused. And the next day, after fierce fighting,

Leipzig was captured. This time Alexander's two Allies had submitted themselves to his orders, having come to the realization, at last, not only of the importance of a single command, but also that the Russian emperor was the only one capable of assuming that command.

While the battle was still raging, Alexander entered Leipzig, a real Agamemnon of a new *Iliad*. The great deed of his life seemed to have been achieved: he had shown the world that he could stand his ground in the face even of such an opponent as Napoleon. The battle of Leipzig freed Germany and Europe from oppression by the modern Attila. But the oppressor took refuge in his haunt, and it was there that Alexander was going now. The second part of his enterprise—the campaign of France—was about to begin. Its goal was Paris.

On the morning of March 31, 1814, Paris awoke with a feeling of perplexity: the sun was too glorious, the city too quiet. The roar of artillery which had kept the Parisians awake at night was no more. A heavy silence hung over the brilliant capital of France. Rumors were born and spread every minute. They were contradictory. The Royalists announced jubilantly that the capitulation had been signed, that a deputation of the municipality had visited Emperor Alexander who had promised to take Paris under his protection. The Bonapartists shouted that it was too soon to herald the return of the monarchy, because the Duke of Vicence was in the city and Napoleon was to make his entrance any minute. Listening to all this the man in the street expressed his fear that the Russians might burn Paris as a year and a half before the French had burned Moscow.

Toward nine o'clock in the morning men wearing white cockades and white scarfs appeared on the Place de la Concorde shouting: "Long live the Bourbons!" At first they were few in number and looked rather frightened, but gradually they filled the large square and lined the whole length of the Champs Elysées. By ten o'clock no one doubted any more that the Allies were soon to enter the town. Toward eleven o'clock the red coats of the Cossacks of the Guard, riding fifteen in a row, appeared at the Pantin Gate. They were followed by the Cuirassier and Hussar regiments of the Prussian Guard and by the Lancers and Hussars of Alexander's bodyguard. Immediately after his own Hussars, Alexander rode on a light gray horse clad in a general's uniform with plumed hat. Prince Schwarzenberg, representing the emperor of Austria, was at his right, Frederick William was on his left. They were accompanied by a suite of a thousand officers of the allied general staffs. Then came the infantry regiments, then the Russian Horse Guards followed by forty-seven squadrons of Russian Cuirassiers. These were the best troops the Allies possessed and the impression they made on the French people was tremendous.

At first the Allies rode through almost deserted streets. Only after they had passed the Saint-Denis Gate did they find the streets lined with people shouting: "Long live Emperor Alexander! Long live the Allies!" As soon as Alexander heard these cries he said in a loud clear voice: "I have come to you not as an enemy, but as a friend. I bring you peace." Paris responded with wild applause. Gradually, as the Allies were nearing the center of the city, the ovations became more and more delirious. Royalists now mingled openly with the common people. White cockades were everywhere; white banners, rapidly manufactured from bed sheets and tablecloths, hung from the windows. Women were waving white handkerchiefs, calling to each other: "They do not look bad at all!" "How handsome Emperor Alexander is!" "How graceful his manners are!" "Let him remain in Paris or let them give us a sovereign who would be like him."

Alexander stopped near the Elysées Palace and reviewed the troops. The crowd around him was so dense that Prince Eugene of Württemberg who stood nearby feared lest the ladies of Paris would leave him completely naked, so ardently they attacked his coat, his boots, his spurs, even the tail of his horse, in order to see better. When the review was over Alexander proceeded to Talleyrand's residence. The clever Prince of Benevent had arranged for Alexander's stay at his house by informing the Russian emperor that the Elysées and Tuileries palaces had been mined and were therefore unsafe, and by offering his own "humble" abode instead. Having Alexander as his guest, it was easier for the former Bishop of Autun to carry out his plans for a restoration, since he had espoused the cause of the Bourbons. The clever diplomat knew that he would have to present convincing arguments to the Russian emperor who was not at all certain that the restoration of a legitimate monarchy would be the best solution for France's political and dynastic crisis. As a matter of fact, Alexander cherished an idea of seeing France a democratic republic. He had spoken of it to Vitrolles, a Royalist agent who had come to see him in the allied camp at Châtillon. He was still toying with this idea when he took up residence in Talleyrand's palace. But his host's disarming manner in which he presented false reports about the popularity of the Bourbons with the French nation finally convinced Alexander and he gave his support in favor of the aged Louis XVIII. The unscrupulous Talley-rand won a major diplomatic victory.

Alexander's stay in Paris was extremely gratifying to him. He had come as a liberator, not as a conqueror. When someone suggested that he should insist upon changing the name of the Austerlitz bridge, he replied: "It will be sufficient for future generations to know that Emperor Alexander crossed the Austerlitz bridge with his army." Europe greeted him now as the leader of a glorious campaign, as the victor of the invincible. Everyone flattered him, called him a new Agamemnon. But the greater the flattery, the more skeptical he was about it. He remembered his triumphant entrance into Dresden a year before. He remembered the jubilations of the Saxons who greeted him as their savior. Only a few weeks later these same Saxons greeted Napoleon with similar jubilations when to the roar of guns and the ringing of church bells the Corsican made his entrance into the city.

Lützen, Bautzen, Dresden, then Kulm, then Leipzig. What a strange calm had dominated him in this Battle of Nations, when everything seemed to be lost, when the armies were on the verge of beating a retreat. Had it not been for his initiative, the Allies would have met with certain defeat. For the first time people saw in him a great captain and obeyed him without murmur. He himself felt, however, that he was being led by a mysterious force. Was it not a new manifestation of divine Providence? After Leipzig he was the master of Europe, but the very nature of the victory made him feel the vanity, the futility of glory. He had not neglected to take the Bible with him. Lying on his hard leather mattress, a leather pillow under his head, he read every night some passage from this ex-

traordinary and enlightening book. Alexander was accused of
ambition, of lust for power and glory, when he started the
campaign of Europe. His critics claimed that he should have
been satisfied with the expulsion of Napoleon from Russia.
Some of them even advanced the thought that Alexander was
jealous of Kutuzov's laurels and wanted to reap glory for himself. These critics could not understand the true motives of
the Russian emperor. Alexander had insisted upon this campaign
because he remembered well what he had learned at Tilsit
when, for a moment, Napoleon had revealed his true self: it
was Bonaparte's conviction that for him to reign meant to
fight, and to fight meant to conquer; he could not possibly
exist as a peaceful ruler. To this Emperor Alexander opposed
his own idea: "to return to every nation the possibility of enjoying its rights and its institutions," to place them all, including
his own Russia, under the obligations of a general alliance, in
order that they might protect themselves against new con-
querors. He had written to La Harpe:

> These are the foundations on which, with the help of
> God, we hope to establish the new system. Divine Provi-
> dence has put us on the road which leads directly to our goal.
> We have already attained a part of it. The other part is still
> surrounded with difficulties. It is imperative that we should
> overcome them.

And he had been confident of the outcome when on New
Year's day, 1814, he had seen his Cossacks cross the Rhine.
They were to overcome the remaining difficulties, but not to
conquer. Indeed, the new campaign was not one of conquest.

It seemed as if Alexander was determined to defeat the enemy not with the force of his armies but with the spread of his charm. His orders to the army announced repeatedly that his troops should be generous with the enemy. And his solicitude was extended not only to the peaceful inhabitants of beautiful France but to the enemy soldiers as well. Lord Castlereagh, representing the British government at allied headquarters, reported this "strange" behavior of the Russian emperor:

At present the greatest danger for us is to be found in the chivalrous attitude of Emperor Alexander. In so far as Paris is concerned, his personal opinions are diametrically opposed to the considerations of military strategy and political expediency. It seems that Emperor Alexander is only looking for the opportunity of entering Paris at the head of his valiant army in order to display the greatness of his soul in retaliation for the destruction of his capital.

Castlereagh had no time to read the Bible and, consequently, could not understand Alexander's motives.

On April 6, Napoleon signed at Fontainebleau a complete abdication for himself and for his heirs. The Allies then sent him into exile on the island of Elba. The way for the restoration of legitimate monarchy in France was now clear.

These important events occurred during Easter week. On Easter Sunday Paris beheld an extraordinary spectacle. At the head of his troops, Alexander proceeded to the exact spot where the weak but kind Louis XVI lost his head on the guillotine. There a temporary altar had been erected. All the Russian clergy that could be found in the French capital were summoned by the emperor to celebrate a requiem service for the unfortunate king of France. Enormous crowds of people gathered for the occasion, people of all walks of life—from the humble workingmen and laborers to Napoleon's marshals and Royalist leaders. It was a truly impressive moment when, in the midst of Paris, melodious Russian chanting sent up to God the prayers of a schismatic nation for the repose of the soul of a Catholic king.

Notwithstanding this touching tribute to a member of the Bourbon dynasty, Alexander accepted the restoration reluctantly. "The Bourbons," he said, "who have not reformed and will never reform, preserve all the superstitions of the *ancien régime*." Alexander could have added, from personal experience, that their haughtiness, incompatible with the times, certainly could not contribute to the consolidation of the new regime. Indeed, Louis XVIII treated even the Russian emperor as an inferior. Upon leaving England, he had declared that he owed his throne, after God, only to the prince regent. He ignored the fact that had it not been for Alexander's troops, he would still be a pensioner of the British crown. At Compiègne, he first received Alexander's ambassador and, later, Alexander himself as if they were some poor relatives humbly requesting favors. Afterward, at a dinner in the Tuileries Palace, to which Emperor Alexander and the king of Prussia were invited, he preceded everyone else into the dining room, and when a court valet had the temerity to serve the Russian emperor before him, the former Count of Provence banged the table with his fist and shouted: "To me first, to me first!" Later, recalling this Bourbon "hospitality," Alexander remarked ironically: "We northern barbarians are more polite with our guests." Inexcusable as it is, this attitude toward Emperor Alexander on the part of the king of France can be explained, perhaps, by the resentment that Louis XVIII felt against the emperor of Russia for having forced him to accept a constitution. Alexander forbade his entrance into Paris unless he took the oath to a constitution elaborated by the French Senate, or made a definite declaration to that effect. Grudgingly, Louis XVIII chose the second alternative and made his entrance into the capital of France on May 3, 1814.

Through all these events, preoccupied as he was with the liberation of Europe from the "infernal" domination of the Corsican, Alexander forgot his own people. He had insisted that the French be granted a constitution by their legitimate king, yet he forgot to care for his own peasants, who in soldiers' uniforms had not only mightily contributed to the achievement of his aim, but had won for him glory never before attained by a human being. The Agamemnon of the *Iliad* was but a faint and feeble predecessor of this new Agamemnon. If, however, Alexander seemed to have forgotten his own people, they did not forget their sovereign. In Bruchsal, Baden, where he had joined Empress Elisabeth Alexeyevna who was sojourning with her mother, Alexander received a deputation of representatives of the Holy Synod, of the Council of State, and of the Senate—the ecclesiastical, legislative, and judiciary bodies of the empire—who begged him humbly to accept from his loving subjects the title of *Alexander the Blessed*.

X

THE HOLY ALLIANCE

WITH Napoleon seemingly safely exiled on the island of Elba, the Allies called a Congress at Vienna to divide the spoils of war and to lay the foundations of a new Europe on the ruins of Napoleon's empire. Alexander arrived in the Austrian capital on September 25, 1814, together with the king of Prussia, and took up his residence at the imperial palace—the Hofburg. He was accompanied by a large suite. Never before had the Hofburg seen such a gathering of royalty as in this autumn of 1814. Besides Emperor Alexander and Empress Elisabeth Alexeyevna there were Alexander's two sisters, Anna Pavlovna and Catherine Pavlovna. The latter, having failed to find a suitable husband at the English court, was now displaying her "Slavic charm" in Vienna. She succeeded in capturing the heart of the crown prince of Württemberg and later became queen of that second-rate German state. Grand Duke Constantine also made an appearance at the Congress but, bored by the proceedings, he soon returned to Warsaw to seek the company of Julia Grudzinska, the future Princess Lowicz, his morganatic wife. The king of Prussia was accompanied by his brother

Prince William and by Prince August. Then there was the king of Denmark with his son-in-law the prince of Holstein-Beck; the king of Bavaria and his queen—the sister of Empress Elisabeth Alexeyevna—together with the two royal princes; the king and crown prince of Württemberg; the former vice-roy of Italy—Prince Eugène de Beauharnais—and almost a hundred petty German princes.

A contemporary wrote:

It is difficult to name them all, and more difficult still to state their pretensions. But their position during the Congress was not an enviable one: no one wanted to listen to them, no one wanted to read and even less to answer their numerous petitions.

All these princes, who would have done much better to have stayed at home but who were attracted like butterflies by the brilliancy of the Congress, played in Vienna merely the part of courtiers.

Indeed they seemed to be courtiers especially in the presence of the Russian emperor, who, casting aside the rules of etiquette, paid more attention to a Swiss landsman or to a pretty Viennese, than to these German princes. . . .

Emperor Francis of Austria remained outside this turmoil as far as the affairs of state were concerned. He had an implicit faith in Metternich's ability. He was very busy entertaining and, even more than that, he was preoccupied with finding the necessary funds for these entertainments. After all, it was a heavy burden upon the Austrian treasury, which was empty, when the daily expenditures at the Hofburg for food alone ran up to fifty thousand florins. New taxes were imposed upon the people of Austria to permit their emperor to play the role of a perfect host.

The luxury which was displayed during the Congress was not limited to the Hofburg. A banquet offered by Alexander at the palace of Count Razumovsky, the Russian ambassador to Austria and one of the plenipotentiaries at the Congress, to three hundred sixty staff officers of the allied armies had cost two hundred thousand florins. Then on November 24, the day of Saint Catherine, a big ball given by Alexander in honor of his sister was followed by a supper, the menu of which included: sterlets (a sort of small sturgeon) from the Volga, oysters from Ostend, truffles from Périgord, oranges from Palermo, pineapples from the imperial hothouses in Moscow, strawberries from the royal gardens of England, and grapes from Burgundy and Champagne. In addition to this, every guest received a plate full of cherries which had come from the imperial gardens in St. Petersburg at a cost of half a dollar for each and every cherry.

Notwithstanding the witty remark of the aged Prince de Ligne that "the Congress dances, but does not advance" all these feasts, banquets, balls did not obscure Alexander's vision of the purpose and aim of the Congress. He fought his way through the innumerable obstacles strewn in his path by the leading statesmen at the Congress—Metternich, Castlereagh, and Talleyrand. At first France was excluded from the Congress, but soon, through the intercession of Metternich and Castlereagh, Talleyrand, who had arrived in Vienna as Min-

ister of Foreign Affairs of Louis XVIII, was granted admission
to the deliberations. The French minister promptly became
the leader of this trio in its opposition to the Russian emperor.
This man, who had betrayed every master he had ever served,
now posed as the defender of the interests of Europe.

What an extraordinary sight it must have been when his
unprepossessing figure, clad in an old-fashioned coat of the
time of the Directory, stooping, heavily advancing on
crooked legs, appeared at some brilliant court gathering. An
enormous mouth filled with rotten teeth above a high collar,
small deep-set gray eyes without any expression in them, a
face striking in its insignificance, cold and calm, incapable
of blushing or revealing any emotions . . . a real Mephi-
stopheles.

When Alexander came to Vienna he had a very definite plan
as to what Russia was to receive as a reward for her actions in
safeguarding and liberating Europe. He wanted Poland, and
in return for the Polish lands then belonging to Austria and
Prussia, he planned to compensate the former by territorial
acquisitions in Italy, and to compensate the latter by the annexation of the kingdom of Saxony. The Italian plan for Austria
did not meet with any objection, because Talleyrand and
Castlereagh had made the interests of Austria their own in
order to counterbalance the might of Russia, but the questions
of Poland and of Saxony met with so much opposition that
Alexander had to use all his ingenuity to reach at least a compromise. Far gone seemed the days when he was acclaimed by
all as the savior of Europe. He was undoubtedly right when

he said, "Human gratitude is found as seldom as a white raven."

Meanwhile the festivities in Vienna continued. Dinners, receptions, dances, masquerades succeeded one another almost without interruption. Such festivities, however, could not prevent the spreading of rumors that the Congress had reached an impasse. Things went so far that England, France, and Austria, having signed a secret treaty of alliance, were actively preparing for a war against Russia. But war clouds were gathering on another part of the European horizon. On March 1, 1815, Napoleon disembarked with his Guard in the Gulf of Juan.

The news of Napoleon's flight from Elba was received by Metternich in the night of March 7. It was contained in a dispatch from the Austrian consul general in Genoa and read:

> The British Commissioner Campbell entered port to obtain information whether Napoleon had not been seen in Genoa as he had disappeared from the island of Elba. As the answer was in the negative the British frigate took to sea without delay.

Not expecting anything important from Genoa, Metternich did not take the trouble to read the dispatch at once and opened it only in the morning. As soon as he had read the short announcement, he realized its importance. He went first to Emperor Francis, then to Alexander, finally to the king of Prussia. In less than an hour a new war was decided upon.

One can easily imagine what it meant to most of the people present in Vienna. The specter of a vindictive Napoleon returning to punish all the traitors presented itself before more than a score of eyes. Talleyrand was one of them. The Prince

Prince Alexander Golitsyn

Count Alexis Arakcheyev

Michael Speransky

Field Marshal Prince Kutuzov

ALEXANDRE PREMIER.

EMPEREUR ET AUTOCRATE DE TOUTES LES RUSSIES.

ROI DE POLOGNE

Emperor Alexander in 1815

of Benevent knew that this time he would not obtain mercy from his twice-betrayed master. His high collar must have seemed to strangle him. He almost felt the cold steel knife of the guillotine on his neck. Such was the magnetic attraction of Napoleon's name, that everyone, forgetting the Corsican's defeats of not so long ago, remembered only his victories, and, trembling, awaited new ones.

Upon landing on the soil of France, Napoleon had proudly announced to his soldiers: "The eagle with the national banner will fly from church steeple to church steeple until it reaches those of Notre Dame in Paris." And he proved to be right.

Twenty days after he had disembarked in the Gulf of Juan, he was in Paris at the Tuileries Palace, without having fired a single shot, while Louis XVIII was hurrying toward Lille and the Belgian frontier. In his haste, the king of France left on his desk the text of the secret treaty directed against Russia. Wanting to open Alexander's eyes to the treacherous behavior of his Allies and thus to secure him as a friend, Napoleon promptly sent this important document to Vienna, hoping to destroy the new coalition formed against him. Alexander, however, considered that his mission would not be fulfilled if he permitted Napoleon's return. His belief in this mission was so strong that he did not hesitate. He called for Metternich and calmly showed him the incriminating document in the presence of a witness:

This was a moment of the greatest importance. Russia's policies had now the opportunity of following an open road in pursuance of their cherished aim, based on the sane principles of state egotism, and not on romanticism. But as was to have been expected mystical romanticism and the real greatness of Alexander's soul primed the sovereign's decision. When Metternich started an explanation Alexander interrupted him by saying: "Metternich, as long as we live, there shall never be a word about this between us. We have other things to do at present. Napoleon has returned; therefore our alliance must be stronger than ever."

With these words Alexander threw the proof of Metternich's duplicity into the flames of an open fireplace.

Napoleon's fate was decided at Waterloo. The Russian troops had time only to reach the Rhine. Alexander made a second entrance into Paris. But this time his feelings were far different from those of a year before. After all, he was right when he supposed that Paris might turn out to be a second Dresden. The same populace which had acclaimed him as its liberator, only a few months later had kissed the boots of the Corsican. In consequence, Alexander did not show much interest in the fate of Paris this time and abandoned it to the vexatious and arbitrary measures of his German allies.

The Hundred Days having strengthened the bonds of common interest among the Allies were also instrumental in bringing the Congress of Vienna to an end. When, after Waterloo, the plenipotentiaries gathered again, they did not retain any of the "fighting" spirit which they had displayed in the early months of the negotiations. The specter of the Corsican still held a strong spell over all of them. Too, summer had come, and the Viennese hostesses had left the capital. So no one remained to dance with, to flirt, or to intrigue with and the final act was speedily concluded on June 9, 1815. A new map of Europe came into being. The nations which did the least, however, obtained the most. They were England and Austria. The whole arrangement was nothing but a compromise of the big powers very similar in result to the dealings that took place a century later and which also brought a new map of Europe into existence. Metternich sacrificed Murat, King of Naples, to the interests of the Bourbons. Frederick William abandoned his ambitious dream of incorporating with Prussia the whole of Saxony. The eastern, i.e., the Balkan, question was completely left out of any settlement despite Alexander's previous desire to have it solved. Alexander had also to give up the complete restoration of Poland.

Notwithstanding the active support that the Poles had given Napoleon during the invasion of Russia, Alexander had not lost his sympathy for the Polish nation. After the capture of Paris, he had received the submission of the Polish corps of Poniatowski, and instead of disbanding it sent it to Poland to form the nucleus of a national army under the command of Grand Duke Constantine. Hearing of this, the veteran Kosciuszko hastened to the French capital to pay homage to the Russian emperor and to offer his services to the new master of his country. At that time Alexander revealed his unselfish intentions with regard to the Poles in a letter to La Harpe: "My intention is to return to them all that I can get of their country, and to give them a constitution the elaboration of which I reserve to myself." But the difficulties he encountered in the realization of his plan were almost insurmountable. Not only did he have to face the stubborn opposition of his Allies, who feared that a restored Poland under a dynastic union with Russia would increase considerably Russia's might and upset the balance of power in Europe, but his own subjects grumbled at the idea of seeing old Russian lands included in a regenerated Poland. Alexander was unquestionably right when he said: "Poland has three enemies, Prussia, Austria, and Russia—and one friend, myself." So he had to be content when finally he was able to restore a Polish kingdom with a much smaller territory than that before 1772, when the first partition of Poland took place.

Of the other countries of Europe, the worst fate was suffered by Italy. She was dismembered once more, put under a multitude of foreign rulers, most of whom were Hapsburgs, with the exception of tiny Sardinia-Piedmont, and became nothing more than "a geographical expression." Belgium was given to the king of Holland in compensation for the lost Dutch colonies taken by England. The only small state that was unexpectedly favored was Switzerland. She received from the powers three new beautiful cantons and the guarantee of perpetual neutrality.

Was all this worth the ruinous wars, the hundreds of thousands killed, the upsetting of the equilibrium of the world? Indeed it was, in the mind of Alexander. If he had failed to realize his "old favorite idea" to restore the kingdom of Poland in all its splendor and to add by doing so a new jewel to the crown of his dynasty, he had achieved two other things, perhaps more important in his own eyes. He had broken the power of Napoleon and had set a moral Christian basis for the government of nations. His determination to bring to an end Napoleon's career as a mighty ruler had never left him for a single moment since the days of Austerlitz, the mere recollection of which still flushed his cheeks, since the days of Tilsit when he had come to know his opponent, since the tragic days of 1812 when he had found a revelation in the Holy Scriptures which opened his eyes to the road he must follow. Even when Napoleon made his spectacular escape from Elba and started his triumphant march across the country to its heart—Paris—he remained firmly convinced of the righteousness of the mission he had undertaken.

When La Harpe, deeply moved by the enthusiasm displayed by the French people toward Napoleon, tried to persuade Alexander that the projected new crusade against the Corsican and France was a violation of the inalienable right of a people to choose their master, and that the enforcement of a rule which had become hateful to the people could not contribute to a lasting peace, Alexander was sympathetic but firm. He could not believe that divine Providence would choose Napoleon as its tool for the welfare of France. Too much blood, too many tears were connected with Bonaparte's career. When later, not satisfied with Alexander's answer, La Harpe addressed his pupil once more, describing what he himself had seen in Paris after the return of the Eagle, he received a personal letter in which Alexander wrote:

I have received your two letters. Forgive me for my frankness, but I completely disagree with you. To submit oneself to the genius of evil means to enforce his power, to place in his hands a tool for the erection of a tyranny much worse than the previous one. It is necessary to have the bravery to fight him, and with the help of divine Providence, through unity and perseverance we shall reach a happy outcome. This is my conviction.

And after Napoleon had been shipped to the distant shores of Saint Helena, Alexander was able to satisfy himself with the thought that the "genius of evil," "the impious king" had received his deserved punishment and it was he, Alexander, the humble servant of Christ the Savior, who had indeed been chosen by divine Providence for the enactment of God's will.

Had Alexander rested upon his military laurels as the man who defeated Napoleon, his fame would have been secure for all time. But it was at this time that his old dream of establishing a new "Respublica Christiana" in Europe took root firmly in his mind. As early as 1804, when he was planning his first encounter with Napoleon, he had entrusted Novossiltsov with the drafting of a document which, composed in the spirit of Christian morals, was to become a first edition of the famous treaty of the Holy Alliance. The prophecy of Sevastianov on the eve of the first campaign in 1805, the memorable days of 1812, the final collapse of Napoleon's power—all led Alexander to resurrect his vague plan of 1804 and to offer to his Allies the most astonishing treaty of all times.

In the early days of September, 1815—probably with the intention of restoring the prestige that the Russian armies had somewhat lost by their absence from the bloodstained field of Waterloo—Alexander decided to display their well-trained strength as a reminder to friend and foe. He had never had much confidence in Austria's faith. As for Prussia, the disappointment with which she had received the settlements of Vienna, accusing Alexander of not having kept his word with respect to Saxony, was rather alarming. So a great review of the entire Russian force was held upon the plain of Vertus, near Châlons.

In the morning of September 10, the magnificent troops of

Alexander's guard and line passed before the Russian sovereign and his guests, the emperor of Austria and the king of Prussia. It was a perfect display of what drilling can accomplish with military units. Not one of the 107,000 parading infantrymen was out of step. The Duke of Wellington, who was present, remarked with admiration: "I could never have imagined that it was possible to bring an army to such an extraordinary state of perfection."

Here also, for the first time, the people of Europe watched the mass of the turbulent ranks of the Cossacks, the wild cavalry of the steppes, whose exploits during Napoleon's retreat had given them a world-wide reputation. But what was perhaps the most remarkable part of this display was the religious ceremony which took place the next day. In the middle of the broad plain which the day before had served as a parade ground seven altars were erected, one for each army corps, and a *Te Deum* celebrated simultaneously at all the altars. The beautiful and imposing ritual of the Russian Orthodox Church with its rich display of sacerdotal garments, with its melodious chanting in the midst of magnificent scenery, impressed Emperor Francis and King Frederick William perhaps as much as the display of sheer military force.

Still under the powerful influence of this significant pageant, the sovereigns present at the review were invited by Alexander to affix their signatures to the famous document subsequently known to history as the Holy Alliance.

By this document the emperor of Russia, the emperor of Austria and the king of Prussia formally declared that henceforth their united policy had but a single object:

To manifest before the whole universe their unshakable determination to take as their sole guide, both in the administration of their respective states and in their political relations with other governments, the precepts of religion, namely, the rules of Justice, Christian Charity, and Peace.

XI

IN QUEST OF SALVATION

ALEXANDER returned to his capital on December 14, 1815 and was acclaimed by his own people as the "victor of the invincible." But the Alexander who now resumed his task of sovereign was a very different one from the Alexander of four years before. It was obvious that even before applying the ideas of the Holy Alliance to his relations with other countries, Alexander was determined to make them the guiding principles of his rule over Russia. In an imperial manifesto promulgated on New Year's day, 1816, after thanking the army and the people for what they had done during the epic fight against Napoleon, whom he called "a criminal of common law," Alexander continued:

But the very greatness of these deeds indicates that it was not solely our work. For their completion, God had given His strength to our feeble hands, His wisdom to our ignorance, His foresight to our blindness. What shall we choose: pride or humility? Our pride would be unjust, ungrateful, criminal before the One who poured on us such great benefits; it would place us on the same level with those whom we deposed. Our humility will better our morals, it will efface our faults before God, will bring us honor, real glory, and will show to the world that we are fearful to none, but also that we fear no one.

While pursuing the "impious king" across Europe, Alexander had left Russia in the hands of incompetent officials who did nothing to further the reforms so wisely begun. These reforms should have been followed by new and more extensive ones, but for four years nothing had been done for the betterment of Russia's internal situation. The French chargé d'affaires in St. Petersburg, Count de La Moussaye, gives an interesting description of Russia at that time:

Russia is enjoying the glory which she won by her victories. Dazzled by these successes the Russian empire puts itself in the front row and proclaims its sovereign the arbiter of Europe and of half of Asia. Meanwhile, the country itself is devoid of laws, of decent administration and is almost completely lacking in industries. . . . Arbitrary authorities govern the interests of ninety-nine per cent of the entire population. . . .

To sum it all up, everything comes up to the decision of this primitive power which is crushed under the burden of its endless attributions; 250,000 unsettled questions await the supreme decision; mistakes and iniquities complement each other and like the courts of justice the administration lags. . . . Four hundred million francs constitute the revenues of this empire which occupies one-seventh part of the entire globe; 300 millions are appropriated for the needs of the army whilst the sciences, the arts, all that which makes peace glorious is left undeveloped.

A tributary of entire Europe for its needs and fantasies, Russia is unable even to clothe her soldiers by whose support alone she exists. . . . Seen from a close angle this country is far from offering the aspect of one of those nations which through a successive development of wise institutions, of virtues and the most noble faculties of mankind have rested their glory and their power on a solid foundation.

For this state of affairs, Alexander alone was responsible. Yet after his return, aware as he was of the need for a wise administration of the affairs of Russia, he could not seem to bring himself to follow the ambitious course set in the first years of his reign. Metternich wrote: "It is from this time that Alexander became visibly tired of living." He found excuse after excuse for abandoning the affairs of state to others. He said:

One cannot do all things at once; events did not permit me to busy myself with the affairs of government as I should have done. . . . The army, the government are not as I should like to see them, but how can one remedy it? One cannot accomplish everything with a single gesture; I have no collaborators.

The great satisfaction he had felt after the defeat of Napoleon had vanished. Qualms of conscience troubled him more and more. He suffered from insomnia and more than once the ghostly recollection of the night of March 23, 1801, made him tremble in cold sweat. His mind was occupied more and more with the problems of his own salvation. General Alexander Mikhailovsky-Danilevsky, who accompanied the emperor on many of his journeys, gives the following characteristic description of Alexander in 1816:

> I spent . . . evenings in the same room with the emperor and not being a lover of dancing nor a seeker of new acquaintances, I was able to observe him constantly and found little sincerity in all his actions. Everything seemed to be nothing but a mask. As usual he was gay and talkative. He danced much, and wanted through his simplicity to have people forget his rank. Notwithstanding his inimitable amiability and the charm of his behavior, I could observe him from time to time casting glances, which indicated that his soul was troubled and that his innermost thoughts were directed to objects far removed from this ball and these women, who seemed to have captured his attention.

This "troubled soul" of Alexander's prompted him to seek refuge from himself in endless travels. During the years from 1816 to 1825, he made fourteen extensive trips through Russia, in addition to a number of visits to localities near St. Petersburg and his European journeys to attend the congresses at Aix-la-Chapelle (Aachen), Troppau (Opava), Lajbach (Ljubljana), and Verona. In fact, he spent two-thirds of these years outside his own capital. When he resided in St. Petersburg, he spent most of his time in the seclusion of his summer residence of Tsarskoye Selo. And he plunged deeper and deeper into the bottomless pit of religious mysticism opened to him in the dark hours of 1812 by Prince Alexander Golitsyn.

It was Golitsyn and Rodion Koshelev who exercised the greatest influence on Alexander's spiritual development. These two men, so different in many respects, possessed a common bond not only in their spiritual philosophy but also in the deep friendship which Alexander had for both of them. The extensive correspondence which the sovereign maintained with them as well as the frequent personal meetings kept Alexander in constant contact with these two men whom he called his "brothers in Christ." Of the two, Koshelev was more profound and better acquainted with the currents and trends of mystical thought in his time. Having married the sister of a well-known Russian mystic, S. I. Pleshcheyev, he became a freemason under the latter's influence. In order to obtain first-hand information on the prevailing trends in Europe, he traveled extensively. During these travels he met personally the leading mystics of the time, Saint Martin, Eckartshausen, Swedenborg, Lavater, and Jung-Stilling, with whom he maintained a lively correspondence. When settled in Russia again, Koshelev undertook to spread the fruit of his knowledge and of his belief among members of St. Petersburg society. To Alexander he sent every new publication of European and Russian mystics, invariably receiving warm acknowledgments in which the emperor humbly recommended himself to his "dear and tender friend's" prayers and signed himself, "Yours, heart and soul in Our Lord the Savior."

Before Koshelev gained his ascendancy over Alexander, he was instrumental in bringing Golitsyn into the fold of mysticism. Scion of an illustrious family descended from Gedimin, grand duke of Lithuania, Prince Alexander Golitsyn spent a frivolous childhood and youth at the court of the Great Catherine, where he was a playmate of Alexander's. During the reign of Emperor Paul he was banished from the capital and resided in Moscow. There he completed his rather haphazard education by extensive reading in the enormous library of Count Buturlin. Upon Alexander's accession to the throne Golitsyn returned to St. Petersburg and to the great surprise of everybody including himself was appointed Procurator of the Holy Synod, which office made him the administrative head of the Russian Orthodox Church. A few years later Alexander added to his duties those of the State Office for Foreign Religions which dealt with the legally recognized faiths outside the Russian Orthodox. Contrary to all expectations, Golitsyn proved to be an able and tactful administrator. During his tenure of office he met Koshelev and, to the astonishment of his friends, soon abandoned his gay and frivolous life to consecrate himself to the study of the Bible and of writers on mysticism. Golitsyn's intimate contact with Alexander can be illustrated best by the fact that during a ten-year period he dined with the emperor 3,635 times, which is almost every day.

Devoted as he was to Golitsyn and Koshelev, Alexander did not confine his quest for salvation to what these two mystics could offer him. He turned to wherever he thought he could find those spiritual values which had been denied him in his youth. With the greatest eagerness he opened his heart and soul to everyone and everything that seemed to have a divine message for him. It was this eagerness to find revelation at each turn of the road that placed him for a brief but eventful year under the influence of one of the strangest personalities of that troubled epoch—Baroness de Krüdener.

In the month of June, 1815, the little town of Heilbrunn

had been chosen for the headquarters of the Russian army, hurrying from the eastern borders of Prussia to the scene of renewed conflict with the returned Eagle. Alexander arrived from Vienna, stopping on his way in Munich and Stuttgart. After the glamor and festivities of the Bavarian and the Württemberg courts, which were intended to outdo the receptions tendered Alexander in Vienna, the emperor sighed with relief when, on June 4, he reached the quiet German city. Alexander was pleased with his modest quarters, with the unintelligent appearance of the inhabitants, with the hot days and cool nights. At other times all this would have annoyed him, but now he felt it was beneficial to him because at last he could collect his thoughts and meditate upon the mysterious ways of divine Providence.

"My first action was to open the Holy Book which I have always with me," Alexander related in later years to Countess Edling, "but my mind could not grasp the sense of what I was reading. My thoughts were incoherent, my heart was oppressed. I put the book aside and started to think what a relief it would have been for me at such a time to have a real talk with a person who would be in spiritual unity with me. This thought made me recall you and what you told me about Madame de Krüdener as well as my desire communicated to you to meet her. 'Where is she?' I asked myself, 'and how could I meet her? Probably never!'

"At that moment I heard a knock at the door. It was Prince Volkonsky. With an air of impatience and discontent he told me that he was sorry to trouble me, but that he did it only to free himself from the insistence of a woman who demanded to see me. He said it was Madame de Krüdener. You can imagine my surprise! It seemed to me as if I were dreaming. Such a sudden answer to my thoughts seemed to me to be more than a coincidence. I received her immediately and she addressed me, as if she were reading my very soul, with strong and consoling words, which calmed the troubled thoughts that had been torturing me for ever so long. Her appearance proved to be a real benefit to me and I promised myself to continue this acquaintance, which was of such obvious importance to me."

Barbara Juliana von Vietinghoff was born in Riga on November 11, 1764. At the age of eighteen she married Baron de Krüdener, a Russian diplomat, almost twice her age. Unbalanced, exalted by nature, she did not find enough attraction in her family life to hold her, and in 1789 formed a passionate attachment for a young French officer. She left her husband and followed her lover to France. In 1798, when Baron de Krüdener was Russian ambassador in Berlin, she returned and for a time was reconciled with him. Her husband's death in 1802 finally released her. In the following two years she lived mostly in Paris where under the influence of Chateaubriand she wrote a sentimental and largely autobiographical novel, *Valérie*. In 1804, she returned to Riga where she underwent "conversion" under the ministrations of a Moravian cobbler. From that time dates her extraordinary career in the execution of her "mission" in Europe as indicated to her by the "conversion."

At Königsberg she met a peasant named Adam Müller who

revealed to her that a man would arise "from the north . . . from the rising of the sun" (Isa. XLI, 25) to destroy the anti-Christ (Napoleon) and that the millenium would then begin. After this the Baroness spent eleven years wandering over Europe before she was able to reveal to Emperor Alexander that he was the predestined man "from the rising of the sun."

She came and conquered. Indeed the hour was hers. She was to become Alexander's inspiration and his judge. She was to follow him to Heidelberg where the general headquarters were soon transferred. She remained with him all through the year 1815, even appearing at the great review of troops at Vertus, where she rode in an open carriage and received attentions of princes and marshals, statesmen and politicians, servants of God and adventurers. Yet she did not accompany Alexander back to Russia, because she lost her balance and began to attribute to her own influence certain acts of the Russian emperor, foremost among which was the organization of the Holy Alliance. In consequence, Alexander was naturally inclined to distrust further activities on the part of the exalted baroness. He did not break with her openly, but gradually freed himself from her entangling influence.

When, in 1821, Baroness de Krüdener went to St. Petersburg to plead the cause of the Greek revolution, the support of which did not enter into Alexander's plans, the man "from the rising of the sun" refused to see her and sent her a letter in which he asked the erstwhile guide of his conscience not only to stop her pro-Greek propaganda, but even to leave the capital of Russia. It was the end of Barbara Juliana von Vietinghoff—Baroness de Krüdener. She went to the Crimea where she died on December 25, 1824. A few hours before her death she said, "The good I have done will endure; the evil I have done the mercy of God will blot out."

Having imposed the spirit of humility on his subjects, in the manifesto of January 1, 1816, Alexander prescribed this spirit also for himself. In September, 1816, he visited Kiev, the ancient southern capital of Russia and a venerated religious shrine, where he went to see the blind monk Vassian, famed for his holy life. There, in the monk's humble cell he spent an entire evening from eight until midnight. As soon as he entered the monk's abode, Alexander said: "Give me your blessing! I have already heard about you in St. Petersburg and I am eager to converse with you. Please give me your blessing." Vassian wanted to bow to the ground before the emperor, as was customary, but Alexander prevented him from doing so and, after kissing the monk's hand, said: "Worship is due to God alone. I am a human being like all the others and a Christian; please hear my confession as you would from any of your spiritual sons."

He showed similar marks of simplicity and humility when he visited, in 1819, the monastery of Valaam in northern Russia. Previous to this he had issued through the Holy Synod an order to all the Russian Orthodox clergy not to glorify him in the Sunday sermons as they were doing, but to forget about the earthly king and to think more about the heavenly king of all.

During these years his whole attitude toward life had changed. He no longer enjoyed festivities. When he was obliged to attend some of them he could scarcely conceal his impatience until such time as he could depart gracefully. His kindness and extreme politeness were still apparent, but any observant onlooker could discern that something was wrong; that deeply hidden somewhere in Alexander's soul burned a scorching flame which threatened to destroy not only his frame but his very essence.

This change in him did not escape the notice of his family. To the inquiries of his beloved sister, Catherine, about his new trend of mind, Alexander responded by sending her a plan of reading about mysticism with a varied and extensive list of books which show his familiarity with a vast number of works on the subject. This plan was prefaced by a general introduction which clearly reveals Alexander's conception of mysticism:

> The origin of the so-called mystic societies is lost in the most remote antiquity. . . . The Christian religion has laid down the link uniting the ancient and the present societies. At its beginning, Christianity was nothing but a mystic society. No one who had failed to pass certain tests and was not purified could enter the Church of Jerusalem. The policy of rulers has transformed this mystic teaching into a universal religion. But having discovered the ritual, their policy could not bring to light its mystery. Therefore at present as ever there is a visible and an invisible Church. The foundation in the teaching of both Churches is the same: the *Bible*. But the first one knows only its *text*, whilst the second reveals its *essence*. . . .

It was in search of the *essence* of Christianity that Alexander devoured text after text of Christian writings. Feverishly he stretched his hands out for that greatest gift of divine Providence—peace to his troubled soul. Not finding solace in the spiritual haven of the Russian Church, Alexander approached other manifestations of the Christian spirit with an almost childlike hopefulness.

Countess de Choiseul-Gouffier wrote in her memoirs:

> The Dominican fathers, who succeeded the Jesuits in St. Petersburg, possess a prayer book which they used to lend to Alexander when he came to pray in their chapel at unfrequented hours. They also conserve the tassels with which this sovereign marked the prayers he had chosen and they were always sad ones. . . . He showed great tolerance in the matter of religious opinion. "I think," he said, "that it is indifferent to God whether one invokes Him in Greek or in Latin; the essential is to do it from the bottom of a sincere heart!"

It was in this spirit that Alexander, in 1818, during his journey through the Crimea, assisted at a religious ceremony of a Russian sect known as Dukhobory and announced to its members that he was their protector. In that same year, 1818, when in Berlin on his way to the Congress at Aachen, Alexander listened with great emotion to a sermon delivered by the Lutheran bishop, Eylert. He invited Eylert to the palace and had a long talk with him on religious matters, and asked Eylert to visit him in Russia. A few years later when, in 1822, he was on his way to the Congress of Verona, Alexander stopped in Vienna especially to confer with Prince Alexander von Hohenlohe, who was a Roman Catholic abbot famed for his exemplary Christian life. Before that trip was undertaken, Alexander had to give his mother a solemn promise not to visit the Pope, as his leanings toward Catholicism were suspected by his family and the dowager empress feared that the Pope might induce him to embrace the Catholic faith.

It was this search for the spiritual treasures of any Christian denomination that prompted Alexander to receive in his capital, in 1819, two representatives of the Society of Friends. The followers of William Penn had made early attempts to approach the rulers of that mysterious country known to them still as Moscovia. In 1698, they had obtained an audience with Peter the Great when the latter sojourned in London. However, this first attempt to establish a contact with Russia was unsuccessful mainly because of the personality of Emperor Peter, who did not favor any mystical inclinations on the part of his people and who, therefore, did not find any use for the offer of the Quakers. Perhaps the personal agnosticism of Peter also had something to do with the failure of this first mission of the Friends. In later years their attempts were doomed also, as eighteenth-century Russia had no use for the Quaker's Christian and philanthropic activities. But in Alexander their hopes to reform Russia seemed to find a sympathetic understanding.

When Alexander visited London, in 1814, William Allen, an Englishman, and Stephen Grellet, a naturalized American of French birth, requested an audience with the Russian emperor, after having obtained one with the king of Prussia. This granted, on the twenty-first of June they presented themselves at Alexander's residence, which was the house rented for his sister, the Grand Duchess Catherine Pavlovna. Grellet left a colorful description of this meeting in his memoirs:

Dear William Allen and another Friend went with me to the Pultney Hotel at the time appointed by the emperor. He came to meet us at the door of his apartment, took us by the hand in a kind manner, and said that for a long time he had wished an opportunity to be with us. Through the empress, who was at Baden when I was at Karlsruhe last winter, he said that he had heard of me and of my visit there. Then he inquired into several of our religious testimonies, principles and practices, to which dear William Allen answered in English, which language the emperor speaks well. Whilst William was engaged in stating the nature of our Christian principles, the emperor said several times, "These are my own sentiments also." We entered fully into the subject of our testimony against war, to which he fully assented. . . . I addressed a few words to him; his heart appeared sensibly and tenderly affected. With tears, he took hold of my hand, which he held silently for a while, and then said, "These, your words, are a sweet cordial to my soul; they will long remain engraven on my heart." We furnished him with a number of Friends' books, which he received with pleasure, and on our taking leave of him, having been together upward of an hour, he took each of us by the hand and said, "I part from you as friends and brethren; feelings which I hope will ever remain with me."

A few days later, Alexander, accompanied by the Grand Duchess Catherine, the Russian ambassador in London— Count Lieven—and William Allen, visited a Friends' meeting at the Westminster Meeting House. Grellet noted:

It proved a good and solemn meeting. The emperor and the grand duchess, by their solemn countenances and religious tenderness, gave evidence that they felt it to be so to them.

Feeling great satisfaction from Alexander's favorable attitude toward the Friends' appeal to end war, Grellet stated:

Alexander especially appeared to feel the subject deeply, and to be sincere in his desire for the promotion of harmony, love and peace throughout the world. He told us that his concern had been great that the several crowned heads might conclude to settle their differences by arbitration and not by the sword.

When parting with the Friends, Alexander invited them to visit him in Russia. It was almost four years before William Allen and Stephen Grellet could undertake this journey. Finally they arrived in St. Petersburg in November, 1818. They were received by the emperor not in an official audience but as "old personal friends," according to Alexander's own words. After a prolonged conversation in which Alexander astounded the two Quakers by his deep knowledge of religious matters, the meeting ended with a silent prayer proposed by the emperor himself.

While Alexander was engaged in his almost desperate quest of salvation, Russia felt a deep disappointment in him. The best, though perhaps not the most profound, minds of the empire were engaged in speculations about a change in the form

of government. Having observed the more democratic systems
of western Europe during the campaigns of 1813 and 1814,
many officers of the guard and line began to discuss the ad-
visability of introducing a constitution in Russia. These men
formed secret societies for this purpose and eventually precipitated the abortive uprising of December, 1825. When informed of the activities and aims of these societies Alexander
remarked: "I cannot prosecute those to whom I have shown the
way." He had not forgotten his youthful dreams nor the intentions of the first years of his reign, but he seemed to be
disenchanted, tired, vanquished by reality, and preoccupied
with a loftier though more personal pursuit. Seeking the salvation of his troubled soul left him little time for the salvation
of Russia's soul. Unfortunately for Russia, he left her to the
care of the man of the hour—Count Arakcheyev, the only
loyal servant Emperor Paul had ever had.

XII

THE HOUR OF ARAKCHEYEV

ON MARCH 23, 1801, at the very hour when Emperor Paul was being murdered, Count Alexis Andreyevich Arakcheyev reached the barrier of St. Petersburg, having been recalled from his exile only the day before. By express orders of Count Pahlen, however, he was not permitted to enter the capital at once. Arakcheyev stepped out of his sleigh and watched silently the turbulent clouds above him. His ugly face lifted toward heaven was expressionless. But his head was filled with thoughts as agitated as the clouds he gazed on. The military governor's orders were not in the least surprising to him. He knew their meaning. He knew that they marked the death hour of his master. But he was not disturbed. He knew that his time would still come and he was prepared to wait for it. With the first rays of a winter sun breaking through the clouds he was permitted to cross the barrier into the city.

Born in 1769, the eldest son of an insignificant and poor country gentleman, Arakcheyev owed his spectacular rise exclusively to himself. At the age of fourteen he was admitted as a cadet to the artillery school for young nobles in St. Petersburg. He soon showed marked ability in his studies, especially in mathematics, and was transferred to the senior classes of the school less than a year after his entrance. He was hard working, punctual, accurate, thrifty. These qualities remained his chief characteristics throughout his life. A hard worker himself, he expected the same from others. Exact in the fulfillment of his duties, he demanded from his subordinates rigid compliance with his orders. No wonder then that he was unpopular with his fellow cadets whom he drilled unmercifully first as a sergeant and later as an officer. However, he was liked by his superiors and, especially, by General Melisino, director of the school, who wrote to him on April 15, 1787:

> From today on you are free to attend classes or to study by yourself. You will draw up a plan of studies for yourself and will render an account of it only to your conscience. . . . Your true friend, P. Melisino.

Though such relations between a student and the head of a school often exist in our days, they were unheard of in the eighteenth century, especially in militarized Russia. When at the end of 1787, Arakcheyev received his commission as lieutenant of artillery, it was Melisino who recommended the young officer as tutor for the sons of Count Nicholas Soltykov. It was Melisino again who appointed Arakcheyev, in 1791, to teach artillery in his alma mater, and when in the following year the good general heard that the Grand Duke Paul was looking for an artillery officer for his small Gatchina troop, Melisino succeeded in persuading the heir to the throne to choose his favorite for that post.

For four years Arakcheyev labored relentlessly at drilling, parading and maneuvering the Gatchina troop. He busied himself also with the modernization of the artillery entrusted to his command, and won continual praise from Paul. In later years, Arakcheyev said that "service in Gatchina was difficult though not entirely unpleasant." His subordinates, however, were of a different opinion. They found service under Arakcheyev almost unbearable, because he was not only demanding but also fiercely brutal. This streak of brutality had already manifested itself at the time when Arakcheyev had been instructor in his own school, where scourging his pupils with birch rods had been his favorite pastime. At Gatchina he applied the same system of punishment to his soldiers, varying it sometimes by striking their faces with his fists or with anything that he had at hand. At one time, in a fit of rage, he bit off the ear of a soldier who had displeased him.

Yet all this did not interfere with Arakcheyev's spectacular rise. On Paul's accession to the throne, the new emperor's favors poured upon Arakcheyev. By that time he had already reached the rank of colonel. On November 18, 1796, Paul appointed him Commandant of St. Petersburg and had him inscribed on the lists of the Preobrazhensky Regiment (the most exclusive of all the regiments of the Imperial Guard). The next day he was promoted to the rank of major general. On December 23 of the same year, the emperor presented him with a landed estate, Gruzino, in the province of Novgorod, with two thousand peasant serfs. On April 16 of the next year, during Paul's coronation in Moscow, Arakcheyev received the Grand Cross of the Order of St. Alexander Nevsky and the title of baron. When the coat of arms of the new baron was presented to Paul for approval, the emperor added to it the inscription: "Devoted without flattery." Through a resemblance of words in Russian this motto offered opportunity to Arakcheyev's enemies to interpret it to mean: "Devil of devoted flattery."

At the beginning of 1797, Arakcheyev was appointed quartermaster general. Soon after that he was also given command of the Preobrazhensky Regiment. He thus became one of the most important and most powerful personages in the empire. However, his brutalities continued, and as a result of one incident during which he had struck a colonel of the Guards in the face and the latter had committed suicide, he was dismissed from active service though with promotion to the rank of lieutenant general. But Paul could not remain long without his favorite, and less than a year after his dismissal Arakcheyev was recalled. He soon regained the confidence of his master, received the appointment of inspector general of all the artillery in the empire, obtained the Commander's Cross of the Maltese Order of which Paul had become the general and protector, was created a count, and thus reached the top ranks of the dignitaries surrounding the throne.

During this period Arakcheyev ingratiated himself with young Alexander. Their relationship had started in Gatchina before Paul's accession to the throne when the latter had ordered Arakcheyev to instruct Alexander in all the refinements of the military service as practiced at the Gatchina court. In November, 1796, when Emperor Paul appointed Alexander Military Governor of St. Petersburg and Inspector General of the Guards stationed in the capital, the young heir to the throne had almost daily contacts with Arakcheyev whose duty it was as commandant of the capital and later as quartermaster general to countersign all orders issued by Alexander. Knowing the demands of the service better than Alexander and often being able to shield him from Paul's anger, Arakcheyev soon became indispensable to the young grand duke. In return Alexander became more and more attached to Arakcheyev, and one of the strangest friendships of history—a friendship between a refined and enlightened ruler and an ill-mannered, narrow-minded and brutal soldier—was formed.

On October 12, 1799, Arakcheyev was dismissed from active service for the second time. And this time his dismissal was accompanied by banishment to his estate from where he returned only on the night of Paul's murder. This second dismissal was caused by a lie which he had told Emperor Paul in order to shield his, Arakcheyev's, brother. A petty theft occurred in the arsenal while this brother, a major of infantry, was on duty. Arakcheyev concealed this fact when reporting the occurrence to the emperor and accused another officer who was promptly put under arrest. Count Kutaisov, Paul's former barber and Arakcheyev's rival for the emperor's favors, revealed the lie. Thereupon Paul's anger knew no bounds. Alexander tried to intervene with his father for his unfortunate friend but to no avail. He wrote to Arakcheyev a pitiful letter in which he expressed his sorrow for not having been able to shield his friend from the emperor's wrath. A few months later Alexander ascended the throne of his ancestors, stained with the blood of his father.

It was precisely because he sensed Alexander's spiritual troubles, arising from the memory of the fateful night of March 23, 1801, that Arakcheyev was able to obtain an almost fantastic hold on his sovereign. He was ingenious in finding ways to remind Alexander that he alone could not possibly have been suspected of ever having plotted against Emperor Paul.

On June 19, 1810, Alexander made his first visit to Arakcheyev's estate. On this occasion the one who called himself Alexander's "faithful friend" took extraordinary pains to impress the emperor with the true nature of his faithfulness. At the entrance to the estate Alexander was met by Arakcheyev whom he embraced warmly. Arakcheyev then led his guest to the church. There they were met by the priest with the cross and the holy water. Alexander ascended the shining white steps and entered the church. The church of Gruzino was simple, austere and cold. After Alexander's eyes had grown accustomed to its semi-darkness, he saw on the left wall a large bas-relief of his father. It was the memorial erected by Arakcheyev to the murdered emperor. Cut in white marble by Martos, Emperor Paul looked down on his son with wide open, surprised eyes as if to say, "I did not expect *you* to come here and disturb my peace." Alexander also noticed an inscription which ran in golden letters along the wall above the memorial: "My heart is pure and my spirit just before you." Alexander stood motionless, breathless, envious of the man who could honestly say that.

Noiselessly, like a cat, Arakcheyev approached the emperor. "Yes, Your Majesty," he said. "And I have *him* always with me." With these words he unbuttoned his uniform and produced a small miniature in enamel. Paul, in a powdered wig, wearing the Grand Cross of the Order of St. John of Jerusalem (Order of Malta), stared at Alexander with his pale blue convex eyes. "Given to me by His Imperial Majesty himself, of blessed memory," Arakcheyev added with a sigh and buttoning his uniform lifted his eyes to the golden inscription on the wall. With trembling fingers Alexander grasped Arakcheyev's hand and pressed it hard. Thus they stood, the servant and the son of Paul I, Emperor and Autocrat of All the Russias, united by invisible yet indissoluble bonds. Arakcheyev had won his greatest victory. He had flicked the ever-bleeding wound in Alexander's heart and, like the perfect charlatan he was, he intended to pose as the only one capable of healing it whenever he wanted to do so.

The rise of Arakcheyev was as gradual as it was steady. During the Napoleonic wars he became Alexander's military secretary. The seventy-seven letters from Alexander to Arakcheyev during 1812 and the nearly one hundred for the years from 1813 to 1814 prove the confidence he inspired in his master. They also prove how much Alexander depended on Arakcheyev. When, in 1814, Alexander went to England, Arakcheyev remained in Germany for a cure. The emperor's letter to him from London, dated June 3, reveals the kind of attachment Alexander had for "the hermit of Gruzino," as Arakcheyev was bitingly nicknamed by Prince Golitsyn:

It was a great sacrifice for me to part with you. Please receive once more my gratitude for the numerous services which you have performed, the memory of which will remain with me forever. After fourteen years of reign, after two years of a ruinous and most dangerous war, I see myself deprived of the man in whom my confidence has always been unlimited. I dare say that no one has ever enjoyed such confidence and that no one's absence has ever been so hard to bear. Ever your faithful friend, Alexander.

Alexander liked order and uniformity. His desk was always kept in perfect order according to the pattern he had set, and he demanded that the papers brought for his signature should always be of the same size. For him, one of the main attractions of Gruzino was, perhaps, the study which Arakcheyev had arranged for him. It was an exact copy of his own study in St. Petersburg. The desk, the writing materials, the candlesticks and accessories had been exactly reproduced and arranged in the same relative positions.

Alexander's love of symmetry was exaggerated to such an extent that he had the furniture in his rooms severely aligned, recalling "the regular beauty of military parades" which had always fascinated him. In the same spirit he preferred the towns of central and western Europe to Russian towns because of their more obvious planning, because of their symmetry. The Russian cities, which looked as if someone had opened a mighty hand and strewn houses over a large space in complete disorder, did not appeal to Alexander. Between the semi-Asiatic Moscow and the symmetrical St. Petersburg, European at least in appearance, Alexander certainly preferred the "paradise" of Peter the Great notwithstanding the terrible memories which it evoked in him.

Alexander often thought how wonderful it would be if he could create a system by which every citizen would have a definite place and a definite role in the complexity of the state's existence. Each one in the empire should work part of his time for himself while devoting the remainder to the state which was

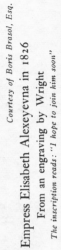

Empress Elisabeth Alexeyevna in 1826
From an engraving by Wright
The inscription reads: "I hope to join him soon"

Emperor Alexander I by Wright
Posthumous engraving

Chapel over the tomb of Fyodor Kuzmich in the cemetery at Tomsk, Siberia

to procure the means for everybody's existence. At regular intervals there would be days of rest, of organized rest and entertainment under the supervision of superiors appointed by the state. Alexander dreamed of seeing the life of civilians emulate that of soldiers. In a regiment every soldier, every officer knows his place and his functions. In the army everything is precise and harmonious. Could not this military organization and discipline be applied to the everyday life of the entire population of the empire?

When Alexander read the book by General Servan entitled, *Sur les forces frontières des états,* he found in it the formulation of his idea. The French general advocated the creation of military colonies along the frontiers of the Napoleonic Empire and, though Napoleon had not found any use for this plan, Alexander intended to give it a thorough test. He ordered Prince Volkonsky to translate this work into Russian so as to make its contents accessible to Arakcheyev who was not versed in the language of Voltaire and Boileau. When the translation was completed, Alexander supplemented it with his own interpretation and sent it to his "faithful friend." The project in its final form was founded upon a humanitarian idea. Its plan was so designed that it would not be necessary to deprive the soldier in time of peace of the benefits of family life. At the same time it would relieve the state's budget from the heavy expenditures that the maintenance of a large armed force incurred, because the soldiers were to provide by their labor not only for their own existence but also for the livestock of the army. It was Arakcheyev whom Alexander chose to execute this plan of state socialism. It was known under the name of "military settlements."

In 1816, Alexander ordered an entire county of the province of Novgorod around Arakcheyev's estate, which had already been militarized since 1810, to be placed under the regime of military settlements. The local peasants became militarized and the troops sent to this county settled down to till the soil. In addition to the regular routine of military service the soldiers had to work as laborers on a "militarized" farm, while the peasants had to don uniforms, have their heads and beards shaved, and learn in their spare time the regulations of military service.

Alexander could rejoice now at the new picture which this part of the country offered to his eyes. The shabby gray houses, the wooden hedges had disappeared. In their stead, neat little houses, all alike, all of the same color, stood in perfect alignment. In addition to these homes the military settlers received advance funds, horses, cows, fowl, new agricultural implements. Yet they had to be dragged in by force, because they refused obstinately to see any "benefits" in this new venture. This puzzled Alexander. He could not understand the obstinacy of his subjects. Why could they not see the numerous advantages of this experiment? Did not the soldiers thus enjoy life with their families? Did not the new houses offer more comfort, better hygienic conditions, a more esthetic outlook when they stood side by side like so many Prussian guardsmen? Did not the new administration care for the peasants in a really fatherly way? Were not all marriageable young men inscribed on special lists so that no girl, no widow, would remain without a life companion? If some of the marriages were arranged by the administration of the settlements, was it not for the good of the inhabitants? After all, their part in the life of the state should

not be selfish; it should be for the benefit of all living and for
that of future generations.

It was with this lofty aim in view that Count Arakcheyev
imposed a fine on every married woman residing on his estate
who did not bear a child every year. How could people speak
of cruelty when all this was done exclusively for their benefit?
Alexander was puzzled. He was so sincerely convinced of the
excellence of his enterprise that he failed to see the reasons of
those who opposed him, though they might have constituted
the entire nation. He considered that his slave-subjects, like
children, did not know what was best for them, and for their
own sake he was determined to carry out his plan. In consequence, the military settlements were expanded. Toward
the end of his reign, thirty-six battalions of infantry and two
hundred and forty-nine squadrons of cavalry were inscribed
on the lists of the military settlements of Little Russia and
ninety battalions of infantry in Great Russia. This constituted
one-third of the entire Russian army in time of peace.

Alexander was pleased with this success although it had been
achieved over rivers of tears and blood. Local revolts were
frequent, but they were quelled in a rapid and radical manner.
Capital punishment having been abolished except for high
treason, the culprits were forced to run the gauntlet between
lines of men wielding birch rods soaked in salt, or ramrods,
and there can be no wonder that many of them died as a result
of such treatment. However, in 1819, a revolt of large pro-
portions occurred in Chuguyev, where more than a thousand
settlers directed their wrath and guns against their oppressors.
Arakcheyev summoned loyal troops and put down the revolt.
He then sent a detailed report to Alexander in which he dis-

coursed at length on the futility and ingratitude of human beings who are always dissatisfied and do not really know themselves what they want. He accompanied his report by a letter in which he wrote:

LITTLE FATHER, YOUR MAJESTY!

In presenting my official report, I write this not to my sovereign, but to my friend, Alexander Pavlovich, and therefore I open here my heart. The recent happenings which occurred here have disconcerted me considerably; I will not hide from you that some of the criminals—the most wicked ones—have died after receiving the punishment prescribed by law and that I am beginning to be tired of all this. . . . Until the end of my feeble life I remain your loyal subject

COUNT ARAKCHEYEV

To this Alexander replied:

My sincere attachment to you, my dear Alexis Andreyevich, is known to you from olden times and therefore you will understand what I felt when reading your papers. On the one hand I was able to understand fully what your tender heart had to suffer under the circumstances described; on the other, I am also able to appreciate the prudence and wisdom which you have displayed during this serious trouble. I thank you sincerely and from the bottom of my heart for all the pains that you have taken.

Toward the end of Alexander's reign the settlers remained peaceful, not because they liked the regime but because they saw no way out. The institution of the military settlements thus continued in operation, although hated by each and every one of the settlers and by the vast majority of the rest of the Russian population; but Alexander was not aware of all this and so remained perfectly content. The only thing that worried him at this time was Arakcheyev's poor health which, in 1822, seemed to have reached an alarming state. Arakcheyev fainted one day at a meeting of the Committee of Ministers. On Alexander's advice he then took a prolonged leave of absence and went to Gruzino, whence he wrote plaintive letters to the emperor until the latter sent his own physician to Gruzino— Sir James Wylie. After such marked attention from his master, Arakcheyev felt noticeably better.

Encouraged by his apparently unlimited influence over Alexander, Arakcheyev began to lay Machiavellian plans for the removal of his most important rival in the emperor's affection—Prince Alexander Golitsyn. The Minister of Spiritual Affairs was still not only Alexander's intimate friend but also his most esteemed adviser in religious matters. Alexander could not forget the spiritual debt he owed Golitsyn for bringing him to the road of mystical Christianity in the tragic hours of 1812. But Arakcheyev knew his victim well, and was prepared to fight Golitsyn with his own weapons. Arakcheyev's tool was Peter Nikitich Spasky, better known as Archimandrite Foty.

Born in 1792, the son of a village sexton, young Peter spent a sad childhood during which his father, often drunk, used to beat him severely. Afterward, when he entered a seminary in preparation for the priesthood, the beatings were resumed by the educators. Having thus received an early training in "mortification" of the flesh, he decided to take orders, and in 1817 became a monk taking the name of Foty. The young monk had the nature of a fanatic. Not content with following the general monastic rules, he mortified his flesh by wearing chains which wounded his body and a hair shirt which prevented the healing of the wounds. He was subject to hallucinations and related in his autobiography how he fought the devil in his own cell. With the passing of years, visions and hallucinations became more frequent. When transferred to St. Petersburg to teach theology, he was tempted by the devil for long months to perform a miracle in order to reveal the power of God. The worst of these temptations was when the devil suggested that Foty should cross the Neva river directly opposite the Winter Palace, walking on the waves like Christ himself. Finally Foty emerged a victor from the midst of these temptations and "wisely declined to perform the miracle."

Foty then applied all his energy to the fight against moral corruption in the capital. In 1820, he "converted" the Countess Anna Orlov-Chesmensky, a superstitious and bigoted spinster, whose immense wealth and powerful influence at the imperial court were to serve well the purpose of the fanatic monk. After that the star of Foty shone brighter with every day. Many people holding high positions in state or society were attracted by the fiery speeches, by the ascetic appearance of the archi-mandrite, and soon they began to think that Alexander should meet him. The candid Golitsyn was one of those who patron-ized Foty and who obtained for him an audience at the Palace. The first meeting took place on June 17, 1822, and Alexander was deeply impressed. In the meantime, Foty became an intimate friend of Count Arakcheyev. While Golitsyn continued to favor the self-styled prophet, the "hermit from Gruzino" and the fanatic archimandrite came closer and closer together. High distinctions were conferred on Foty: Alexander sent him a diamond cross, the dowager empress presented him with a golden watch, and Prince Golitsyn obtained for him the wealthy and important Yuriev monastery in Novgorod, not far distant from Gruzino. There Foty planned how to defend the Russian Orthodox Church from its imaginary enemies. There Count Arakcheyev visited the archimandrite more than once and "helped" him to formulate his plans. It was not difficult for Arakcheyev to persuade Foty that the true enemy of the church was Golitsyn. The benign Minister of Spiritual Affairs had never been very orthodox in his Christian beliefs and was suspected of being a freemason. This was enough to inflame the imagination of the fanatic monk. He needed now only an opportunity to discredit the Minister of Spiritual Affairs in the eyes of Alexander and the Russian people.

In May, 1824, on the occasion of a visit by Prince Alexander Golitsyn to Foty, the archimandrite pronounced the venerable prince "anathema," thus excluding him from the spiritual benefits of the church. The news spread quickly. All St. Petersburg lived in breathless expectation. Though Foty was not quite sure of the consequences of this bold act, Arakcheyev knew that his enemy was crushed. Indeed, three days later, Prince Golitsyn was relieved of his duties as Minister of Spiritual Affairs and the ministry itself was abolished.

Foty was jubilant. He wrote to the archimandrite of a neighboring monastery:

Rejoice with me, Very Reverend Father! The evil is destroyed, the devil's army is no more; all these atheistic societies are suppressed. Our minister now is Our Lord Jesus Christ, in the name of the Father, of the Son and of the Holy Ghost. Amen. . . . Pray for Arakcheyev: he came like Saint George the Victorious to fight for the Holy Church and our faith.

But Foty and his fellow conspirators were soon to find out that there was no reason for rejoicing. It was not Jesus Christ who became the new minister; it was Arakcheyev. All the affairs of the church were to be submitted to him before presentation to the emperor. Arakcheyev immediately militarized the whole church organization. Priests, bishops, archbishops and metropolitans did not dare even to protest. They all regretted the kind Prince Golitsyn.

Soon after these memorable events a new icon was placed in the church of Gruzino facing the memorial to Emperor Paul. It represented Our Savior holding the Gospel. The icon was covered with heavy silver trimmings. One of these silver plates, representing a page of the Gospel, could be moved on an almost invisible silver bolt disclosing another icon—an apotheosis of Count Alexis Andreyevich Arakcheyev in a general's uniform bedecked with decorations, reclining on clouds, as if coming in all his glory to judge the living and the dead.

Arakcheyev was now supreme. But he did not enjoy the fruit of his treachery for long. On September 22, 1825, household serfs in Gruzino murdered Arakcheyev's housekeeper, Anastasia Minkina. For twenty-five years she had been his mistress and companion. For twenty-five years the foremost personage in Russia had remained under the spell of a vulgar, illiterate, soldierlike female. And for twenty-five years Anastasia Minkina had terrorized Arakcheyev's serfs. Finally their patience had been exhausted. One night, they had gone into her bedroom and slit her throat. Two days later, Arakcheyev wrote to Alexander:

LITTLE FATHER, YOUR MAJESTY!
The misfortune of losing a faithful friend who had lived in my house for twenty-five years has disturbed and weakened my health and mind to such an extent that I only want to die and look for death to come; and therefore I am unable to occupy myself with any affairs. Good-by, Little Father, remember your servant who was. Household serfs murdered my friend in the night and I do not know where to rest my poor head, but I am leaving this place.

This letter shows the depth of the sorrow that no one had ever thought the brutal militarist capable of feeling. At the same time, Count Arakcheyev forgot his duty and relieved himself of his functions as Commander of the Independent Corps of Military Settlements. By a letter, dated September 23, he ordered Major General Eiler to take over the military affairs of the corps. On the same day he transferred all the civil affairs of the military settlements to the Secretary of State, Muravyov. Arakcheyev seemed to have forgotten that only the emperor had the right to relieve a military commander of his office. On this occasion, General Aide-de-Camp Baron Diebich made the following remark:

Of course, no one in the empire, regardless of how high his position might be, could ever have acted so lawlessly with impunity. But this man has always been an exception from the general rule.

Instead of censure, Count Arakcheyev received a long personal letter from Alexander in which the emperor sympathized with his "dear friend's loss." After urging him not to despair, but to trust in God's mercy, Alexander continued:

You tell me that you want to leave Gruzino, but that you do not know where to go. Come to me. You have no friend who loves you more sincerely than I do. The place here is quiet. You can live here as you please. And a talk with a friend who shares your sorrow will help you. But for God's sake do not forget your country, do not forget how useful and, I may add, how absolutely necessary your services are to it. And my country and I are one. I need you. . . . My dear friend, I pity most of all your tender heart. . . . Good-by, my dear Alexis Andreyevich, do not desert a friend, your faithful friend.

It was obvious that the hold that Arakcheyev had on Alexander was not in the least weakened by the former's act of insubordination. A few days after sending this letter, Alexander wrote another one. In this new message the emperor implored Arakcheyev to take care of himself and not to forget to inform him about his health by couriers. The letter was signed: "Ever thy loving Alexander."

Such was Alexander's solicitude for the man to whom he

had entrusted the government of Russia, the "vice-emperor." Since the shrewd and unscrupulous Metternich had relieved Alexander of his concern for the affairs of Europe, Alexander could have shown more interest in the affairs of Russia instead of abandoning her to a merciless executioner in the person of the "faithful friend." Friendship and confidence in the man alone are not sufficient to explain such disinterestedness; the invisible bonds which had joined Alexander and Arakcheyev on June 19, 1810, did not presuppose the surrender of power to the "hermit of Gruzino." There must have been some other reason. There was. Alexander was tiring of his heavy crown.

ESCAPE

ALEXANDER had not fulfilled the expectations that had heralded the opening of his reign. He had deserted the liberalism of La Harpe, the statesmanship of Speransky, the wise councils of Novossiltsov, Kochubey, Stroganov and Czartoryski only to fall into the dark pit of mystic piety wherein he lost his bearings and followed the road to reaction instead of the road to liberty. When the tragic hour on March 23, 1801, had come and he had been forced to decide whether or not to accept the bloodstained crown of his father, he had been afraid not to accept it; and he was willing to bear the heavy burden of this crown in order to better the conditions of life in his country. Now that he had not succeeded, now that he really saw no chance to succeed, he was ready to face abdication.

In 1817, while in Kiev, Alexander had visited the venerated Monastery of the Caves for a second time. There he had had long talks with the hermit fathers. At dinner, on September 20, he broke into a conversation about the duties of citizens including crowned heads, saying loudly:

When anyone has the honor to be at the head of such a nation as ours, he has to have the courage to be the first to face danger. He must not remain in his place any longer than his physical strength will permit him nor, one might say, longer than he is able to mount a horse. After this he must retire. As for me, I feel well at present, but in ten or fifteen years, when I shall be fifty, then . . .

Two years later, his readiness to abdicate received further emphasis in two memorable interviews.

In the summer of 1819, Alexander reviewed the Second Brigade of the First Division of the Imperial Guards commanded by his brother, the Grand Duke Nicholas. The perfect alignment, the flowing march of giants, each one over six feet in height, the color of their uniforms, their glittering rifles and accouterments, the gay fluttering of banners in the warm summer air, and above all the able command exercised by his brother pleased Alexander. The emperor felt a natural pride because it was he who had trained his brother, who day after day had spent hours in teaching him and the youngest of the family, the Grand Duke Michael, those elements of military command which do not serve as very effective weapons in war time but are so spectacular when displayed on a parade ground. Now he was able to view with pride the fruits of his painstaking efforts. No wonder that he was exceptionally amiable with his brother and the latter's wife, the Grand Duchess Alexandra when, after the review was over, they dined together. Suddenly, in the midst of a most friendly and animated conversation, Alexander changed his whimsical tone to one of extreme seriousness and said that he was doubly pleased with the success of the grand duke because the day would come when Nicholas would have to assume a much heavier burden than that of a brigadier general, for he was considering him as his successor and that the succession would come about much sooner than anyone anticipated; it would happen while he was still living.

The grand duchess wrote in her diary:

The emperor continued: "You seem to be surprised, but you must know that my brother Constantine, having never cared much about the throne, has now firmly decided to renounce officially his right of succession in favor of his younger brother Nicholas and of his descendants. As for myself, I have decided to free myself from my present obligations and to retire from this sort of life. More than ever, Europe needs young monarchs, strong and energetic, and I am no longer what I was. Therefore, I deem it my duty to retire in time." Seeing that we were almost in tears, he tried to comfort us by saying that this would not take place immediately, that still a few years would go by before he would be able to realize his plan. Then he left us. One can imagine the state we were in. We had never even dreamed of such a possibility. It was as though we had been struck by lightning. This was a memorable moment in our lives.

In the autumn of the same year, Alexander visited Warsaw. He was accompanied for a short part of the return journey by his brother Constantine, still commander in chief of the troops in Poland. During this drive together Alexander said to his brother: "I must tell you, brother, that I want to abdicate; I am tired and I have no more the strength to carry the burden of government. I tell you in advance so that you may decide what to do under these circumstances."

The grand duke replied: "In this event I shall ask for myself the position of your second valet. I will serve you and I will, if necessary, clean your boots. If I were to do it at present, people would term it vileness on my part, but when you will no longer be on the throne, then I shall be able to show my faithfulness to you, my benefactor."

"When I had spoken these words," Constantine Pavlovich related, "the Emperor kissed me more heartily than he had ever done before during all the forty-five years of our life." Alexander closed this conversation by saying: "When the time to abdicate comes, I shall let you know and you will then inform mother." On this the two brothers parted.

These two revelations make the year 1819 a memorable one in Alexander's life. They were prompted, most probably, by the death on January 9 of the same year of the Grand Duchess Catherine, then queen of Württemberg, after a short illness. The death of that beloved sister affected Alexander deeply. The dear Bissiam was gone! What a turmoil of thoughts must have gripped Alexander at the recollection of all the years during which Catherine had occupied such a prominent place in his heart. Was it not a warning? To die in sin was to lose one's future felicity. Was the sum total of earthly pleasures worth that? The short illness which had carried Bissiam Bissiamovna to her premature death might occur in anyone's life—in his own. Would he be able to face death unprepared? Could he ever expiate his sins whilst crowned, whilst wearing the purple? Obviously not. The one way to save his immortal soul would be to free himself from all those obligations that weighed so heavily on his stooping shoulders and from those dreadful bonds that make a human being a slave, a prisoner of a principle.

Alexander the Blessed, By the Grace of God, Emperor and Autocrat of All the Russias wanted to free himself from those magnificent, but ever so heavy, chains which he had borne stoically through almost twenty years. Still he could not do it at once. Were he to abdicate, he would still remain a former emperor in the eyes of the people. His youthful dream to retire and live the simple life of an ordinary citizen "somewhere on the Rhine" could not be carried out now. This was not his aim; he needed an escape. He must wait for a propitious moment when he could disappear, when he could continue to live unobserved, unknown.

On January 24, 1824, Alexander became seriously ill. High temperature, a severe headache and nausea were the signs by which the doctors decided that he had "glowing fever." A few days later they also discovered erysipelas in his left leg, where he had been kicked by a horse, which for a time had endangered his thigh bone. Alexander was ill for over two months. The suddenness and the seriousness of this illness must have made him think once more of his decision. This time, however, he must have felt that circumstances were pressing.

Alexander had never shirked responsibilities. To him the performance of his duty was paramount and he demonstrated this when death robbed him of his beloved daughter—Sophie Naryshkin. In June, 1824, the regiments of the Guards had entered their summer quarters at Krasnoye Selo. Alexander, though not completely recovered from his recent illness, had left his residence in Tsarskoye Selo and joined the troops. Sophie was critically ill, suffering from tuberculosis. The emperor had received, every day, a bulletin of her health by special courier. On June 23, Alexander was to review the Guards' Artillery. On that particular morning, the courier brought the sad news of Sophie's death and handed the dispatch to Prince Peter Volkonsky. All the generals of the Guards were assembled in the palace, awaiting the emperor in order to accompany him for the review. Sir James Wylie and Dr. Tarasov were also present. Tarasov was awaiting a summons to the emperor's room to change the bandage on Alexander's leg. Upon the receipt of the dispatch Prince Volkonsky approached Wylie, and whispered into his ear the bad news, asking him to break it to the emperor. At first the English physician refused, but he was persuaded by Volkonsky to accept this painful mission.

Tarasov entered Alexander's room and was told by the emperor to hasten the dressing as he was already late. While Tarasov busied himself with the emperor's leg, Volkonsky and Wylie entered the room. Sir James had come close to the emperor, inspected his leg and said in French: "Everything is all right." During this time Prince Volkonsky remained near the door, silent. Alexander cast a quick glance at him and became alarmed. "What is the news?" he asked. Volkonsky dropped his head, but did not answer. Then turning to Wylie, Alexander repeated his question in English. Sir James answered: "It is the end: she is no more." Tarasov had just finished his task when he saw that the emperor was silently shedding tears. He wept so profusely that he had to change his shirt, the front of which had been drenched with tears. Thereupon Volkonsky, Wylie, and Tarasov left the room. It seemed to them that the emperor would not be able to review the troops that day. However, a quarter of an hour later, Alexander appeared in the waiting room and after greeting his generals mounted his horse and galloped toward the aligned regiments.

Nothing revealed to the assembled men what was going on in Alexander's heart. No one except Volkonsky, Wylie, and Tarasov knew of the sad news. The emperor performed his duties admirably. He was amiable as usual, questioned his generals, commented on their answers, greeted the men. Then he stood and watched his soldiers march past him. Their heavy tread reverberated like distant thunder. They marched past him as they had done many times before going into battle. Many of them wore medals. Medals purchased with blood. They had no families and looked upon their emperor as their father. He did not, he could not disappoint them although his own heart was bleeding, although his own child was no more. "Long live the emperor!" Alexander smiled. Alexander waved his plumed hat. The review was over.

After thanking his generals, Alexander returned to the palace. There he quickly changed from his dress uniform to a simpler one, jumped into an open carriage drawn by four horses and ordered his coachman to go at full speed to Naryshkin's home whose threshold he had not crossed for ten years. He returned to Krasnoye Selo in the afternoon, silent, tired, an aged man. His carriage was now drawn only by two horses, the other two having fallen on the road from exhaustion. He did not dine that evening, but locked himself in his study and spent the whole night without sleep. He had done his duty, the duty that service demands.

The loss of his sister, Catherine, in 1819 and now of his beloved child robbed Alexander of the last ties with this world.

He was becoming more restless than ever and sought forget-fulness in continuous travels. All the time he was looking for the opportunity to find an escape from that narrow circle of life in which he, an emperor, felt himself a prisoner. Finally that ardently desired opportunity came.

At 3:30 A.M. on the night of September 13, 1825, a lonely figure descended the front steps of the white palace on Ka-menny Ostrov. Clad in a simple green uniform and a military cap with a coat thrown over his shoulders, Alexander stepped quickly into the waiting open carriage drawn by three horses. Through the deserted and silent streets of the sleeping town Ilia, the emperor's personal coachman, drove the open carriage to the monastery of St. Alexander Nevsky, reaching it at 4:15 A.M. Met at the entrance of the cathedral by the Metro-politan Seraphim, the clergy and all the monks, Alexander alighted swiftly, kissed the crucifix and after being sprinkled with holy water, received the benediction of the metropolitan. He then entered the cathedral and ordered the doors to be closed.

Once in the cathedral the emperor went straight to the cas-ket of St. Alexander Nevsky, his patron saint, and stood before it as the *Te Deum* began. He seemed to be completely under the spell of religious emotion, praying devoutly, and yet there was in his eyes a curious expression of determination and even of victory, reflecting a strange inner light which filled his light blue eyes with extraordinary animation. When the *Te Deum* came to an end, the emperor prostrated himself before the relics of the saint, kissed his image and bade good-by to all that were present.

Upon leaving the cathedral, Alexander went to the metropolitan's quarters. There he entrusted to Seraphim a sealed package to be delivered to his successor on the throne of Russia. It contained the documents relative to the change in line of succession brought about by the Grand Duke Constantine's renunciation of his rights to the throne.[1]

When Alexander stepped into his carriage, his eyes were filled with tears. Before departing, he asked the metropolitan who stood surrounded by the clergy and monks: "Pray for me and for my wife." He remained bareheaded until the gates of the monastery were reached. On his way he often turned back, bowed and crossed himself, looking all the while at the cathedral where on the large stone steps the gorgeous sacerdotal garments of the metropolitan, the clergy, and the dark mass of monks clad in black formed a picture full of brilliancy and contrast, of light and of shadow. When he reached the barrier, Alexander ordered his coachman, Ilia, to stop. He stood up in the open carriage and contemplated the town for a long time as if bidding it a last good-by. There lay his capital, which had witnessed glory and decadence, triumph and downfall, which had been filled with terror and with jubilant shouts of praise.

Twenty-five years before, there had stood another man at this barrier, who watched the clouds and waited for the sun to rise. That man had been patient; in time he had gotten what he wanted. Decidedly, Count Arakcheyev was stronger than Alexander. Count Arakcheyev ruled Russia while Alexander only played his role. Now Alexander was leaving the stage, for good. With a deep sigh the emperor sat back in the carriage and said to Ilia: "Go with God!" And a lonely traveler was sped down the road leading south to Taganrog.

[1] A similar package had been left with the President of the Senate, Lopukhin.

The journey to Taganrog, a small town on the shores of the Azov Sea in southern Russia, was undertaken for the sake of Empress Elisabeth Alexeyevna who, the council of physicians had recommended, should spend the winter in a more temperate climate than that of St. Petersburg. The choice of Taganrog was made by Alexander himself for reasons of his own, for in the medical men's recommendation that place was not indicated, the recommendation containing simply the mention of Italy, the south of France, or southern Russia. The choice of Taganrog was a curious one, for the town was known for its fierce northeast winds and storms in winter and was not at all an appropriate place for a person needing a temperate, even a mild, climate. However, Taganrog suited Alexander's plans, so the choice was made.

Alexander remembered this city, having visited it in May, 1818, and readily brushed aside all objections to his choice. To the remark that the only house available for his residence in Taganrog was much too modest to accommodate the emperor, he made an enigmatic reply: "It is necessary that the passage to private life should not be too abrupt." And, as soon as the journey was decided upon, Alexander displayed feverish activity. He countermanded the review of troops of the Second Army which had been gathered especially for this purpose at Belaya Tserkov; he ordered his personal friend, Prince Peter Volkonsky, to accompany the empress, notwithstanding the fact that the prince had just returned from Paris where he had assisted at the coronation of King Charles X; he personally worked out the itinerary and noted in a little book the exact route and the schedule to be followed. In planning the route, he took especial care to avoid Moscow and all large cities, giving strict orders that there should be no receptions, parades, reviews of troops or any ceremony whatsoever. Finally, when everything was ready, he set the date of his departure for September 13 and that of Empress Elisabeth for September 16.

A few days before his departure, Alexander asked Prince Golitsyn to put his private papers in order. Notwithstanding the abrupt ending of Golitsyn's career the year before, Alexander turned to him for this intimate task, because he felt that he could trust his life-long friend and adviser. During this work Golitsyn asked Alexander whether it was not unwise in view of his departure to conceal any longer the arrangements concerning the succession to the throne. To this the emperor gave the following reply: "Let us commend ourselves to the will of God; He shall dispose of things much better than we poor mortals could ever do."

What reason prompted Golitsyn to ask such a question? Alexander had traveled all his life and the some fifteen hundred miles separating St. Petersburg from Taganrog were really no great distance for him. Why should this particular journey have provoked Golitsyn to touch upon such a disturbing topic? Probably no other reason than that Golitsyn knew of Alexander's plan as well as the fact that it was Nicholas and not Constantine who was to succeed Alexander as Emperor and Autocrat of All the Russias.

Alexander's journey to Taganrog was uneventful. He had always liked rapid transportation and this time, too, hurried south as if his very life depended upon his reaching the goal in time. He seldom stopped even to spend the night, preferring to sleep in his carriage while moving along the road. But at every

station marked on the schedule, he inspected in detail the ac-
commodations prepared for the passage of Empress Elisabeth.

He arrived in Taganrog on September 25, true to his schedule.
On October 5, he was joined by Empress Elisabeth.

The house chosen for Their Majesties' stay in Taganrog was
a one-story stone building, very simple in line, containing a
basement for the accommodation of servants. That part of
the house reserved for Empress Elisabeth contained eight small
rooms, two of which were to be occupied by the ladies in waiting. The center of the house formed a large hall which was to
serve as reception and dining room. A small chapel was arranged
in the empress' apartment. The other half of the house contained two rooms to be occupied by Alexander. One of them,
a bright spacious room, was the emperor's study which was to
serve also as his bedroom. The other was small, of semicircular
shape, with one window opening onto the yard. This was to
serve as the emperor's dressing room. A corridor between the
rooms would accommodate the valet on duty. The estate contained a large yard and a small park with fruit trees. The fur-
nishings of the house were of the very simplest kind.

At the beginning of his stay in Taganrog, Alexander seemed
to be perfectly pleased with his choice of the place. Every day
he took the empress out into the garden and walked with her
up and down the alleys and paths. Perfect peace reigned at
last between these two who had been so unhappy in their married life. Later in the day Alexander would go out and walk
about the town, alone, as he had done during the first years of
his reign. But this idyll did not last long. Alexander was soon
overcome by his mania for traveling and first went into the

region of the Cossacks of the Don, where he spent five days
from October 23 to October 27. After this he prepared for a
longer journey to the Crimea.

He left Taganrog on November 1. The journey delighted
him. Really he had never been as happy as when rushing from
one place to another. At this time Alexander was in exceptionally good spirits. After visiting Mariupol, the Mennonite colonies on the river Molochnaia, Simferopol, Gursuf, he stopped
at Oreanda, an estate which he had recently purchased. He
could not find enough words of praise to express his delight
over this place. He walked around the beautiful gardens with
Prince Volkonsky, then suddenly turned to him and said: "I
shall soon settle down here to live the rest of my life as a private
citizen. I have served for twenty-five years and even a simple
soldier can retire after that much service.[2] You too will retire
from service and be my librarian."

Deeply moved, Prince Volkonsky fell to his knees and said:
"Wherever you go, sire, I will follow you."

It would seem that Alexander had made up his mind in January that time was pressing, for in that month he had told his
brother-in-law, the Prince of Orange, that he intended to abdicate soon and to live his own life at last. When the heir to the
throne of Holland had protested, he merely told him not to
divulge the secret as yet. And there, in Oreanda, he confirmed
to Prince Volkonsky what had always been his dream and what
had now become a firm and irrevocable decision.

From Oreanda, Alexander went to Alupka where he visited
Count Vorontsov. From there he went on horseback to Baidary.

---

[2] A soldier in the Russian army during Alexander's time served for twenty-
five years.

He countermanded the dinner that was awaiting him in Sevastopol and went to Balaklava. From Balaklava he traveled in an
open carriage to that point where the road makes a turn to the
monastery of St. George. There he mounted a horse, sent his
entourage to Sevastopol and, taking only a cabinet courier with
him, went to the monastery. This took place on November 8,
at 6 P.M. Alexander did not wear an overcoat, because the day
had been very warm, but when night fell a strong northeast
wind brought almost freezing temperature. When the emperor
returned to Sevastopol he felt shivery, refused to dine and took
only a hot cup of tea, obviously having caught a cold in the
mountains. This seems to have been the turning point in his last
days as emperor. The different accounts that we possess of
Alexander's journey in the Crimea and of his last days in Taganrog are contradictory to such an extent that it is almost impossible to follow them clearly unless one adopts as evident that
the official records did not tell the truth. The most reliable ac-
count is to be found in the recollections of Dr. Dimitry Tarasov, court physician, and the description of the events to follow
is based mainly on his story.

The day of November 9 was spent by the emperor in inspecting the fortifications, the hospital, the arsenal, in passing
in review the fleet. Later the emperor gave a big dinner and
nothing disturbing could be noticed in the state of his health.
The next day Alexander crossed the Bay of Sevastopol and,
after inspecting the fortifications on the north coast, went in
an open carriage to Bakhchisaray where he stayed in the Khan
Palace, as in 1818. There he had asked Tarasov to prepare for
him a rice potion similar to that which he had taken in 1824
when he had suffered from fever and an inflammation of his leg.

Tarasov carried out the order immediately and deemed it his duty to let Wylie know that the emperor had a slight gastric disturbance. However, Alexander did not complain of any illness either to Tarasov or to Wylie. He did not take any rest, but spent the whole day in visiting places in the vicinity of Bakhchisaray, obviously in good spirits. He conversed with everyone in his usual charming manner.

On November 13, he went to Eupatoria where he spent the night after having visited churches, mosques, synagogues, arsenals and quarantines. The next day he proceeded to Perekop where he visited the hospital. Early in the morning of November 15, he continued his journey according to his itinerary and, in the village Znamenskoye, passed in review a brigade of artillery, visited the local hospital, where he had his meal and was very well satisfied with the food, especially with a barley soup of which he took more than one helping. Since leaving Bakhchisaray where Alexander had ordered the rice potion, he seems to have been in perfect health and did not complain of anything either to Tarasov or to Wylie.

That same day, at the last station before Orekhovo, where he was to spend the night, Alexander met the courier Maskov, who had brought papers from St. Petersburg and Moscow. Having received the papers, Alexander ordered Maskov to accompany him to Taganrog. On the road to Orekhovo a serious accident occurred. Maskov's coachman let his horses go too fast and at a sharp turn of the road the courier's carriage overturned. Maskov fell to the ground and remained motionless. Alexander immediately ordered Tarasov to take care of the wounded and to report to him personally about Maskov's condition in Orekhovo.

It was after midnight when Tarasov arrived in Orekhovo. General Diebich was still awaiting him and told him to go immediately to the emperor who was anxious to hear about the wounded courier. Tarasov proceeded to the emperor's apartment. He described his visit in the following dramatic passage:

> After the valet had announced my arrival, I entered the emperor's bedroom. His Majesty sat near an open fire, his shoulders covered with a coat, reading some papers. I noticed that the emperor looked worried and that he was trying to warm himself by the open fireside. As soon as I stepped into the room he asked me hastily: "How is Maskov?"—"He received in his fall a heavy blow on the head that provoked a cerebral concussion and a large fracture at the base of the skull; when I reached him I saw that he had stopped breathing and that all medical help was already useless." Having listened to my report the emperor stood up and said in tears: "What a terrible thing! How I pity this man!" Then turning to the table he rang the bell. On this I left the room. I could not fail to notice an extraordinary expression on his face, a face which I knew well, having studied it for so many years; his face revealed I do not know what of hidden excitement and the emperor was shaken by a nervous chill.

The next day, November 16, Alexander reached Mariupol at seven o'clock in the evening. At ten o'clock he asked for Wylie, who found that he was suffering from a paroxysm of fever. Sir James displayed unusual anxiety and recommended that the emperor remain in Mariupol for some time, but Alexander refused saying that he had promised the empress to be back the next day. So at 10 A.M. on November 17, wrapped in a warm overcoat, his feet covered with a bear skin, Alexander left Mariupol in a closed coach. He arrived in Taganrog the same day at 7 P.M.

And the body of courier Maskov followed him at a little distance.

XIV

JOURNEY'S END

THE LAST two weeks that Emperor Alexander spent in Tagan-rog, before his official death, have been recorded in the diaries of Empress Elisabeth, Prince Peter Volkonsky, Sir James Wylie, Dr. Dimitry Tarasov, and in an unsigned manu-script entitled "Official History of the Illness and Death of Emperor Alexander I." We possess also the recollections of some of the emperor's servants, especially those of his valets, Anisimov and Fyodorov, but they do not contain a day-by-day record of events and very often give way to the temptation of recalling stories based upon hearsay and therefore of no historical value. Prince Peter Volkonsky kept a day-by-day record and his description is the most complete if not always the most accurate. However, as a whole, the four principal wit-nesses have left us four different stories full of the most ob-vious contradictions. This state of affairs can be explained only by two suppositions: (1) that they had to write something about Alexander's illness in view of the emperor's determina-tion to use it as a means of escape and, obviously, did not arrange among themselves all the details of their narratives; and

(2) that some of these diaries, and especially Volkonsky's, were written *post factum*.

On the morning of November 18, Prince Volkonsky notes that the emperor had just spent a good night. Wylie on the other hand writes: "The night from the seventeenth to the eighteenth was bad. I am afraid that it may all turn for the worse." In his description of the day of November 18, Volkonsky states that Wylie and he had to interrupt their dinner at 3:00 P.M. because the emperor felt feverish. He tells us that they went together to the emperor's room and remained there. This is contradicted by the empress who writes that Wylie was alone in Alexander's room and that she herself went in later, not mentioning Volkonsky at all, while the latter omits to note the presence of Empress Elisabeth. Then, too, Volkonsky writes: "At *seven o'clock* in the evening the emperor thanked Wylie who left his room. Later came the empress and stayed until *ten o'clock*." [1]

Empress Elisabeth contradicts this statement by saying: "I had been with the emperor until *seven o'clock* and then returned to my apartment. He slept all evening and *did not call for me*." On November 19, Volkonsky writes: "The emperor has spent a good night. In the morning at about eight o'clock he got up and dressed as usual. About 11:00 A.M. he took a laxative and felt relieved, but toward the evening his temperature rose again *because he refused to take any more medicine*."

For this day, the empress gives many more details, while Volkonsky's diary contains only the short statement mentioned above. The empress writes: "He had come to my apartment between 11:00 and 12:00 A.M. and told me that he was feeling

[1] All italics in the diaries are the editor's, not those of the original writer.

much better . . . He was still looking rather yellow, but was much happier. We busied ourselves in sorting sea shells that I had gathered. I begged him not to work too much as he had done the day before, to which he answered that work with him was a habit, that when he did not work he felt that his head was empty and that if he abdicated he would devour entire libraries, because otherwise he would go insane."

The empress further relates that she dined that day with Alexander and after dinner he visited her again. Toward 7:00 P.M. she was called to the emperor. She found him lying on a couch clad in a dressing gown. He told her that *he had taken his medicine* which had acted so violently that it had caused cramps, but that Wylie had given him some tea which had relieved the pain. He said that he was feeling fine. He talked with great animation and laughed heartily. Volkonsky and Wylie went in at nine o'clock. Wylie asked the emperor how he was feeling. Alexander answered smilingly: "Fine!"

Wylie's notes are a complete contradiction of the long and detailed description of Empress Elisabeth. He writes: "The emperor is apathetic. Spells of vertigo and attacks of fever repeat themselves too often. I dare not declare that it is *hemitritacus semitertiana*, although everything seems to indicate that it is."

On November 20, the empress, Volkonsky and Wylie all state that Alexander's health was satisfactory. Only the anonymous author of "The Official History of the Illness and Death of Emperor Alexander I" comes out with an alarming statement: "He is so ill that Doctor Stoffregen has been called to his bedside." This statement is very strange not only because it contradicts the previous three but also and especially because it mentions Stoffregen, court physician to the empress. Alexander had his own two medical men—Wylie and Tarasov, in both of whom he placed great faith. Were there need for the opinion or help of another physician, would it not have been more natural to call for Tarasov, who had attended the emperor for so many years but had not been called to his bedside since his return to Taganrog, than to call in Dr. Stoffregen? And if Stoffregen had really been called to Alexander's bedside, would the empress and Volkonsky not have mentioned this fact in their detailed description of that day?

The date of November 20 contains also an important statement in Volkonsky's diary. He relates that the emperor wrote a letter to St. Petersburg addressed to his mother, the Dowager Empress Maria Fyodorovna, and ordered this letter to be antedated by two days, forbidding everyone to write to the capital about his illness. To this Volkonsky remarked that it would be better to tell the truth because some of the townspeople might write and exaggerate the real situation. This is particularly astounding when one recalls that Alexander had returned to Taganrog only three days before and that nothing alarming could have been said about his state of health, since he arose and dressed every morning at eight o'clock, as usual, receiving couriers, listening to the daily reports of General Diebich, moving around the house, suffering apparently only from a slight indisposition.

The next day, November 21, the empress writes: "The night was satisfactory and, although perspiration continued, the emperor felt better and spent the day without any further change in his health . . . As another courier was leaving this day for St. Petersburg, the emperor asked me to write about his illness to the dowager empress and ordered General Aide-de-Camp Diebich to inform the Grand Duke Constantine, in Warsaw, that after his return from the Crimea, where he had contracted a slight fever, he had been compelled to remain in his room."

Prince Volkonsky mentions the same fact, but adds in the margin: "This order to General Diebich was given not on the 21st but on the 23rd." Wylie states also that there was an amelioration in the condition of the emperor's health.

It is important to note the emperor's sudden decision to inform Constantine, then still considered heir to the throne notwithstanding the fact that he had formally renounced his rights long before, and this announcement to Constantine was to be made through the medium of a third person while the letter to his mother, though written by the empress, was signed by Alexander himself. This was in accordance with what he told his brother in Warsaw some time before: "When the time to abdicate will come, I shall let you know and you will inform mother of your decision." It seems evident that the Dowager Empress Maria Fyodorovna served as an intermediary in the secret correspondence between her two sons concerning the question of their mutual abdication.

Up to November 22 the statements of the witnesses were noticeably contradictory, but those describing that day are most peculiarly so. The empress writes that on that day Alexander fainted in the morning, but that in the afternoon he was feeling very well and conversed animatedly with her until evening. Volkonsky states, however, that all through the day the emperor felt badly, that toward the evening he was completely prostrated and hardly spoke during the whole day, and Wylie makes an extraordinary statement under this same date.

He writes: "I notice that since November 20 the emperor is preoccupied with something other than his health. These thoughts seem to dominate him completely."

But it is the next day, November 23, which seems to be the most important of all. This date decidedly marks the turning point in Alexander's last days as ruler of the Russian empire. Both Volkonsky and Empress Elisabeth note distinct amelioration in the condition of the emperor's health. Wylie still expresses his grave concern while the empress contradicts him when writing: "About five o'clock in the afternoon I asked Wylie to come to see me and to tell me how things were. Wylie was jovial and told me that although the emperor still had some fever, I should go to see him, because he was distinctly better."

The empress spent the whole evening with Alexander and later wrote a letter to her mother in which she exclaimed: "Where can one find refuge from this life? When one thinks that one has arranged everything for the best and is able to enjoy it, a new and unexpected trial arises which upsets all one's plans and takes away the faculty of enjoying the fruit of so much effort."

Is not this mysterious outcry of despair in contradiction to Elisabeth's statement in her diary? And is it not strange that her diary ends under this date? What could be the reasons for all this? What other explanation could one find than that the emperor had told Elisabeth that very evening that the fulfillment of his decision was near and had asked her to help him to carry it out? Did Elisabeth then find that there was no reason to continue her diary, since she knew that what was going to take place was merely stage play? Or did she continue to write and was the rest of her diary destroyed?

This possibility is quite admissible because Alexander's brother and successor, Emperor Nicholas I, destroyed the diary kept by his mother, Empress Maria Fyodorovna, and in general "liked to destroy many things having any connection with his brother," according to a statement made by the well-known Russian historian, the Grand Duke Nicholas Mikhailovich in a letter to Prince Vladimir Bariatinsky. One thing is quite clear: something must have happened in the course of the evening of November 23 to make Empress Elisabeth write to her mother as she did. And the only thing that could have happened was Alexander's announcement of the imminent fulfillment of his decision, of which he had spoken earlier to Elisabeth during their stay in Taganrog.

On November 24, one finds another contradiction between the statement of Prince Volkonsky and that of "The Official History." Volkonsky writes: "Toward evening the emperor felt *better*" while the anonymous author states: "Toward the evening the emperor felt *worse*." On November 25, Volkonsky, Wylie, and the anonymous author concur in their opinion that the situation is hopeful for the first time. On November 26, Wylie makes the following important statement: "The situation is critical . . . I wanted to give him some medicine, but the emperor refused saying, 'Go away!' Then, when he saw that I was crying, he said, 'Well, dear friend, I hope that you do not mind. *I have reasons of my own.*' "

The same day at about nine o'clock in the evening, Dr. Tarasov was called to the emperor for the first time since the latter's return to Taganrog. Tarasov spent over an hour alone with Alexander. When he left, Alexander went to sleep and spent a good night. Of what did they converse? And what had Tarasov been doing during all these days since their return from the Crimea?

The night was pitch dark when the body of courier Maskov arrived in Taganrog. The small town was fast asleep. Tarasov, who had been waiting at the entrance to the town, gave orders to take the body to his house where he was to perform the autopsy. Soon the body lay naked on a table in a back room of the house occupied by the court physician, and Tarasov began to perform his duty. He could not help admiring the perfect form of the deceased courier and must have compared it with that of the emperor. No doubt if the face were hidden the body could easily be taken for that of Alexander himself. Tarasov also noticed that Maskov's right leg bore a scar, probably from an old wound. He must have thought: "What a pity it is not the left leg." The emperor's scar as a result of a horse's kick was on his left leg.

Through the remainder of the night Tarasov busied himself with the dead body. But if anyone could have spied upon him, he would have been astounded by the discovery that it was not an autopsy that the surgeon was performing. Tarasov was embalming the body of courier Maskov. This work continued for two more days and nights until the corpse was well preserved from decay. Then Tarasov waited to be called to the emperor in order to announce to him that he could then "die" safely. He took this news to Alexander in the evening of November 26. Five days earlier, a simple ceremony had taken place at the local cemetery. Courier Maskov was buried with military honors. There were few people present besides a detachment of infantry, because Maskov's family lived too far away to be able to come to the funeral. When the grave was closed, the officer commanding the detachment of infantry had deposited on the small mound a large wreath, bearing the imperial crown and Alexander's initials. This attention on the part of the emperor had touched the hearts of the officers and soldiers who were present at the funeral ceremony. But what would they have thought if they had known that the casket supposed to contain the body of courier Maskov was empty?

The days immediately following November 26 precipitated the crisis. Everything seemed ready for the passing of Emperor Alexander into another world. The accounts of the witnesses continue, however, to be as contradictory as before. On November 29, Prince Volkonsky states that the end was approaching, the emperor remaining fully prostrated. Tarasov, too, remarks that the illness had reached its paroxysm. And Wylie makes a remarkable revelation. He writes: "Things are getting worse and worse. Prince Volkonsky has been occupying my bed in order to be nearer to the emperor." This is the most significant statement of all that had previously been made by the court physician. It is hardly conceivable that at a time of extreme danger, such as was revealed by the records, it should be a personal friend of the emperor who would occupy the nearest place to Alexander's bedroom instead of his own physician. One can understand, however, that in order to carry out his plans it was more important for Alexander to have near him not Wylie but Volkonsky. On November 30, the witnesses indulge in their usual contradictions. However, they all state that the situation was so critical that one could expect the worst. Wylie writes more plainly than the others: "No hope to save our beloved sovereign. I hastened to inform the empress as well as Prince Volkonsky and Baron Diebich."

Then came the night, the last night in the life of Emperor Alexander I. Contrary to the rule, it was Tarasov who was on duty in Alexander's bedroom. Prince Volkonsky occupied the bed in the corridor between Alexander's bedroom and dressing room. There were, therefore, no other persons besides Volkonsky and Tarasov in the emperor's apartment during the night of November 30–December 1. Diebich and Wylie remained in the basement with the servants. It was around midnight that Tarasov left the emperor's room and went to see Prince Volkonsky. The prince was ready. They cautiously went to the door leading into the courtyard, opened it, and waited. Soon they saw four men carrying something heavy that looked at first glance like a coffin. It was, however, a bathtub. The four men deposited their burden in the emperor's dressing room and went away. Volkonsky followed them to the door and told them to return in an hour in order to take the bathtub back. In the meanwhile, Tarasov removed a linen sheet covering the bathtub and revealed the body of courier Maskov. An hour later, the four men came back and carried the bathtub away. Little did they suspect that they were then carrying their master, Emperor and Autocrat of All the Russias! And on the emperor's bed reposed, calm and serene, the unfortunate courier Maskov, whose accidental death had made his emperor's escape possible.

The morning of December 1 was gray and somber. The space before the emperor's residence was crowded. People who had attended the early Mass offered for the recovery of His Imperial Majesty went straight from church to the emperor's residence in order to get the latest news about their master's illness. No one except the empress and Prince Volkonsky had been in

the emperor's room since dawn. Tarasov had left the house
early in the morning in order to obtain a little rest after his
sleepless night on duty. At 10:50 A.M., the news of the emper-
or's death reached the crowd. Soon after, the mournful ringing
of church bells announced the sad tidings to the whole city.

During the whole day of December 1, no one but those of
the emperor's closest entourage was permitted to enter Alexander's bedroom. The same precautions were taken the following day. In the evening of December 2, the body was placed in
the emperor's dressing room and Wylie together with Stoffregen began to make preparations for embalming it. Tarasov
refused to assist his colleagues in this part of their duty,
probably because he felt that he had already done more than
his share and did not care to be involved any further. During
the entire process of embalming the body its face was kept
constantly covered so that not one of Wylie's and Stoffregen's
attendants saw it. This continued all through the night and on
the following day the body, dressed in a general's uniform, was
viewed by the awe-struck people. But the face was already un-
recognizable.

There is a strange mystery about the autopsy of the body.
Wylie has declared that he performed it and described its
results in a *procès-verbal* which, as an official document, bore
the signatures of nine people including also that of Tarasov.
However, Tarasov assures us that, though it was he who composed the document, he did not sign it. Such contradictions
in the statements of as important personages as Wylie and Tarasov can lead only to an obvious conclusion, if one bears in mind
the part played by Tarasov since Alexander's return to Taganrog after his Crimean journey. This conclusion can be nothing

but that the document in question described the autopsy of courier Maskov and not that of Emperor Alexander. And it is confirmed by the statement that the body had a scar on its right leg.

The empress did not remain in the same house where the body lay in state. She had moved in the morning of December 1 to a near-by house belonging to some people by the name of Shikhmatov, who had been prepared to receive her on the day before, when they were told by Prince Volkonsky to have quarters ready for the empress. This indicates that Volkonsky *knew* of the forthcoming change. From the Shikhmatovs' house, Elisabeth addressed a number of letters. On December 2, she wrote one to the Dowager Empress Maria Fyodorovna in which one finds a peculiar sentence: "When he goes I will go too if permitted. I will go with him as long as I shall be able to. I still do not know what will become of me."

Two days later, she wrote to her mother and repeated almost the same sentence that she had written in the letter to her mother-in-law: "I stay here as long as he is here; when he goes, I shall go too, but I do not know when . . . I feel well, do not worry too much about me, but, if I dared, I would like to follow the one who has been my very life."

Meanwhile, couriers had been dispatched to Warsaw and to St. Petersburg to announce the fatal news to the Grand Duke Constantine, still officially heir to the throne, and to the imperial family. The courier sent to Warsaw reached Constantine in the evening of December 7. As soon as the grand duke read the news, he ordered the preparation of papers to be dispatched to St. Petersburg announcing the renunciation of his right of succession in favor of his next brother, Nicholas. It took all night to have the papers written, copied, and executed, and in the morning of December 8, Constantine entrusted the documents to his younger brother, Michael, who was staying with him in Warsaw, and sent him off to St. Petersburg.

While Grand Duke Michael was on his way, the courier from Taganrog reached St. Petersburg on the morning of December 9. At that time the Dowager Empress Maria Fyodorovna, the Grand Duke Nicholas, his wife, and members of the court were attending a *Te Deum* in the palace chapel for the recovery of Emperor Alexander. The news was delivered to Nicholas who interrupted the service and then and there took the oath of allegiance to the new Emperor Constantine followed by members of the court. Later Nicholas, as the senior member of the imperial family in St. Petersburg, issued a formal proclamation announcing the death of Alexander and the succession of Constantine and the taking of an oath of allegiance to the new emperor by members of the government and the troops stationed at the capital.

It was only on December 15 that Grand Duke Michael arrived in St. Petersburg and threw his brother, Nicholas, into consternation by the decision of Constantine. Nicholas feared that the country would not accept such "family arrangements" and immediately sent a courier to Warsaw informing Constantine that the capital had already taken an oath to him and imploring him to reverse his decision. Later, Nicholas sent Michael to Warsaw again with instructions to try to persuade Constantine by a personal appeal. But it was all in vain. And while couriers were galloping day and night during the next ten days between St. Petersburg and Warsaw, Russia had no sovereign. Finally Nicholas reluctantly decided to ascend the throne. This decision was reached late in the night of December 25, at the end of a long session of the Council of State and after the President of the Senate, Lopukhin, pleaded eloquently with the grand duke, pointing to the documents which Alexander had left with him as proof that such was the desire of the late emperor. So the members of the government and high officials of the empire were ordered to assemble the next morning in the Winter Palace to take a new oath of allegiance, this time to Nicholas. At the same time, orders were issued to the troops to take the new oath in their quarters.

This was the occasion that the members of the secret Northern Society seized to attempt a revolution. All through the night they went from regiment to regiment trying to persuade the soldiers that Nicholas was a usurper and that Constantine was held captive in Warsaw. These tactics partially succeeded and in the morning of December 26 some units in defiance of orders marched to the Senate Square near the Winter Palace demanding to be shown the will of Emperor Alexander. There they stood all day in the bitter cold, abandoned by most of the conspirators, defiant, but leaderless. When the Military Governor of St. Petersburg, General Count Miloradovich, a hero of the War of 1812, rode up to the rebellious troops in an attempt to persuade them to return to their barracks, he was shot and killed by one of the minor conspirators. And further entreaties by Grand Duke Michael and the metropolitan, Seraphim, were to no avail. While the rebels counted three thousand, they represented but a small proportion of the garrison of the capital. Finally, when evening was setting, and after a cavalry attack on the rebels had been repulsed by their rifle fire, Nicholas ordered artillery to be brought up. The rebels were quickly dispersed by cannon shot, leaving many dead and wounded. And in the night that followed, most of the would-be revolutionaries of the Northern Society were arrested. Thus ended the so-called "Decembrist revolt." In quelling it, Nicholas showed moderation and a strength of character that no one suspected in him. And having disposed of his "friends of the 26th of December," the new emperor was ready to proceed with the ceremonial funeral of his brother and predecessor.

During all this time the body of Alexander had remained in Taganrog. Finally the arrangements for transporting it to St. Petersburg were completed and the funeral procession left Taganrog on January 10, 1826. It moved slowly across the vast expanse of Russia, stopping each night in a village or town where the coffin, always closed, was invariably placed in a local church or cathedral where it was viewed by the multitudes, not in the least suspicious that it might contain the body of a common mortal and not that of a crowned and annointed sovereign.

After a stop in Moscow from February 15 to February 18, the procession reached Tsarskoye Selo on March 12. Here at midnight on March 13, the coffin was opened (after a preliminary inspection by Dr. Tarasov) so that the body could be viewed by the members of the imperial family. Special precautions were taken so that the soldiers and servants who lifted the lid of the casket would not see the body. And they were kept at a considerable distance during the time when the Dowager Empress Maria Fyodorovna, Emperor Nicholas, and his Empress Alexandra, and Grand Duke Michael each in turn ascended the steps and viewed the body. But they could hear as the dowager empress exclaimed: "Yes, this is my dear son, my dear Alexander. Oh, how he has changed!"

On March 18, the body, now reposing in a bronze casket, was moved to St. Petersburg. There it stayed in the Cathedral of Our Lady of Kazan until March 25. On that morning it was taken to the church in the fortress of Saints Peter and Paul where it received the final burial. It was a gray, cloudy morning and the procession, which included Emperor Nicholas, moved slowly on foot through the slush of half-melted snow along streets lined with quiet, solemn people, many of whom sobbed. The journey took two hours. Finally, when the casket was lowered into the vault, the thunder of cannon announced to the people of St. Petersburg that Alexander the Blessed, who had reigned over them for twenty-five years, had reached his last resting place. And soon he was to be followed by his spouse.

Empress Elisabeth Alexeyevna had remained in Taganrog throughout this trying winter. But on May 3, she left the tragic little city going north to Kaluga where she was to meet her mother-in-law, the Dowager Empress Maria Fyodorovna, who was coming the long way from St. Petersburg. For what purpose? Was Empress Elisabeth going to reveal the secret? Or was she to confirm the dowager empress' suspicions? We will never know, for before reaching Kaluga, Elisabeth died in the small town of Belev, in the province of Tula, in the early morning of May 16, and the dowager empress, who had hastened beyond Kaluga to meet her daughter-in-law, arrived in Belev a few hours later only to find a corpse. Elisabeth's wish "to follow the one who was my very life" seems to have been fulfilled. Or was it? Because strange things had happened in the town of Taganrog not only preceding but also following the official death of Emperor Alexander I.

During the last days of November, the beautiful Bay of Taganrog, always gay with vessels from many foreign countries, gradually became deserted. Every ship hastened to leave port in time to clear the entrance to the Sea of Azov before it was blocked by ice. And by December 1 there was only one boat which had fearlessly remained at anchor on the steel-gray waters of Taganrog Bay. This vessel was a private yacht and she bore a British flag. Her owner was the Earl of Cathcart, former ambassador of His Britannic Majesty at the Court of St. Petersburg. When the sad news of the emperor's death rang through the town, hardly anyone paid attention to the belated stay of this yacht in Taganrog waters. The people of Taganrog, the people of Russia were alarmed. And the people of Taganrog did not display their usual curiosity, and failed even to notice the day when the lonely ship left the harbor. Nor could the actual date of her sailing be ascertained from her log, because for some perhaps obvious reasons her skipper neglected to make any entries until the end of December. By that time the yacht was sailing lazily through the blue waters of the Mediterranean. She had performed an important mission after leaving Taganrog with a distinguished visitor on board. She had been to the Holy Land, where the distinguished visitor had gone to pray at the tomb of the Savior, as reported by the British Consul at Jerusalem. Then she had taken him back to the land of "barbarians" where even a once-crowned head still had a conscience and was ready to expiate with Christian resolution and fortitude a voluntary, or even an involuntary, crime in order to save his immortal soul.

XV

EXPIATION

Over ten years had passed since the day the bronze casket bearing the inscription "Emperor Alexander I the Blessed" was lowered into the vault of the church of Saints Peter and Paul. On September 16, 1836, a stranger, mounted on a beautiful white horse, followed the trail of exiles to Siberia. He rode his superb mount in silence. The autumn days were clear and sunny. The roads were deserted. The air was filled with the fragrance of pine and cedar trees and with that little something of sadness that is so characteristic of a northern autumn. In the early mornings, frost, the first messenger of winter, spread a silver veil over the green grass and the yellow sand of the road. It was obvious that summer had gone.

Late in the evening of that day the stranger reached Krasnoufimsk. Stopping at an inn, he silently dismounted, entered the large, low-ceilinged room and made the sign of the cross before the icons. He was tall and had a military bearing notwithstanding his very simple civilian clothes. He appeared to be a man of about sixty years of age and wore a gray beard. He remained silent most of the time as if in deep thought. When addressed, he made short and enigmatic replies, but he did not start a conversation himself. The innkeeper did not ask him who he was, because in Siberia only the authorities are interested in the names or deeds of people. So the stranger passed a quiet night at the inn. The next morning, however, the police demanded to see his papers. He had none. They asked him who he was. He refused to answer them. The police then arrested him as a tramp and took him to court on the charge of vagrancy. In accordance with the existing laws, he was sentenced to twenty lashes of the whip and to deportation, because he was too old to serve in the army. And on April 7, 1837, under the number 117, which had been assigned to him, he was sent to Bogoyavlensk with a party of other prisoners. This time he could not ride, because he had given his horse to the innkeeper in payment for his stay. He walked through the deep snow rubbing shoulders with thieves and murderers. And in a small bundle containing his belongings there was an icon of Our Lady of Pochayev bearing on one side the letters A.I. surmounted by the imperial crown.

In Bogoyavlensk, the stranger remained for five years until 1842. From then on he was known by the assumed name of Fyodor Kuzmich. Very often people would ask him to tell them his real first name so that they could pray for him to his patron saint, but invariably he refused, once even adding that it was not necessary because the church prayed for him.

Very soon after this deportation to Bogoyavlensk, Grand Duke Michael came to Krasnoufimsk where Fyodor Kuzmich had been sentenced. When the grand duke learned that the stranger had been punished with twenty lashes of the whip, he became furious. He went to the judge who had pronounced the sentence and threatened to inflict upon him a lashing also and to send him to Bogoyavlensk to take the place of Fyodor Kuzmich. But later, after he had visited the stranger himself and spent a long time in conversation with him, he seemed to be pacified and did not carry out his threat to the unfortunate judge.

During Fyodor Kuzmich's stay in Bogoyavlensk it happened that Afanasy, Archbishop of Irkutsk, when passing through the town desired to visit the stranger. Fyodor Kuzmich met the archbishop at the entrance to his modest dwelling and bowed to the ground. The archbishop did likewise. Then they kissed each other's hands and entered the house, where they remained closeted for many hours and talked in a foreign language. This puzzled the good people of the small town, but they were not accustomed to asking too many questions. After the archbishop's visit, Fyodor Kuzmich's landlord, calling his attention to the icons and engravings which were visible on the walls of his room, asked if it was not the archbishop who left them for him. Fyodor Kuzmich replied that he had possessed them for a long time and that he had received them as a gift from a certain Peter Volkonsky, a very good friend of his.

In 1842, Fyodor Kuzmich left Bogoyavlensk and for some time moved from place to place until he settled in a village near Krasnorechensk. There he lived for eight years in the depths of the forest in a small hut which had been built for him by a rich peasant named Ivan Latyshov. Its interior contained only a narrow wooden couch, a few wooden benches and some icons including one of St. Alexander Nevsky, the patron saint of Emperor Alexander. Fyodor Kuzmich felt very happy here. During the summer he lived in the small hut among the dark and massive cedar trees. He kept bees and was always very proud to be able to offer his landlord or his guests some of the honey that his bees had collected during the short summer. For the winter months he abandoned his small hut and took quarters in his landlord's house. In the course of the long winter evenings he told the people who came to see Latyshov and Latyshov's family innumerable stories about court life and historical events that had occurred at the beginning of the nineteenth century.

It appears that he recalled with the greatest pleasure the times of Empress Catherine II. Stories about her, about the Turkish campaigns, about the exploits of Field Marshal Suvorov delighted his simple listeners. Then he told them also about the famous men of a more recent period, about Kutuzov and how the old soldier emerged victorious from the campaign of 1812. But he never mentioned the name of Emperor Paul I and very seldom that of Emperor Alexander I. Only once did he recount the following anecdote: "When Napoleon was marching on Moscow, Emperor Alexander went to pray at the casket of Saint Serge of Radonezh. The cathedral was dark and he was alone. Abundant tears streamed down the cheeks of the praying emperor. And suddenly he heard a voice which said distinctly, 'Go, Alexander, and trust Kutuzov. God be with you.'"

Although not belonging to any of the orders, Fyodor Kuzmich led the life of a monk. He slept on a thin mattress placed on boards. He wore only the simplest garments of unbleached linen. His food never included meat and he fasted often. He kept up a large correspondence with people in Russia. However, he wanted to keep this a secret and therefore hid carefully his paper, pen and ink, destroying the letters that he received or locking them in a small wooden box. He visited the local church upon every occasion prescribed by the Russian Orthodox religion, but constantly refused to receive Holy Communion. This fact at the beginning alarmed the local priest, but the latter very soon received word from his bishop to the effect that he should not worry about it and that Fyodor Kuzmich was a very holy man. The stranger, although apparently unknown to everyone, seemed to have protectors of importance.

One day when Latyshov's farm hands began to sing a soldiers' song about the white tsar and how he fought the French, Fyodor Kuzmich suddenly became deeply moved and went away, his eyes full of tears. Later on he begged Latyshov to ask his farm hands not to sing songs about Alexander I.

On another day, when workmen who were repairing his hut made such an infernal noise that he could not say his prayers, Fyodor Kuzmich stepped out with fiery eyes and burning cheeks and shaking his fist at them shouted with rage: "If only you knew who I was, you would not martyr me like this. I have but to write one word to St. Petersburg and you would cease to exist." Soon afterward, however, he realized that he should not have behaved as he did and begged the workmen to forgive him and to forget what he had said.

During these eight years he was twice recognized by former soldiers of his. "One day," relates the priest, George Belousov, "an old soldier who had been condemned to be deported to Siberia, but whose name I cannot recall, told me that when he met Fyodor Kuzmich he recognized in him Emperor Alexander and fell to his knees. Fyodor Kuzmich treated him very kindly, but begged him not to tell anyone about what had happened."

On another occasion he was recognized by an old soldier by the name of Olenev, whom Alexander had known personally. Fyodor Kuzmich was a guest at the house of a man named Paramonov who had been the chairman of the board of trustees of the local church. It was there that Olenev saw him and immediately exclaimed, "This is our Little Father, Tsar Alexander Pavlovich!" This time Fyodor Kuzmich became angry and said, "I am a tramp. Do not tell anyone that I am a tsar, because you would be put in prison and I would have to flee."

During his stay with Latyshov, Fyodor Kuzmich was taken ill and his landlord placed him in the nearest hospital. At that time, the hospital was visited by General Count Kleinmichel, former chief of staff of the military settlements, who was on a tour of inspection in Siberia. Kleinmichel, of course, knew Alexander well enough to recognize him even after all these years. As soon as Fyodor Kuzmich heard about Kleinmichel's impending visit, he took every precaution to avoid being seen by him. Finally, when Kleinmichel entered the ward where Fyodor Kuzmich occupied a cot, the latter drew the sheets over his face and pretended to be asleep, thus avoiding recognition.

Years went by. The gray beard of the stranger had turned quite white. His hair, also white and rather thin on the crown of his head and temples, flowed down his neck in long curly streams. He stooped rather heavily although when he walked with his two hands thrust in his belt he seemed to be taller, revealing without a doubt his former military training. And his light blue eyes ever remained alive as if age did not dare touch their beauty.

All through these years he had continued to lead a simple and uneventful life among simple people. Important events had taken place in Russia and in Europe. Emperor Nicholas I had attempted to undertake the emancipation of the serfs by two laws promulgated on April 14, 1842, and November 20, 1847. They had perhaps as much the nature of half-measures as the famous law promulgated by Emperor Alexander in 1803. Nevertheless, they were conscientious attempts to solve that all-important problem. Then came the year 1848. Europe was once more in the throes of revolutionary convulsions. Russia alone stood out like an invulnerable giant. But it was already evident that the giant had feet of clay. News of these events reached Siberia also and became a topic for regular comment on the part of Fyodor Kuzmich. He invariably praised the attitude of Emperor Nicholas I, but never compared it with that of Emperor Alexander. Only once did he make a direct allusion to the past. When commenting on the downfall of Prince Metternich (he called him always "Count" Metternich, and we know that the Austrian diplomat and statesman received his princely title only after 1825) he said, "If that had happened during the reign of Emperor Alexander, it would have pleased him, because Alexander did not like the old fox of Vienna."

Then came the news of the Hungarian rebellion and of Russia's intervention in order to help Emperor Francis-Joseph retain his crown. Fyodor Kuzmich followed the news of Rus-

sian victories with a great deal of excitement and praised the
Russian soldier as the best in the world.

It was in this year, 1849, that he had given his blessing to a
young woman who was going to make a pilgrimage to the
venerated shrines and monasteries of Russia. This young woman
was named Alexandra Nikiforovna and was the daughter of
a peasant from Krasnorechensk. Born in 1827, she had lost
her parents while still in her infancy and had been educated by
a priest, Father Polikarp. She was very religious and it was
not surprising that when, at the age of twelve, she first met
Fyodor Kuzmich she soon began to regard him almost as a
saint. With passing years this admiration turned into a profound attachment and affection. The girl became a real companion to Fyodor Kuzmich. She helped him in whatever she
could and served as his regular messenger. But most of her
time she spent listening to the old man's stories of the past.

Of all that Fyodor Kuzmich told her, she liked best his
descriptions of different Russian monasteries, and began to
dream of a regular pilgrimage to the holy shrines of Russia.
When she was getting ready to leave, she said to Fyodor Kuzmich: "But above all I should like to see the tsar." And when
the old man inquired of her why she was so anxious to do so,
she replied, "Well, Little Father, everyone says, 'the tsar this'
and 'the tsar that' and no one knows exactly how he looks."
To this Fyodor Kuzmich remarked pensively: "Wait, perhaps
you will see more than one tsar. If it be the will of God, you
might even talk to them and would then see that tsars are human
like everyone else."

When Alexandra Nikiforovna arrived in Russia, at first she

wanted to go directly to the monastery of Our Lady of Pochayev, but remembering that Fyodor Kuzmich had told her to visit the town of Kremenchug and to find there Count Dimitry Osten-Sacken, she did so and spent several months in the count's house. While she was there, Emperor Nicholas I came to Kremenchug and also stopped at the house of Count Osten-Sacken. There he learned of the presence of Alexandra Nikiforovna and asked to see her. She came and was received by the emperor in the presence of their host. Nicholas immediately began to ask her about life in Siberia and about Fyodor Kuzmich. Alexandra Nikiforovna replied frankly to all his questions. Some of her replies amused the emperor, who said to Count Osten-Sacken: "You have a brave guest here. She is not even afraid to answer any questions of such a powerful man as I." To this the girl replied at once: "Why should I be afraid when God is with me and I am protected by the holy prayers of Fyodor Kuzmich?" The emperor then became pensive and said, "Indeed, Fyodor Kuzmich is a holy man."

Upon leaving, Nicholas gave Alexandra Nikiforovna a personal note and told her to come to visit him in St. Petersburg. "You will have but to show this note at the entrance to the palace and you will be brought to me at once. And do not forget to ask me for anything you need. Friends of Fyodor Kuzmich are my friends."

But Alexandra Nikiforovna did not go to St. Petersburg, and in 1852 she returned to Siberia. There she was eagerly awaited by Fyodor Kuzmich who asked her to describe to him all of her journey. When she described her meeting with Emperor Nicholas and repeated what he had said to her about Fyodor Kuzmich, the old man could not restrain his tears. For many

days Alexandra Nikiforovna entertained her protector by relating to him in detail all that she had done and seen during
the two years of her absence. One day, while he was listening
to her apparently absorbed in his own thoughts, the girl suddenly exclaimed, "Little Father, Fyodor Kuzmich, how like
Emperor Alexander Pavlovich you are!" No sooner had she
pronounced these words than Fyodor Kuzmich jumped to his
feet. His eyebrows were menacingly drawn together, his blue
eyes were flaming. "How do you know it? Who told you so?"
he demanded sternly. Alexandra Nikiforovna became frightened and explained: "No one told me, Little Father, I said it
without thinking. I saw a portrait of Alexander Pavlovich
at Count Osten-Sacken's and it seemed to me that you are
like him and that you hold your hand on your belt exactly as
he did in the portrait."

Fyodor Kuzmich did not reply to this, but went into the
next room in order to hide the sudden emotion that over-
whelmed him.

For five more years Alexandra Nikiforovna remained with
Fyodor Kuzmich. In the course of this time the old man received an important visit. One day an open carriage stopped
near his modest house. A young man wearing the uniform of
an officer of the Hussar Regiment of the Guards stepped out
and gracefully assisted a young and attractive woman to alight.
They entered the house and spent over an hour in animated
conversation conducted in a foreign language. When they
were leaving, the young officer kissed Fyodor Kuzmich's hand,
a thing that the latter had never before permitted anyone to
do. The old man accompanied them to their carriage and afterward stood for a long time in the middle of the road gazing in

the direction where they had disappeared. When he returned to his dwelling he smiled and said: "A long time ago I was known by my grandparents and now it is the turn of my grandchildren." Fyodor Kuzmich concealed his true relationship to the visitors, because the young officer was his nephew, the Grand Duke Alexander Nikolayevich, the future Emperor Alexander II, and the young woman who accompanied him was his wife, the Grand Duchess Maria Alexandrovna.

On March 2, 1855, Emperor Nicholas I died. When this news reached Fyodor Kuzmich, he was deeply moved. He could not remain in his room and went outside. He walked slowly down a narrow path in the snow, along the river, and into the dark forest. His thoughts must have been troubled. So, after all, he had outlived his younger brother, and many others. Where now were Pahlen, Kutuzov, La Harpe, Napoleon, Arakcheyev? For a moment he visualized what would have happened if he had not fled from the throne, but he soon drove these thoughts away. God had willed it thus and he had but to thank Him for His mercy.

Late in 1857, Alexandra Nikiforovna again left for a pilgrimage to Russian monasteries. She was never to see her protector again. Soon after her departure, Fyodor Kuzmich accepted the invitation of a wealthy merchant by the name of Simeon Khromov and went to live with him. At first he settled on Khromov's small estate three miles from the town of Tomsk, but later he moved into Tomsk where Khromov had a hut built for him in his own garden containing a similarly simple interior as that at Latyshov's. Here Fyodor Kuzmich spent the last years of his life as a recluse. He now became even less communicative than before and spent most of his nights in

prayer. Khromov once saw that the old man's knees were cal-
loused from kneeling for hours on the hard floor. The stranger's
health failed visibly during these years. No doubt it was the
result of the hermitlike existence that he was leading but of
course old age also had something to do with it: he was eighty.

In Tomsk he aroused the natural curiosity of people. Some
of them, not aware of his dislike of being questioned, bothered
him with attempts to discover his real identity. One day a
young woman by the name of Natalia Popova asked him to
tell her the names of his parents so that she might order a
requiem mass for the repose of their souls. "You need not
know them," Fyodor Kuzmich replied, "because the Holy
Church prays for them. If I told you my name, I would have
to disappear and heaven would mourn, while hell would rejoice and celebrate a victory."

In the summer Fyodor Kuzmich spent most of his time in
the large fruit grove adjoining Khromov's garden. There too
he kept bees as he had done before when he had lived at Latyshov's. Khromov used to tidy his hut personally, because Fyodor Kuzmich did not like to employ servants. One day a woman
by the name of Olga Balakina, who often went to see Fyodor
Kuzmich, entered the old man's abode, but found only
Khromov. When Balakina entered, Khromov was bending
over a wooden box in which the hermit kept all his papers. At
the sound of steps, Khromov turned abruptly, but seeing it
was not Fyodor Kuzmich, he produced a large blue sheet of
paper bearing seals and many signatures and said: "They all
say that Fyodor Kuzmich is a tramp but, see, here is a marriage
certificate of the Grand Duke Alexander Pavlovich and Elisabeth Alexeyevna."

When the news reached Tomsk that Emperor Alexander II had freed the serfs, it caused great excitement among the people, although there were no serfs in Siberia. Fyodor Kuzmich, however, refrained from discussing this subject, although in previous years he had always been ready to comment on all important events. It was not until the evening of the day when this news had arrived that he told Khromov: "It has always been a cherished dream of Emperor Alexander I."

In January, 1864, Fyodor Kuzmich became very ill. He could not take any food and subsisted only on water. His strength was failing, but he kept a clear head up to his last hour. During this time, Khromov slept in his room in order to be near him should he need anything in the night. On January 31, Fyodor Kuzmich awoke in the night, raised himself on his cot and said distinctly: "The end is near." Then he lay back and slumbered until morning. When Khromov left the old man's room in the morning, he said as usual: "Give me your blessing, Little Father." Fyodor Kuzmich replied: "Go with God!" and then added: "Now give me your blessing." At first Khromov protested, but when the old man insisted, he said: "God bless you, Little Father." Fyodor Kuzmich smiled and lay back on his bed.

The whole day of February 1 he remained silent. From time to time his lips moved, but his eyes were closed. Khromov understood that he was praying. He had not the strength to get up. Toward nine o'clock in the evening Khromov noticed that Fyodor Kuzmich was nearing his end. He was suffering great pain, but not a murmur escaped his lips, and his eyes were extraordinarily bright and luminous. People hearing that the old man's life was ebbing came into his cell and stood there

holding lighted candles. With a trembling hand Fyodor Kuzmich motioned for a candle. He held it for but a few moments;
then he let his hand fall and a deep sigh marked his passing.

His body clad in a simple white shirt of unbleached linen
was buried in the grounds of the Bogoroditsko-Alexeyevsk
monastery in Tomsk on February 4, 1864. A simple cross
marked his grave. The cross bore the inscription: "Here rests
the body of the Great and Blessed Father Fyodor Kuzmich."

Many years later, when the last Russian Emperor Nicholas II, then still only heir to the throne, traveled through
Siberia on his way to the Far East, he visited the simple grave.
Noticing the poor wooden cross he ordered a marble slab to
replace it and a chapel built over the grave.

Few things remained in the modest hut in Khromov's garden
that had belonged to the departed old man. They had all been
gathered together, carefully sealed, and sent to St. Petersburg
by special command of the governor general at Irkutsk. Khromov had kept only a small sachet which he had taken from the
hermit's neck after his death, and which contained the old
man's secret, as Fyodor Kuzmich had told Khromov on more
than one occasion. The sachet contained only a note in cipher.
For many years it kept its secret until it was recently deci-
phered. It read:

ANNA VASILIEVNA: We have discovered a terrible flaw in
our son: Count Pahlen informs me of Alexander's participation in the conspiracy. We must hide, tonight, wherever it is possible.
Saint Petersburg.

23—III. 1801   PAUL

APPENDIX

AUTHOR'S NOTE

THE MYSTERY that to this day surrounds the events concerning the official death of Emperor Alexander I in 1825, as well as the hypothesis that he survived in the person of Fyodor Kuzmich, form problems of history for scholars and students to solve as fascinating as those connected with the Dauphin Louis XVII and Marshal Ney in France, or the Roanoke Colony in America. The statements in this Appendix are presented to the reader in order to amplify the main body of the work and to acquaint him with the difficulties confronting the historian. The statements contain at times certain contradictions, which at first glance would appear to invalidate the author's thesis. However, it is the author's belief that such a wide range of statements, often based on the testimony of witnesses, might of itself constitute a partial proof of the veracity of the thesis, as in the saying, "Where there is smoke there is fire." But the author's contention that Emperor Alexander I not only did not die in Taganrog in 1825, but lived under the name of Fyodor Kuzmich in Siberia until 1864, is largely based on negative evidence, because no historian has ever been able to identify Fyodor Kuzmich. It is self-evident that Fyodor Kuzmich was no common hermit for he knew too well the details of court life during the reign of Alexander I (this is admitted even by those historians who have discarded the author's thesis as sheer imagination), yet *every* person at the time who might have had such knowledge is well accounted for—everyone except Alexander himself.

It is the author's surmise that the proof of his thesis can be found in the private papers of the Cathcart family in England, access to which has been refused to every investigator including the late Grand Duke Nicholas Mikhailovich. Such a refusal was registered as late as 1925, the year that marked the centenary of the emperor's official death, when Prince Vladimir Bariatinsky made a futile attempt to obtain access to the Cathcart papers on the ground that a century is the longest known period for keeping archives closed to investigation. Granting that one hundred years is a safe period after which secrets may be divulged and believing in the identity of Emperor Alexander I and Fyodor Kuzmich, the author is convinced that the truth will be known in 1964 when one hundred years will have elapsed since the death of Alexander in the guise of the Siberian hermit. And the author hopes that the Cathcart papers will then be made available. Until then the author invites the reader to weigh the evidence presented and to draw his own conclusion.

LEONID I. STRAKHOVSKY

1. FROM AN ARTICLE BY JACQUES CERVIER IN THE FRENCH
NEWSPAPER "LIBERTÉ," JULY 18, 1926

News from Russia reveals the sacrilegious opening by the Moscow vampires of the tomb of Emperor Alexander I. It was empty.

2. EXCEPTS FROM A STATEMENT BY MADAME A. DUBASOV [1]
IN THE RUSSIAN DAILY "VOZROZHDENIE"
[PARIS], APRIL 11, 1926

In the autumn of 1919 I made the acquaintance in Simpheropol of General Balinsky. He often used to spend the evenings at the house of my son-in-law, Tatishchev, then governor of the province of Taurida. One evening the conversation touched upon the subject of his preoccupation: the possible sale of a manuscript which represented the results of his lifelong efforts. Convinced of our real interest in the subject he then told us, i.e., N. A. Tatishchev, his wife (my daughter) and myself, the following:

General Balinsky was the son of a well-known psychiatrist, Professor Balinsky, who for many years had been the director of a psychiatric clinic in St. Petersburg. The janitor of the clinic had been appointed in a strange fashion. Emperor Alexander II once had expressed the desire that a retired soldier, whom he knew, should be given the position of janitor at the clinic. This soldier proved to be an excellent man, with a kind

[1] The contents of this statement are confirmed by the Grand Duke Andrey Vladimirovich in a letter addressed to Prince Vladimir Bariatinsky and published by the latter in his book *Le mystère d'Alexandre Ier*.

257

heart, but with a rather taciturn disposition. General Balinsky, the son of the professor, knew him from childhood and was his friend. Professor Balinsky did not know why the emperor was interested in this soldier until the latter's death hour. When dying, the janitor desired to see the professor and found it necessary to communicate to him the following [the Grand Duke Andrey Vladimirovich complements here the statement of Madame Dubasov by saying that the reason for this confession lay in the fact that the old soldier had willed to his daughter the sum of ten thousand roubles, which he had received from the emperor, and that he did not want Balinsky to wonder how he became the owner of such an important sum]: Many years ago (1866) he was sent one night together with other soldiers for special duty at the cathedral of Saints Peter and Paul [which contained the family vault of the Romanov dynasty]. There they found the emperor and a group of generals. The soldiers first had to take an oath not to reveal to anyone what they were going to witness. Then they were ordered to open the tomb of Emperor Alexander I. The human remains were removed from the tomb, placed in a simple coffin and buried the same night in a lonely spot in one of the capital's cemeteries. All this performance was closely supervised by the emperor himself. . . . Here lies the explanation of the fact that when the Bolsheviks opened the tomb of Emperor Alexander I they found it empty.

When General Balinsky learned from his father the contents of the janitor's confession, he became ardently desirous to solve the riddle of Alexander's death and of the life of Fyodor Kuzmich and ever since he has devoted much time, effort and money to it.

Being convinced by now that the emperor's death had been
faked, first of all he carried out research in order to establish
the means of his disappearance. Investigating the circumstances,
Balinsky came to the conclusion that there must necessarily be
a relation between the manner of disappearance and the place
chosen for it: it was necessary to "die" in a seaport, because
only a sea route does not leave any traces. Therefore it was
obviously this consideration which had prompted the choice of
Taganrog, a lively seaport, visited by many *foreign* ships. . . .
Balinsky then made an inquiry at Lloyd's and found that after
November 25, there was only one foreign ship in Taganrog. It
was the yacht of the former British ambassador at the Court
of St. Petersburg, the Earl of Cathcart. With this the officials
of Lloyd's had established a strange fact: the yacht's log did
not contain either the date of her departure from Taganrog or
her destination; only after a lapse of a few weeks an entry
placed her as navigating in the Mediterranean. This is particularly strange because according to rules and custom the
log is kept day by day. Thus on the basis of the presence of the
yacht in Taganrog, of the lack of entries in the ship's log and
of the friendship which had existed between the emperor and
the Earl of Cathcart, Balinsky came to the conclusion that
Alexander I "disappeared" on this yacht. . . . Continuing
further his research, Balinsky found traces of the presence of a
mysterious traveler in Palestine and then established the arrival
of this traveler at Kiev. At the time when General Count
Dimitry Erofeyevich Osten-Sacken (the hero of Sevastopol)
was governor or governor general of Kiev, he received the
visit of this mysterious traveler and entertained secret *pourparlers* with him. As the result of this, the mysterious traveler

obtained identification papers in the name of Fyodor Kuzmich [both names common to the family of Osten-Sacken], received indications as to the routes to follow to Siberia and a white horse on which he departed.

After this Balinsky continued his research in another direction. It is known that, before leaving St. Petersburg for Taganrog, Alexander had entrusted the metropolitan of the capital with a sealed envelope to be delivered to his successor. As this envelope had never been delivered to Emperor Nicholas I, Balinsky began to look for it. The metropolitan whom Balinsky had told of his aim replied that he had never heard of such an envelope. Nevertheless, he gave Balinsky permission to search the archives of the Laure [the residence of the metropolitan of St. Petersburg] and presently, after much hard work, Balinsky discovered the envelope in question and brought it to the astonished prelate. . . . However, the metropolitan refused to give Balinsky permission to break the seals and ordered him to deliver the envelope to Sabler, the Procurator of the Holy Synod, who, after some time, declined to tell Balinsky what happened to it.

These are the contents in a few words of Balinsky's manuscript backed by numerous documentary evidence. . . . As far as I know General Balinsky was shot by the Bolsheviks in 1920.

3. EXCERPTS FROM A LETTER OF PROFESSOR SERGE GRUZDYOV OF THE IMPERIAL UNIVERSITY OF ODESSA IN THE RUSSIAN DAILY "VOZROZHDENIE" [PARIS], MAY 31, 1926

. . . At a certain time—before the Russian-Japanese war—I had under my orders (in the Naval Hospital at Cronstadt) a

Dr. Martens, nephew and namesake of the famous professor
of international law at the Imperial University of St. Petersburg. . . .[2] One day during the meal hour, our conversation
touched upon the question of the date of Emperor Alexander's
death. When I mentioned the year 1825, Dr. Martens interrupted me and asked, to my great surprise, whether I really
believed that the emperor died in Taganrog at that time.
I answered affirmatively basing my statement on events
known. . . . But he said: "No. My uncle, the professor, *knows
of irrefutable documents* showing that Emperor Alexander I
did not die in 1825 at Taganrog, but that he disappeared, ex-
changing the life on the throne for that of a hermit, and that
he died much later, already in the reign of Emperor Alexander
Nikolayevich [Alexander II]. These documents remain secret
at present, because according to the laws of the empire they
cannot be made public before one hundred years after the date
of his death, but they are known to more than one person!"

4. EXCERPTS FROM A STATEMENT MADE BY NICHOLAS GRIGORIEVICH MESHCHERINOV TO P. N. KRUPENSKY [3]

When I was sixteen years of age I lived in Omsk in the house
of my father, General Aide-de-Camp Meshcherinov, then gov-
neror general of western Siberia. In the autumn of 1881 an
aide-de-camp, whose name I have forgotten, arrived from St.
Petersburg to my father with a special mission to collect and to
bring to the capital all the documents and effects which be-

[2] Professor Frederic Martens, member of the Institute of International Law
and of the Institut de France, solicitor of the Russian Ministry of Foreign
Affairs and Russia's representative at a number of international conferences
from 1874 (Brussels) until 1899 (The Hague).

[3] P. N. Krupensky: "The Emperor's Secret" (in Russian), pp. 88–91.

longed to Fyodor Kuzmich. My father then sent the vice-governor, Gregory Baklashin, and a clerk by the name of Kassagovsky to the locality where Fyodor Kuzmich had died. They returned with a number of articles and I was present when these were being sorted. Among them was an icon on the back of which I saw some kind of inscription, also the initial A surmounted by an imperial crown. Then there were three packages of letters written all in English and representing the correspondence which Fyodor Kuzmich had conducted with different people. My mother, who knew English well, read them to us, but being too young I did not pay much attention to their contents. My father placed all the objects in a package, sealed it with his personal as well as his official seal, and dispatched it personally to Emperor Alexander III. Some time later an acknowledgment of receipt reached my father, after which he declined to talk about the identity of Emperor Alexander I and of Fyodor Kuzmich, even forbidding us to talk about it, although up till then we often spoke about it and were convinced as to that identity. This question did not trouble me then at all, because I thought that it belonged to such historical facts as the manner of Emperor Paul's death, about which it was not the custom to talk. I remember also that in 1882 a certain Galkin-Vrasky, who was to be later director of all the prisons, arrived in Omsk from St. Petersburg and made a special trip to the grave of Fyodor Kuzmich, although it was about two hundred miles distant. . . .

I have also heard something about this question from a certain Lashkov, secretary to Governor Count Medem. Lashkov was entrusted by the Grand Duke Nicholas Mikhailovich to collect material about the person of Fyodor Kuzmich. . . . When he returned from his trip to Siberia he was thoroughly convinced of the identity of Emperor Alexander I and of Fyodor Kuzmich. But when the book about Fyodor Kuzmich, written by Grand Duke Nicholas Mikhailovich, was published we all asked Lashkov how could it have happened that the grand duke opposed the "legend." By way of an answer Lashkov only made an indecisive gesture; as for us we now believed that such was the order from higher authorities.

5. EXCERPTS FROM "SAINTS AND SINNERS," MEMOIRS BY A. V. BOLOTOV, FORMER GOVERNOR OF THE PROVINCE OF PERM [4]

After returning from Siberia where he had been on a tour of inspection and where he had visited the grave of Fyodor Kuzmich, Galkin-Vrasky made his report to Emperor Alexander III and told him that everyone in Siberia believed in the identity of Emperor Alexander I and Fyodor Kuzmich. The emperor became pensive, then he got up and pointed to the wall of his study where Galkin-Vrasky saw between the portraits of Alexander I and Nicholas I that of Fyodor Kuzmich.

[This story was told personally to A. V. Bolotov by Galkin-Vrasky.]

6. STATEMENT BY K. N. MIKHAILOV, RUSSIAN HISTORIAN [5]

On July 18, 1901, one of my very highly placed correspondents, very competent in the historical questions of the period of Em-

[4] Quoted after P. N. Krupensky: *op. cit.*, pp. 62–63.
[5] K. N. Mikhailov: *Emperor Alexander I—Staretz Fyodor Kuzmich* (in Russian), pp. 22–25.

peror Alexander I [Grand Duke Nicholas Mikhailovich?],
wrote to me from his estate that for reasons unknown to him,
K. P. Pobiedonostsev[6] is taking all possible measures to draw
a veil over the question of Fyodor Kuzmich, although he is
obviously interested in it. With this aim in view he has "robbed" the archives of the former Third Department [the political
secret police] of all the documents relating to Fyodor Kuzmich and has hidden them somewhere. My correspondent
obtained this information from a former director of the
Department of Police. This last source was obviously quite
reliable.

About three years later when my book on Moscow
antiquities was published, I received unexpectedly an invitation from an "old Moscovite"—K. P. Pobiedonostsev,
whom I had never met before, to come to see him for a talk
about my book. K. P. Pobiedonostsev gave me excellent information concerning Moscow antiquities which I later used.
. . . During one of my next visits when Pobiedonostsev discussed the period of Emperor Paul in comparison with that of
Ivan the Terrible and started to speak about Alexander I, I
suddenly asked him: "What do you think about Fyodor Kuzmich?" This put him on his guard. "But what do *you* think
about him, young man?" he asked in turn and stared at me.
His whole being, angular, with big ears and large dark spec-
tacles, seemed to be set on me like the barrel of a pistol. I felt
uneasy.

"I do not have any personal opinion about him," I answered,
"but I have heard that the documents relating to Fyodor Kuz-

[6] The famous procurator of the Holy Synod and personal adviser to the
emperors Alexander III and Nicholas II.

mich have been stolen. After this it will be indeed difficult to know exactly who he was."

"Stolen . . . stolen!" Pobiedonostsev repeated with visible anger.

"But he was Alexander?" I became suddenly bold. "Alexander I?"

"I cannot . . . say it!" he answered, and the last words came almost in a whisper, as if against his will.

"Then can you deny it? Can you deny it categorically, absolutely?" I insisted.

"To deny it? I do not know . . . one should study the time better, the events, the customs . . . perhaps . . . there are some contradictions . . . some obscurity . . . some mystery. Nevertheless, I recommend that you do not busy yourself with this question," he said, hardly concealing his anger. "It will be better if you will study more thoroughly the Moscow historical and judicial antiquities; there you will certainly find more material for your erudition."

"But Alexander I is also an antiquity," I insisted.

"Yes," he said, and getting up looked sternly right into my eyes. "An antiquity, but it is yet too soon to study it. The time has not come. When the time comes . . . then everything will be clear. Meanwhile—good-by."

This conversation took place in the Little Palace in Tsarskoye Selo where he was spending the summer. The very tone of voice and the meaning of Pobiedonostsev's words became strongly imprinted in my mind and they still trouble me. This conversation left no doubt to me as to who Fyodor Kuzmich was as well as to the fact that Pobiedonostsev knew it.

Later I was informed by the same very highly placed person

that Pobiedonostsev had studied and put in order all the documents taken from the Third Department and handed them over to Emperor Alexander III. It is said that these documents contain the entire life story of Fyodor Kuzmich from 1825 to 1864 (the date of his death) and that K. P. Pobiedonostsev as well as Arakcheyev knew how Alexander I had disappeared.

7. "THE MYSTERY OF THE DEATH OF EMPEROR ALEXANDER THE FIRST: HAS IT AT LAST BEEN SOLVED?" FROM THE BELGIAN NEWSPAPER "NATION BELGE," MAY 20, 1929

Riga, 19th May

The death of a certain Victor Basilevsky, descendant of a noble Tartar family, is announced from Hungersburg, a little town in Estonia. When quite young, Basilevsky, who died at the age of ninety, had inherited from his father important Siberian gold mines, which had made him one of the richest men in Russia. When the Bolshevik revolution broke out he was stripped of all his goods and sought refuge in Estonia. In dying, he leaves sensational memoirs which are being published and which bring to light the mystery of the death of Alexander I, on the subject of which Russian historians have given themselves up to suppositions of a most varied and least likely nature. Let us remember that the tomb of the tsar was found empty and that never has it been discovered what became of the embalmed body of the emperor.

About 1860, Basilevsky rented an estate which he possessed in Siberia to a merchant Khromov. The latter, some time later, went to see Basilevsky, who was at that time residing in southern Russia, and, under the stress of a great emotion related that, on the farm which he was exploiting lived for many years a very pious Russian, who called himself Fyodor Kuzmich, but whom the people had christened *sviatoy staretz* (the holy settler).

The mysterious personage was said to accomplish miracles and was greatly beloved by all the peasants of the vicinity. One day Kuzmich fell seriously ill, and feeling his end was coming he sent for Khromov to whom he confessed that he was the Emperor Alexander I, whom everyone believed to have died of malaria at Taganrog in 1825.

Before his death the supposed Kuzmich entrusted to Khromov documentary proofs of his identity, begging him to give them as well as a portrait of his to Emperor Alexander II.

Khromov obtained an audience with the tsar, who kept him for two hours and when he left the palace he hastened to reach Siberia without speaking to anyone about the interview he had just had with the emperor. Basilevsky, however, had the impression that the latter had been convinced that Kuzmich and Alexander I were one and the same person, hence the formal injunction made by the emperor to Khromov not to reveal anything of their conversation.

An especially important chapter of the memoirs is the one treating of the confidences made to Basilevsky by his confessor, Metropolitan Isidor, who revealed to him under the vow of secrecy that, on the order of Emperor Alexander II, the body of a soldier had been exhumed from the imperial mausoleum of Saints Peter and Paul and buried in a cemetery in St. Petersburg.

And lastly, let us add, that Basilevsky, who had devoted all his life to this all-absorbing mystery, had written to the Grand Duchess Olga Alexandrovna, sister of Nicholas II, who was at that time in Copenhagen, begging her to tell him whether the interview between Alexander II and Khromov had in reality enlightened the mystery. The grand duchess replied that to her, as well as to the rest of the members of her family who were still living, there was not the slightest doubt as to the identity of Fyodor Kuzmich and Alexander I. Only the Dowager Empress Maria Fyodorovna, recently deceased, never replied categorically to the questions which were put to her on this subject.[7]

8. "THE MAN WHO KNEW THE SECRET OF FYODOR KUZMICH."
TRANSLATION FROM THE RUSSIAN DAILY "NOVOYE RUSSKOYE
SLOVO" [NEW YORK], SEPTEMBER 15, 1932

Victor Ivanovich Basilevsky, considered to have been one of the richest men in old Russia, died recently in his cottage on the shore of the Finnish Gulf, twenty versts from Narva. He was ninety years of age.

Basilevsky was an extraordinary personality. Of an old Russian noble family, a millionaire, benefactor, high among the powerful, he had outlived the reigns of four emperors. He had owned large estates and gold mines in the Ural Mountains and in the Lena district, in Siberia.

In the eighties of the last century he established his residence on his estate, Velikino, in the district of Yamburg, from where he would go only for the summer to a cottage in Hungersburg [now in Estonia]; there he died after having lost all his estates in Russia and after Hungersburg ceased to be a Russian watering place.

[7] So far as we know, the Basilevsky memoirs have not as yet been published.

A great figure of old Russia, a witness of four wars, and of four most significant reigns, has gone to the grave in the person of this millionaire benefactor. He witnessed the reforms of Emperor Alexander II—the liberation of the serfs, the introduction of the jury in the courts, the formation of local self-government.

Well educated, talented, an aristocrat, both by birth and by family relations, immensely rich, courted by members of the imperial family, Basilevsky might have made a brilliant career, had he so desired. But he had remained a private citizen all his life, refusing any position in the government.

V. I. Basilevsky possessed the key to the unraveling of the mystery which surrounded the death of the Emperor Alexander I. He never doubted the identity of Fyodor Kuzmich with Emperor Alexander Pavlovich.

In the sixties of the last century, V. I. Basilevsky leased some land in Siberia from a merchant by the name of Khromov, who had extended hospitality to Fyodor Kuzmich. During the reign of Emperor Alexander III (1881–1894) Khromov, very much perturbed, arrived in Velikino and told V. I. Basilevsky the following:

Feeling the approach of his end, he said, he wanted to share a great secret as he knew Basilevsky, having entry to court, could help him. Handing over to Basilevsky a picture of Fyodor Kuzmich and a roll of papers, tied together with a string, Khromov told Basilevsky that on his deathbed Fyodor Kuzmich confessed that he was Emperor Alexander I, and begged Khromov to deliver the picture and papers into the hands of the reigning emperor.

Khromov failed to execute the last will of Fyodor Kuzmich,

though he had preserved the picture and the papers. Now he had decided, however, to fulfill the promises he had given to the hermit. Basilevsky reassured Khromov and promised to obtain for him an audience with the emperor.

Through the good offices of the Grand Duke Vladimir Alexandrovich, Basilevsky arranged the desired audience, but Khromov failed to return to Velikino, after seeing the emperor, as he had promised Basilevsky he would do.

This Basilevsky explained as the result of an express order of Emperor Alexander III, who, no doubt, convinced of the identity of Fyodor Kuzmich with Emperor Alexander I, preferred not to have the news divulged.

Not long before his own death, Basilevsky revealed that the Metropolitan Isidor, as a go-between for Khromov and Emperor Alexander III, had confided to him that the tomb of Emperor Alexander I in the Cathedral of Saints Peter and Paul had been opened and the embalmed body taken out of it and buried in one of St. Petersburg's cemeteries.

As is known, when the Bolsheviks opened the coffin of Alexander I, it was found to be empty.

9. EXCERPTS FROM A BOOK BY LEV LIUBIMOV:
"THE MYSTERY OF EMPEROR ALEXANDER I" (IN RUSSIAN)

On December 31, 1825, Princess Sophie Volkonsky, the wife of Prince Peter Volkonsky, wrote a letter to the Dowager Empress Maria Fyodorovna in which she said: "I must not be afraid to let the mother of our sovereigns know the contents of the letters received from my husband [these letters have never been discovered] because she cannot be angry at my decision to reveal the painful happenings about which she could inform the person [Emperor Nicholas I] whose interest it is to know of these intimate observations about the emotions of our beloved never-to-be-forgotten monarch. I must add that my husband does not know and will never know that I am writing this letter . . . But I am consoled by the thought that what he has seen and what is his firm conviction on the matter shall not be lost. Everything that concerns your beloved son is a deep remembrance for me and I should like to cherish it until my death, after which it will disappear with me." *p.* 138.

Dr. Tarasov's nephew, who was a professor at the Yaroslavl Lyceum, told his colleague, Professor Behrens, later a senator, that his uncle while living in retirement in Tsarskoye Selo never attended the requiem services for Alexander I. Only in the middle sixties when newspapers reported the death in Siberia of the hermit Fyodor Kuzmich did Dr. Tarasov order a requiem service for Alexander in the palace church at Tsarkoye Selo and attended it in full uniform. When questioned by his family, he replied that only now was the time to pray for the repose of the soul of Emperor Alexander, and added that it is a great secret which will die with him. *p.* 155.

Colonel Count N. V. Osten-Sacken, grandson of Count Dimitry Osten-Sacken, tells that his grandfather never attended requiem services for Emperor Alexander I. But when he received news of the death of Fyodor Kuzmich, he donned his full uniform and ordered a requiem service to be performed in his house chapel. *p.* 174.

K. F. Resnikov sheds some light on why Alexander chose the name of Fyodor Kuzmich:

"Before the revolution my family possessed a ring which had been given by Emperor Alexander I. Perhaps even now it is preserved by some member of my family in Soviet Russia. Its story was told to me by my father who died in 1897. When Emperor Alexander I was on his way to Taganrog he stopped overnight in the little provincial town of Bely in the province of Smolensk. Our house, which was the largest and best in town, was requisitioned for his rest. During his short stay, the emperor wanted to meet my grandfather and his family. My father was then a little over one year old. The emperor took a liking to the baby and taking him in his arms he inquired what his name was. My grandfather answered: 'Fyodor.' The emperor also asked my grandfather's name, which was Kuzma. Then, still holding the child, the emperor repeated pensively his name and patronymic: 'Fyodor Kuzmich.' Before leaving the next morning the emperor called my grandfather again and presented him with a ring saying that he was giving it to his son, Fyodor Kuzmich, and that it should always pass to the eldest in the family. When I was still in high school I remember how my father gathered us children together, took the ring out of a strong box and told us its story. Later when I was already an officer and came for a visit from St. Petersburg, I examined the ring several times. It was fairly large, with a large stone in the middle surrounded by small diamonds. It was in a leather case with the initial of Emperor Alexander I surmounted by a crown embossed in gold."

This story was confirmed to the author by other residents of the town of Bely. *pp.* 180–181.

Countess A. I. Shuvalov, daughter of Count I. I. Vorontsov-Dashkov, former Minister of the Court and later Viceroy of the Caucasus, tells that one day in the late eighties her father came home late, visibly agitated. He told his wife and daughter that he had just been with the Emperor Alexander III in the church of Saints Peter and Paul, because the emperor wanted to open the tomb of Alexander I (Count Vorontsov-Dashkov's presence was necessary because as Minister of the Court he kept the keys of the vault). When the casket was opened in the presence only of the emperor, the Count Vorontsov-Dashkov and of four soldiers, who had lifted the lid, it was found to be empty. Count I. I. Vorontsov-Dashkov told his wife and daughter that what he had revealed was a secret which should not be divulged. *p. 202.*

The late Duke Michael of Mecklenburg, who was a grandson of the Grand Duke Michael Pavlovich, said that in his opinion there is very little doubt that the so-called "legend" about Fyodor Kuzmich is actually the truth. *p. 213.*

BIBLIOGRAPHY

Abbot, John S. C., *The History of Napoleon Bonaparte*, New York, 1883. 2 vols.

Abrantes, Duchesse d', *Mémoires*, Paris, 1838. 4 vols.

——, *Memoirs of Napoleon, His Court and Family*, New York, 1895. 2 vols.

Adams, John Quincy, *Memoirs, 1795–1848*, Philadelphia, 1874–1877. 12 vols.

——, *Writings*, New York, 1913–1916. 6 vols.

Adrianov, N., *The Ministry of the Interior*, St. Petersburg, 1901. (in Russian)

Aksharumov, D., *Description of the War of 1812*, St. Petersburg, 1819. (in Russian)

Alexander I and His Collaborators, St. Petersburg, 1845. 2 vols. (in Russian)

Alexeyev, G. N., *Alexander I, His Personality, His Government and His Intimate Life*, London, 1908. (in Russian)

Allen, William, *The Life of William Allen*, London, 1846–1847. 3 vols.

Allonville, Comte A. d', *Mémoires secrets*, Paris, 1838–1845. 6 vols.

Angeberg, Comte d', *Le Congrès de Vienne et les traités de 1815*, Paris, 1863. 4 vols.

Arndt, F. M., *Erinnerungen*, Leipzig, 1840.

Aster, H., *Die Gefechte bei Leipzig*, Dresden, 1852–1853. 2 vols.

Baden, Charles-Frederic, Prince of, *Politische Korrespondenz*, Heidelberg, 1888–1901. 5 vols.

Bailleu, P., *Briefwechsel König Friedrich-Wilhelms III und der Königin Luise mit Kaiser Alexander I*, Leipzig, 1900.

——, *Königin Luise*, Berlin, 1908.

——, *Preussen und Frankreich von 1795 bis 1807*, Leipzig, 1880–1887. 2 vols.

Barante, Baron de, *Notes sur la Russie*, Paris, 1875.

——, *Souvenirs, 1782–1866*, Paris, 1890–1891. 8 vols.

Bariatinsky, Prince Vladimir V., *A Royal Mystic: Emperor Alexander I—Fyodor Kuzmich*, St. Petersburg, 1912. (in Russian)

——, *Le Mystère d'Alexandre Ier, 1825–1925*, Paris, 1925; 2nd ed., Paris, 1929.

Bartienev, P. I. (editor), *Eighteenth Century*, Moscow, 1869. 4 vols. (in Russian)

——, *Nineteenth Century*, Moscow, 1872. 2 vols. (in Russian)

Beauvollier, Comte P. de, *Mémoires sur l'expedition de Russie*, Paris, 1825.

Bennigsen, Comte L., *Mémoires*, Paris, 1907. 2 vols.

Biedermann, K., *Funfundzwanzig Jahre deutscher Geschichte, 1815–1840*, Breslau, 1890. 2 vols.

Bignon, L., *Souvenirs d'un diplomate*, Paris, 1864.

Bilbasov, B., *Archives of Count Mordvinov*, St. Petersburg, 1902. (in Russian)

Blagovidov, F. V., *The Procurators of the Holy Synod*, Kazan, 1900. (in Russian)

Blumenthal, M., *Die Konvention von Tauroggen*, Berlin, 1901.

Bobrovsky, P., *The Russian Greek-Catholic United Church under the Reign of Alexander I*, St. Petersburg, 1890. (in Russian)

Bogdanovich, M. I., *A History of the Reign of Emperor Alexander I and of Russia during That Time*, St. Petersburg, 1869–1871. 6 vols. (in Russian)

Bogerianov, I. N., *Grand-Duchess Catherine Pavlovna*, St. Petersburg, 1888. (in Russian)

Boigne, Comtesse de, *Mémoires*, Paris, 1907.

Borodkin, M., *A History of Finland*, St. Petersburg, 1909. (in Russian)

Boudou, Adrian, S. J., *Le Saint-Siège et la Russie*, Paris, 1922.

Braun, J. W., *Luise, Königin von Preussen in Ihren Briefen*, Berlin, 1888.

Brückner, A. (editor), *Materials for a Biography of Count N. P. Panin, 1770–1837*, St. Petersburg, 1888–1892. 7 vols. (in Russian)

Cassagnac, Paul de, *Napoléon, pacifiste*, Paris, 1933.

Castlereagh, Lord Robert Stewart, *Correspondence, Despatches and Other Papers*, London, 1848–1852. 12 vols.

Caulaincourt, A. de, Duc de Vicence, *Souvenirs*, Paris, 1837–1841. 3 vols.

——, *Mémoires du Général de Caulaincourt duc de Vicence*, Paris, 1933. Tome I and III.

——, *With Napoleon in Russia*, New York, 1935.

————, *No Peace with Napoleon*, New York, 1936.

Cazalas, E. (translator), *La Guerre patriotique de 1812*, Paris, 1903–1911. 7 vols.

Centenary of His Majesty's Own Chancery, St. Petersburg, 1912. (in Russian)

Centenary of the Ministry of War, St. Petersburg, 1904. 8 vols. (in Russian)

Chaadayev, P., *Complete Works*, St. Petersburg, 1914. 3 vols. (in Russian)

Chapuisat, E. (editor), *Journal du Congrès de Vienne de J. Eynard*, Paris, 1916.

Chateaubriand, R., Vicomte de, *Mélanges historiques*, Paris, 1874.

————, *Mémoires d'outre-tombe*, Paris, 1849. 12 vols.

————, *Oeuvres complètes*, Paris, 1857–1858. 20 vols.

Choiseul-Gouffier, Comtesse de, *Mémoires historiques sur l'empereur Alexandre I*, Paris, 1829.

————, *Reminiscences sur l'empereur Alexandre I et sur l'empereur Napoléon*, Paris, 1862.

Chulkov, G., *The Last Autocratic Tsars*, Leningrad, 1927 (in Russian). French edition: *Les derniers tsars autocrates*, Paris, 1928.

————, *The Rebels of 1825*, Leningrad, 1925. (in Russian)

Comfort, W. W., *Stephen Grellet*, New York, 1942.

Coudray, H. du, *Metternich*, London, 1935.

Crehange, D., *Histoire de Russie depuis la mort de Paul I*, Paris, 1882.

Cresson, W. P., *The Holy Alliance*, New York, 1922.

Cruzenstolpe, M., *Der russische Hof vom Peter I bis auf Nicolaus I*, Hamburg, 1856. 6 vols.

Cunningham, John, D.D., *The Quakers from Their Origins till the Present Time: An International History*, Edinburgh, 1868.

Czartoryski, Prince Adam, *Mémoires du prince Adam Czartoryski et correspondance avec l'Empereur Alexandre I*, Paris, 1887. English edition: London, 1888.

Czartoryski, Prince L. (editor), *Alexandre Ier et le Prince Czartoryski: correspondance particulière et conversations*, Paris, 1865.

Danilevsky, P., *History of the Founding of the State Council*, St. Petersburg, 1859. (in Russian)

Dashkov, Princesse C., *Mémoires*, Paris, 1859. 2 vols.

Dmitriev, M. A., *Recollections*, Moscow, 1869. (in Russian)

Documents for the History of Russia's Diplomatic Relations with the Western European Powers since the Conclusion of the Peace of 1814 and to the Congress of Verona of 1822, St. Petersburg, 1823. 2 vols. (in Russian)

Dokert, W., *Die Englische Politik auf dem Wiener Congress*, Weide, 1911.

Dolgoruky, Prince P., *History of the Dolgoruky Family*, St. Petersburg, 1840. (in Russian)

———, *La vérité sur la Russie*, Paris, 1860.

Dovnar-Zapolsky, M., *Memoirs of the Decembrists*, Kiev, 1906. (in Russian)

———, *The Secret Societies*, Moscow, 1906. (in Russian)

———, *Ideals of the Decembrists*, Moscow, 1907. (in Russian)

Driault, E., *Napoléon et l'Europe*, Paris, 1910–1912. 2 vols.

Du Casse, Baron A., *Mémoires et correspondance du Prince Eugène de Beauharnais*, Paris, 1858–1860. 10 vols.

Dubrovin, N. F., *Historical Materials from the Archives of His Majesty's Own Chancery*, St. Petersburg, 1876–1901. 11 vols. (in Russian)

———, *Correspondence of the Principal Collaborators of Emperor Alexander I (1807–1829)*, St. Petersburg, 1883. (in Russian)

Dumas, Comte Mathieu, *Souvenirs*, Paris, 1839. 3 vols.

Dyrin, N., *History of the Semyonovsky Regiment of the Imperial Guard*, St. Petersburg, 1883. (in Russian)

Dzhivelegov, A. K., *Alexander I and Napoleon: Historical Essays*, Moscow, 1915. (in Russian)

Edling, Comtesse R., *Mémoires*, Moscow, 1888.

Engelhardt, L., *Memoirs*, Moscow, 1868. (in Russian)

E. R., *The Last Days of Emperor Alexander the Blessed*, Moscow, 1877. (in Russian)

Eylert, R., *Charakterzüge aus dem Leben des Königs Friedrich-Wilhelm III*, Magdeburg, 1843–1847. 3 vols.

Eynard, C., *Vie de Madame de Krüdener*, Paris, 1849. 2 vols.

Fatéev, A., "Le problème de l'individu et de l'homme d'état dans la personalité historique d'Alexandre I, empereur de toutes les Russie," in *Notes of the Scientific-Research Union*, Praha, 2, 1927.

Ferlindin, P., *Historical Outline of Higher Education in Russia*, Saratov, 1894. (in Russian)

Filipov, A., *A History of the Senate*, Yuriev, 1895. (in Russian)

Firsov, N., *Emperor Alexander I*, St. Petersburg, 1910. (in Russian)

———, *Emperor Alexander I and His Spiritual Drama*, St. Petersburg, N.D. (in Russian)

Fisher, J., *Finland and the Tsars, 1809–1899*, London, 1899.

Ford, C., *The Life and Letters of Madame de Krüdener*, London, 1893.

Fournier, A., *Napoleon I*, Wien, 1905. 3 vols.

Fusil, L., *L'incendie de Moscou*, London, 1817.

Gagarin, Prince J., S.J., *Les archives russes et la conversion d'Alexandre Ier*, Lyon, 1877.

Galaktionov, I. A., *Emperor Alexander I and His Reign*, St. Petersburg, 1877. (in Russian)

Gentz, F. von, *Mémoires et Lettres*, Stuttgart, 1841.

Gershenzon, M., *A History of Young Russia*, Moscow, 1908. (in Russian)

——, *The Decembrist Krivtsov*, Moscow, 1914 (in Russian). 2nd ed., Moscow-Berlin, 1923.

Glinka, S., *Memoirs*, St. Petersburg, 1837. (in Russian)

Golitsyn, Prince A. (editor), *The Youth of Alexander I*, Leipzig, 1862. (in Russian)

Golitsyn, Prince P., *The First Century of the Senate*, St. Petersburg, 1910. (in Russian)

Golovin, I., *Histoire d'Alexandre Ier*, Leipzig-Paris, 1859.

Goriainov, S., *1812. Documents of State and of the Principal Archives of St. Petersburg*, St. Petersburg, 1912. (in Russian)

Gorsky, A., *Diary*, St. Petersburg, 1885. (in Russian)

Gotze, P. von, *Fürst A. N. Golitsin und seine Zeit*, Leipzig, 1882.

Grech, N. J., *Biographie de l'Empereur Alexandre I*, Stockholm, 1836.

——, *Autobiographical Notes*, St. Petersburg, 1886. (in Russian)

Gribble, F. H., *Emperor and Mystic: the Life of Alexander I of Russia*, New York, 1931.

Grigoriev, V., *The First Fifty Years of the University of St. Petersburg*, St. Petersburg, 1870. (in Russian)

Grot, I. (editor), *The Correspondence of Catherine II with Grimm*, St. Petersburg, 1884. (in French and Russian)

———, *Letters of Baron I. Grimm to Empress Catherine II*, St. Petersburg, 1886. (in French and Russian)

G[. . .]v, K., *The Noteworthy and Mysterious Siberian Staretz Fyodor Kuzmich*, St. Petersburg, 1905. (in Russian)

Handelsmann, M., *Napoléon et la Pologne*, Paris, 1909.

Helldorf, von, *Aus dem Leben des Prinzen Eugen von Württemberg*, Berlin, 1861–1862. 4 vols.

Herzen, A., *Works*, St. Petersburg, 1905. 6 vols. (in Russian)

Hildt, J. C., *Early Diplomatic Negotiations of the United States with Russia*, Baltimore, 1906.

Historical Documents from the Reign of Alexander I, Leipzig, 1880. (in Russian)

Hohenlohe, Prince Alexander, *Mémoires*, Paris, 1835.

Ikonnikov, V., *Count N. Mordvinov*, St. Petersburg, 1873. (in Russian)

Iscander (A. Herzen), *La conspiration russe de 1825*, London, 1858.

———, *Emperor Alexander I and V. N. Karazin*, St. Petersburg, 1862. (in Russian)

Jacob, *Madame de Krüdener*, Paris, 1881.

Joyneville, C., *Life and Times of Alexander I*, London, 1875. 3 vols.

Karamzin, N., *About Ancient and Modern Russia*, Berlin, 1861. (in Russian)

———, *Works and Letters*, St. Petersburg, 1862. (in Russian)

Karnovich, E., *Grand Duke Constantine Pavlovich*, St. Petersburg, 1899. (in Russian)

Kiesewetter, A., *Historical Essays*, St. Petersburg, 1913. (in Russian)

Kobeko, D., *The Lyceum of Tsarskoye Selo*, St. Petersburg, 1911. (in Russian)

Konovalova, E. I. (editor), *The Mysterious Staretz Fyodor Kuzmich*, Moscow, 1898. (in Russian)

Korff, Baron M., *L'avénement au trône de l'Empereur Nicolas I*, Paris, 1857.

———, *Life of Count Speransky*, St. Petersburg, 1861. 2 vols. (in Russian)

Korff, Baron S., *A History of the Governing Senate*, St. Petersburg, 1911. 5 vols. (in Russian)

Kornilov, I., *Prince Adam Czartoryski*, Moscow, 1896. (in Russian)

Koshelev, A. I., *Memoirs*, Berlin, 1884. (in Russian)

Kotliarevsky, N., *Literary Tendencies at the Time of Alexander I*, St. Petersburg, 1907. (in Russian)

Kovalevsky, E., *Count Bludov and His Time*, St. Petersburg, 1871. (in Russian)

Krüdener, Baronne de, *Le camp de Vertus*, Paris, 1815.

Krupensky, P. N., *The Emperor's Secret*, Berlin, 1927. (in Russian)

Kudriashov, K. V., *Alexander I and the Mystery of Fyodor Kuzmich*, St. Petersburg, 1923. (in Russian)

Kulomzin, A., *Minutes of the Committee of Ministers, 1802–1812*, St. Petersburg, 1888–1891. 2 vols. (in Russian)

La Ferronays, Comte A. de, *Souvenirs, 1777–1814*, Paris, 1900.

La Garde, Comte de, *Souvenirs du Congrès de Vienne*, Paris, 1901.

La Harpe, F. C. de, *Mémoires*, Paris, 1864.

———, *Le gouverneur d'un prince*, Lausanne, 1902.

Lacombe, Bernard de, *Talleyrand the Man*, London, 1910.

Langeron, Général Comte de, *Mémoires*, Paris, 1902.

Lee, R., *The Last Days of Alexander and the First Days of Nicholas*, London, 1854.

Lelevel, J., *Novossiltsov à Wilno*, Bruxelles, 1844.

Leuchtenberg, Duc G. de, *Le Prince Eugène de Beauharnais à la tête de la grande armée*, Paris, 1913.

Liubimov, L., *The Mystery of Emperor Alexander I*, Paris, 1938. (in Russian)

Lloyd, H. E., *Alexander I, Emperor of Russia*, London, 1826.

Lopukhin, I., *Memoirs*, London, 1860. (in Russian)

Lutteroth, H., *La Russie et les Jésuites*, Paris, 1845.

Maistre, Joseph de, *Correspondance diplomatique 1811–1817*, Paris, 1860.

———, *Mémoires politiques et correspondance diplomatique*, Paris, 1864.

———, *Oeuvres complètes*, Lyon, 1880–1887. 14 vols.

Marbot, General Baron de, *Mémoires*, Paris, 1891. 3 vols.

Maria Fyodorovna, Imperatrice, *Correspondance*, Moscow, 1883–1885. 2 vols.

Masson, C. F. P. H., *Mémoires secrets sur la Russie*, London, 1802. 3 vols.

Mazour, Anatole G., *The First Russian Revolution*, Berkeley, 1937.

————, "Le Comte Aleksej Andreevich Arakcheev," in *Le Monde Slave*, June, 1936.

Merkle, J., *Katharina Pavlovna, Königin von Württemberg*, Stuttgart, 1890.

Metternich, Prince de, *Mémoires, documents et écrits*, Paris, 1880–1884. 8 vols. English edition: New York, 1880–1884.

Miakotin, V. A., *Out of the History of Russian Society*, St. Petersburg, 1906. (in Russian)

————, *A. S. Pushkin and the Decembrists*, Prague-Berlin, 1923. (in Russian)

Michelsen, E. H., *The Life of Nicholas I, Emperor of All the Russias*, London, 1854.

Mielgunov, S., *Free-masonry in the Past and in the Present*, Petrograd, 1915. (in Russian)

Mikhailov, K. N., *Emperor Alexander I—Staretz Fyodor Kuzmich*, St. Petersburg, 1914. (in Russian)

Mikhailovsky-Danielevsky, A., *Description of the First War against Napoleon*, St. Petersburg, 1844. (in Russian)

————, *Description of the Second War against Napoleon*, St. Petersburg, 1846. (in Russian)

————, *History of the Campaign of 1814 in France*, St. Petersburg, 1845. (in Russian)

————, *History of the Patriotic War of 1812*, St. Petersburg, 1840. 4 vols. (in Russian)

————, *Memoirs of the Campaign of 1813*, St. Petersburg, 1834. (in Russian)

Miliukov, P. N., *Essais sur l'histoire de la civilization russe*, Paris, 1901.

———, *Essays on the History of Russian Culture*, St. Petersburg, 1905. 3 vols. (in Russian). English edition: *Outlines of Russian Culture*, Philadelphia, 1942. 3 vols.

———, *Le mouvement intellectuel russe*, Paris, 1918.

Miliutin, Count D. A., *The History of Russia's War with France in the Reign of Emperor Paul I in 1799*, St. Petersburg, 1852–1853. 5 vols. (in Russian)

Ministry of Finance, The, 1802–1902, St. Petersburg, 1902. (in Russian)

Modzalevsky, V. L., *A. F. Labzin*, St. Petersburg, 1904. (in Russian)

———, *The Romance of the Decembrist Kakhovsky*, Leningrad, 1926. (in Russian)

———, (editor), *Archives of the Rayevsky Family*, St. Petersburg, 1908. (in Russian)

Mordovtsev, D., *Russian Women*, St. Petersburg, 1871–1874. 3 vols. (in Russian)

Moroshkin, Rev. Mikhail, *The Jesuits in Russia*, St. Petersburg, 1867. 2 vols. (in Russian)

Nadler, V. K., *Emperor Alexander I and the Idea of the Holy Alliance*, Riga, 1886–1892. 5 vols. (in Russian)

Napoléon I, *Correspondance*, Paris, 1858–1870. 32 vols.

———, *Correspondance inédite*, Paris, 1912.

———, *Lettres inédites*, Paris, 1897. 2 vols.

Nesselrode, Comte C. de, *Lettres et papiers*, Paris, 1904–1907. 6 vols.

Nicholas Mikhailovich, Grand Duke, *Correspondence between Emperor Alexander I and His Sister the Grand-Duchess Catherine Pavlovna*, St. Petersburg, 1910 (in Russian and

French). English edition: *Scenes of Russian Court Life*, London, n.d.

———, *Correspondence of the Members of the Imperial Family with Countess A. Protasov*, St. Petersburg, 1913. (in Russian and French)

———, *Count Paul Alexandrovich Stroganov, 1774–1817*, St. Petersburg, 1903. (in Russian)

———, *Diplomatic Relations between Russia and France, 1808–1812*, St. Petersburg, 1905–1908. 6 vols. (in Russian and French)

———, *Diplomatic Reports of Lebzeltern, Minister of Austria at the Russian Court, 1816–1826*, St. Petersburg, 1913. (in Russian and French)

———, *Emperor Alexander I*, St. Petersburg, 1912. 2 vols. (in Russian). 2nd ed: St. Petersburg, 1914. 1 vol. French edition: *Le tsar Alexandre Ier*, Paris, 1931.

———, *Empress Elisabeth Alexeyevna*, St. Petersburg, 1908–1910. 3 vols. (in Russian)

———, *Generals Aide-de-Camp to Emperor Alexander I*, St. Petersburg, 1913. (in Russian)

———, *The Legend about the Death of Emperor Alexander I in Siberia in the Person of Fyodor Kuzmich*, St. Petersburg, 1907. (in Russian)

———, *The Princes Dolgoruky*, St. Petersburg, 1901 (in Russian). German edition: Leipzig, 1902.

———, *Russian Portraits*, St. Petersburg, 1905–1909. 5 vols. (biographical notes in Russian and French)

Nikitenko, A. V., *Memoirs*, St. Petersburg, 1904. 2 vols. (in Russian)

Obolensky-Neledinsky-Meletsky, Prince, *Archives of Prince*

Obolensky-Neledinsky-Meletsky, St. Petersburg, 1876. (in Russian)

Oginski, M., *Mémoires*, Paris, 1826–1827. 4 vols.

Outline of the History of the Ministry of Foreign Affairs, 1802–1902, St. Petersburg, 1902. (in Russian)

Paléologue, Maurice, *The Mystic Czar*, New York, 1938.

Patriotic War and Russian Society, The, Moscow, 1911–1912. 6 vols. (in Russian)

Philaret, Metropolitan, *Correspondence and Opinions*, Moscow, 1884–1888. 8 vols. (in Russian)

Pierling, Rev. Father, S.J., *L'Empereur Alexandre Ier est-il mort catholique?* Paris, 1901. 2nd ed., Paris, 1913.

Pietrov, A., *Count Arakcheyev and the Military Settlements*, St. Petersburg, 1871. (in Russian)

Pingaud, L., *Un agent secret, le comte d'Antraigues*, Paris, 1893.

——, *Bernadotte, Napoléon et les Bourbons*, Paris, 1901.

Pokrovsky, S., *The Power of Ministers in Russia*, Yaroslavl, 1906. (in Russian)

Polovtsov, A. (editor), *Correspondance diplomatique des ambassadeurs et ministres de Russie en France et de France en Russie de 1814 à 1830*, St. Petersburg, 1902. 2 vols.

Popov, A. N., *Russia's Relations with European Powers before the War of 1812*, St. Petersburg, 1875–1876. (in Russian)

Popov, N. A., *Russia and Serbia*, Moscow, 1869. 2 vols. (in Russian)

Potapov, V., *Alexander the First*, Moscow, 1845. (in Russian)

Pozzo di Borgo, Comte C., *Correspondance diplomatique*, Paris, 1890–1897. 2 vols.

Pushkin, A. S., *Complete Works*, St. Petersburg, 1907–1915. 6 vols. (in Russian)

Rabbe, A., *Histoire d'Alexandre I*, Paris, 1826. 2 vols.

Rain, Pierre, *Alexandre Ier et les révolutions nationales*, Paris, 1912.

———, *Un tsar idéologue: Alexandre Ier, 1777–1825*, Paris, 1913.

Rappoport, A. S., *The Curse of the Romanovs: a Study of the Life and Reign of Paul I and Alexander I of Russia*, London, 1907.

Razumovsky, Graf C., *Fürst A. K. Razumovsky, Lebenskizze*, Halle, 1912.

Renaut, F. P., *Les relations diplomatiques entre la Russie et les États Unis*, Paris, 1923.

Romanov, D. G. (editor), *The Mysterious Settler Fyodor Kuzmich in Siberia and Emperor Alexander I*, Kharkov, 1912. (in Russian)

Romanovich-Slaviatinsky, A., *Nobility in Russia*, St. Petersburg, 1870. (in Russian)

Rozhdestvensky, S. V., *An Historical Outline of the Activity of the Ministry of Public Instruction, 1802–1902*, St. Petersburg, 1902. (in Russian)

Rusov, N. N., *Russia of the Landowners*, Moscow, 1911. (in Russian)

Ryleyev, K., *Works and Letters*, St. Petersburg, 1872. (in Russian)

Savary, Général, Duc de Rovigo, *Mémoires*, Paris, 1901. 5 vols.

Schiemann, Th., *Geschichte Russlands unter Kaiser Nikolaus I*, Berlin, 1904–1919. 4 vols.

Seebohm, B. (editor), *Memoirs of the Life and Gospel Labours of Stephen Grellet*, London, 1861. 2 vols.

Seeley, J. R., *Life and Times of Stein*, Cambridge, 1878. 3 vols.

———, *A Short History of Napoleon the First*, London, 1886.

Ségur, Comte de, *Vie du Comte Rostoptchine*, Paris, 1873.

Sementowski-Kurilo, N., *Alexander I. Rausch und Einkehr einer Seele*, Zürich, 1939. Spanish edition: *Alejandro I; euforia y recogimiento de un alma*, Madrid, 1941.

Shcheglov, V., *The State Council in Russia*, Yaroslavl, 1903. 3 vols. (in Russian)

Shchegolev, P. E., *Decembrists*, Moscow-Leningrad, 1926. (in Russian)

———, *A. Griboyedov and the Decembrists*, St. Petersburg, 1905. 2 vols. (in Russian)

Shilder, N. K., *Emperor Alexander First*, St. Petersburg, 1897–1898. 4 vols. (in Russian)

———, *Emperor Nicholas I*, St. Petersburg, 1903. 2 vols. (in Russian)

———, *Emperor Paul I*, St. Petersburg, 1901. (in Russian)

Shtraikh, S. Y., *Revolts in the Army under Alexander I*, St. Petersburg, 1922. (in Russian)

Shubinsky, S., *Characters and Anecdotes from the Life of Emperor Alexander I*, St. Petersburg, 1877. (in Russian)

Smietletsky, N., *Prince A. N. Golitsyn*, Kiev, 1901. (in Russian)

Soloviyov, S. M., *Emperor Alexander I*, St. Petersburg, 1877. (in Russian)

Sorel, A., *L'Europe et la Révolution Française*, Paris, 1903–1909. 8 vols.

Stählin, Karl, *Geschichte Russlands*, Berlin, 1935. Vol. III.

Staretz Fyodor Kuzmich, 1837–1864, Tomsk, 1907. (in Russian)

Strakhovsky, Léonid, *L'Empereur Nicolas I et l'esprit national russe,* Louvain, 1928.

Sukhomlinov, M., *Frédéric-Caesar La Harpe,* St. Petersburg, 1871. (in Russian)

Svatikov, S., *The Social Movement in Russia,* Rostov-on-Don, 1905. (in Russian)

Sverbeyev, D., *Memoirs,* Moscow, 1899. 2 vols. (in Russian)

Talleyrand, Prince M. de, *Mémoires,* Paris, 1891. 3 vols.

Tarasov, D. K., *Emperor Alexander I,* Petrograd, 1915. (in Russian)

————, *Memoirs,* St. Petersburg, 1872. (in Russian)

Tarle, E., *Bonaparte,* New York, 1937.

————, *The Continental Blockade,* Moscow, 1913. (in Russian)

————, *Napoleon's Invasion of Russia,* New York, 1942.

————, *Talleyrand,* Moscow, 1939. (in Russian)

Tatishchev, S., *Alexandre et Napoléon,* Paris, 1891.

————, *From the Past of Russian Diplomacy,* St. Petersburg, 1890. (in Russian)

Thomas, B. P., *Russo-American Relations, 1815–1867,* Baltimore, 1930.

Törngren, Adolf, "Mystiken Kring Alexander I:s död," in *Finsk Tidskrift,* 1938. Vol. CXXIV.

Tolstoy, Comte L., *Physiologie de la guerre: Napoléon et la campagne de Russie,* Paris, 1888.

Touchard-Lafosse, G., *Histoire de Charles XIV (Jean Bernadotte),* Paris, 1838. 3 vols.

Tourgenev, N. I., *La Russie et les Russes,* Paris, 1847. 3 vols.

Ulmann, H., *Russisch-Preussische Politik unter Alexander I und Friedrich-Wilhelm III,* Leipzig, 1899.

Umaniets, F. M., *Alexander I and Speransky*, St. Petersburg, 1910. (in Russian)

Vandal, A., *Napoléon et Alexandre I: l'Alliance russe sous le premier Empire*, Paris, 1898–1903. 2 vols. 5th ed.

Vasilich, *Emperor Alexander I and Fyodor Kuzmich*, Moscow, 1910. (in Russian)

Vereschchagin, V., *Napoléon en Russie*, Paris, 1897.

Vernadsky, G., *La charte constitutionnelle de 1820*, Paris, 1933.

Viazemsky, Prince P., *Complete Works*, St. Petersburg, 1878–1886. 10 vols. (in Russian)

Viegel, V. V., *Memoirs*, Moscow, 1864–1865. 7 vols. (in Russian). 2nd ed., Moscow, 1891–1893. 7 vols.; same under editorship of S. Y. Shtraikh, Moscow, 1928. 2 vols.

Villèle, Comte de, *Mémoires et Correspondance*, Paris, 1887–1890. 5 vols.

Vitrolles, Baron de, *Mémoires*, Paris, 1884. 3 vols.

Volkonsky, Prince S., *About the Decembrists*, Paris, 1921. (in Russian)

Vorontsov Archives, Moscow, 1870–1885. 30 vols. (in Russian)

Voyensky, K., *The Patriotic War of 1812*, St. Petersburg, 1911. (in Russian)

Waliszewski, K., *La Russie il y a cent ans: Le règne d'Alexandre I*, Paris, 1923–1925. 3 vols.

Walsh, Robert (editor), *Correspondence respecting Russia*, Philadelphia, 1813.

Webster, C. K., *The Congress of Vienna, 1814–1815*, London, 1919.

———, *The Foreign Policy of Castlereagh 1813–1815 and 1815–1822*, London, 1925 and 1931. 2 vols.

Wilson, Sir Robert, *Narrative of the Events during the Invasion of Russia*, London, 1860.

——, *Private Diary*, London, 1861. 2 vols.

Winkler, M., *Zarenlegende. Glanz und Geheimnis um Alexander I*, Berlin, 1941.

Württemberg, Prinz Eugen von, *Memoiren*, Frankfurt, 1862. 3 vols.

X. (editor), *Correspondance inédite de l'Empereur Alexandre et de Bernadotte pendant l'année 1812*, Paris, 1909.

Yakushkin, I. D., *Memoirs*, Leipzig, 1874. (in Russian)

Yakushkin, V., *Speransky and Arakcheyev*, Moscow, 1905. (in Russian)

Yermolov, A. P., *Memoirs*, Moscow, 1863–1864. 2 vols. (in Russian)

Zakharov, E. Z., *The Legend about the Life and Labors of Staretz Fyodor Kuzmich*, St. Petersburg, 1897. (in Russian)

Zatvornitsky, N., *Centenary of the Ministry of War*, St. Petersburg, 1903. (in Russian)

Znamensky, P., *Lectures on the History of the Russian Church under Alexander I*, Kazan, 1885. (in Russian)

INDEX